DATE DUE

WITHDRAWN

DE PROPRIETATIBUS LITTERARUM

edenda curat

C.H. VAN SCHOONEVELD

Indiana University

Series Practica, 108

THE HOMELY WEB OF TRUTH:

A Study of Charlotte Brontë's Novels

by

LAWRENCE JAY DESSNER
The University of Toledo

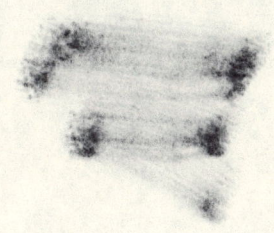

1975
MOUTON
THE HAGUE - PARIS

© Copyright 1975 in The Netherlands
Mouton & Co. N.V., Publishers, The Hague

No part of this book may be translated or reproduced in any form, by print, photo print, microfilm, or any other means, without written permission from the publisher

I acknowledge with appreciation the permission granted me to use and reproduce in this work materials in the posession of the Pierpont Morgan Library and the Henry W. and Albert A. Berg Collection of the New York Public Library, Astor, Lennox and Tilden Foundations.

L.J.D.

ISBN 90 279 334 3

Printed in The Netherlands by Intercontinental Graphics, Dordrecht

ACKNOWLEDGMENTS

The Henry W. and Albert A. Berg Collection, New York Public Library,
   Astor, Lenox and Tilden Foundations.
Reference Collection, New York Public Library.
The Library of New York University.
The Pierpont Morgan Library.

Professor Gordon N. Ray.
Miss Winifred Gérin.
Research Grants Committee, Graduate School, The University of Toledo.
The Graduate English Faculty, New York University.
Mouton and Company.
Mr. and Mrs. William B. Dessner.
Gerald H. Dessner.
Mr. and Mrs. Dessner.
Susan Leona and Daniel Adam
Dedicated, with gratitude and love, to Phyllis.

BIBLIOGRAPHICAL NOTE

Except when otherwise noted, all quotations from the novels are taken from the Shakespeare Head Brontë, edited by T.J. Wise and J.A. Symington, Oxford, 1931. Chapter numbers precede volume and page numbers in my references.
"Letters", in my notes, refers to *The Brontës: Their Lives, Friendships and Correspondence*, edited by T.J. Wise and J.A. Symington, four volumes, Oxford, 1932.

I use the following standard abbreviations:

BST   *Transactions of the Brontë Society*

CE   *College English*

CHEL   *Cambridge History of English Literature*

NCF   *Nineteenth-Century Fiction*

OED   *Oxford English Dictionary*

RES   *Review of English Studies*

VN   *Victorian Newsletter*

TABLE OF CONTENTS

Acknowledgments V
Bibliographical Note VII
   I.   Introductory 1
  II. Literary Culture 12
 III. George Sand and Walter Scott 33
 IV. The Professor 49
  V. Jane Eyre 64
 VI. Shirley 82
VII. Villette 98
Selected Bibliography 120
Index 124

I

Introductory

1

"There has been a tendency on the part of almost all those who have written about the Brontës, to lose their heads", says Mr. Delafield fresh from the researches which resulted in his useful compilation of comtemporary references to the famous family. (1) And Delafield is hardly the only student of the Brontës whose reaction to the size and quality of the mammoth Brontë bookshelf is one of bemused dismay. May Sinclair felt that an apology was needed for her own addition of "another Brontë book" to the massive accumulation available by 1912 (2) - an accumulation dwarfed by comparison with that of 1969. But it is quality not quantity that brought forth the tone of stoic hopelessness with which G. F. Bradby debunked the more flamboyant "Brontë Legends", (3) and quality too that prompted Henry James, lecturing on "The Lesson of Balzac" in 1905, to this almost angry outburst:

> The romantic tradition of the Brontës, with posterity, has been still more essentially helped, I think, by a force independent of any one of their applied faculties - by the attendant image of their dreary, their tragic history, their loneliness and poverty of life. That picture has been made to hang before us as insistently as the vividest page of Jane Eyre or Wuthering Heights. If these things were "stories", as we say, and stories of a lively interest, the medium from which they sprang was above all in itself a story, such a story as has fairly elbowed out the rights of appreciation, as has come at least to impose itself as an expression of the power concerned. The personal position of the three sisters, of the two in particular, had been marked, in short, with so sharp an accent that this accent has become for us the very tone of their united production. It covers and supplants their matter, their spirit, their style, their talent, their taste; it embodies, really, the most complete intellectual muddle, if the term be not extravagant, ever achieved, on a literary question, by our wonderful public. The question has scarce indeed been accepted as belonging to literature at all. Literature is an objective, a projected result; it is life that is the unconscious, the agitated, the struggling, floundering cause. But the fashion has been, in looking at the Brontës, so to confound the cause with the result that we cease to know, in the presence of such ecstasies, what we have hold of or what we are talking about. They represent, the ecstasies, the high-water mark of sentimental judgment. (4)

And the "most complete intellectual muddle" has since been enhanced not only by more of the same, but by some remarkable performances of an altogether new kind. We have what amounts to a comic parody of scholarly source-hunting in the seriously intended books of Florence S. Dry. (5) Here we find that "many of the passages in Jane Eyre are mere paraphrases" from Scott's Heart of Midlothian, this based on the sort of thinking that finds a conclusive similarity in the names of "Old Mother Blood and Grace Poole" (6) and that discovers a deliberate acknowledgment of Charlotte Brontë's debt to Scott in Rochesters's remark to Mason, "We shall get you off cannily, Dick." (7)

James was also spared the amateur Freudianism, supported by the uncritical use of the more suspect biographical theories, of Miss Rosamond Langbridge, (8) and the jargon with which Barbara Hannah relates the Brontës' fiction to

Jung, (9) not to mention more scholarly excursions (10) into the "intense inane". (11) The method is to apply the terms of some elaborate metaphoric account of individual or social consciousness to the persons and relationships in, most often, Jane Eyre. Yet these post-Jamesean modernist approaches are commonly grounded in and supported by James's old abhorrence: undue reliance on biography.

Biographical criticism with a good deal of biographical speculation - not always so labeled - has been the dominant mode of approach to Charlotte Brontë until well into this century. Even before Mrs. Gaskell's Life of Charlotte Brontë (1857), even before the identity of "Currer Bell", the "Editor" of Jane Eyre's "Autobiography", (12) was known to more than a handful of people, biographical speculation was rife. Within weeks of its publication by Smith, Elder, and Company, Thackeray, with what seems a studied casualness, asked William Smith Williams to betray his client's anonymity: "It is a woman's writing, but whose?" (13) and later, despite Miss Brontë's protestations prefacing Jane Eyre's third edition (April, 1848), Sydney Dobell gave the readers of The Palladium for September 1850 his solution to the mystery of the three novel-writing Bells: Currer Bell wrote them all. (14)

As biographical information became available and the public interest aroused, especially by Mrs. Gaskell's biography, a score of investigators followed "In the Footsteps of the Brontës", (15) and were able to show the multifold correspondences between the life and the novels. All too often gaps in biographical knowledge were filled in by recourse to the fictional biographies in the novels, and on occasion great liberties were taken with this suspect procedure in order to support some overriding speculative premise. (16)

The earliest objection to biographical curiosity and speculation was Charlotte Brontë's own: "To such critics I would say, 'To you I am neither man nor woman - I come before you as an author only. It is the sole standard by which you have a right to judge me - the sole ground on which I accept your judgment.'" (17) Another and more common objection to the equating of fact and fiction was concerned, not with the method, but with some of its results. Preëminent in this category are the acrimonious public debate on the accuracy of the portrayal in Jane Eyre of the Clergy Daughters' School at Cowan Bridge, (18) and the heated polemics on the question of Miss Brontë's relationship with the Hegers of Brussels.

The publication in the London Times, in 1913, of four letters from Charlotte Brontë to Constantin Heger provided substantial support to previous speculation that this relationship was pivotal to an understanding of her life and work. To others the letters are felt to disprove the theory that the pupil loved the Master. Heger used the back of the letters for his laundry and shopping lists. (19) Does this prove him disinterested in their contents or merely thrifty? Did he find them worthy of neither the fire nor the vault, or did he carry them in his pockets so long for sentimental reasons? However one chooses to define this perplexing relationship, it has increased the flow of Brontë biographies, of which Winifred Gérin's exhaustive works are perhaps the culmination. (20)

Thesis-ridden as Miss Gérin's books sometimes are, they profit, especially her Charlotte Brontë, from the use of the mass of juvenile and other unpublished materials which has come to light only in this century. Forty years to the day after Charlotte Brontë's death, her husband, Rev. Arthur Bell Nicholls, handed over to Clement K. Shorter "countless manuscripts written in childhood, and bundles of letters". (21) Shorter's series of books, the efforts of private collectors and of the Brontë Society (founded in 1893), and subsequent scholarly research and publication, have made students familiar with the extant correspondence and aware of the secret literary life of the young Brontës. While the volume of Charlotte Brontë's contributions to the juvenile material is greater than that of her published works, its literary value is negligible. But as an index to her development as a writer, knowledge of the "Angrian" material provides a basis for studies which show her casting off, with more or less success, the world of uncontrolled "Fancy" and "Imagination", and coming to terms with the mundane and the "Real". (22)

Miss Ratchford's survey of the juvenilia (23) draws comparisons of this kind, elucidates some of the many hidden references to the juvenilia in the later novels and letters, and most remarkably, casts doubt on the long tradition of finding real-life models for the fictional characters. She shows, and generally convincingly, that prototypes for the characters in the novels are to be found in the juvenile fiction written, for the most part, before Miss Brontë met the people who have long been considered their prototypes or "sources". (24) The argument is complicated however by Miss Brontë's own statements naming living models for some of her characters, (25) and by the fact that the juvenile tales, like anything else, had their sources too.

2

Without having achieved any large areas of general agreement on interpretative matters, or in fact having produced a widely accepted "definitive" biography of Charlotte Brontë, the biographical school of criticism, and the psychological school, which in most cases requires biography as its starting point, have faded as the focus of academic Brontë studies. The followers of Henry James, Percy Lubbock, Joseph Warren Beach, and others, armed as well with the tools of the "New Critics" of poetry, have developed methods and terminology most readily of value with twentieth-century works, but which have been increasingly brought to bear on the standard novelists, one must say rather the standard novels, of the nineteenth century. As if Jane Eyre were a short poem by John Crowe Ransom in Cleanth Brooks's textbook, critics arise from most careful readings of the text to point out heretofore unnoticed patterns of imagery which provide new meanings for the novel and disclose parts "of the rich substratum of the work". In one case, Charlotte Brontë's use of the word "nature" is followed as a "guide" to the conflict between "Romantic" and "Victorian" elements in her psyche. (26) Robert B. Heilman surveys the appearances of the moon, (27) Mark Schorer explicates the use of trees as poetic symbols, (28) and David Lodge discovers that the four elements, fire, air, earth, and water, with roughly their Elizabethan meanings, play a large part in unifying and enriching the novel. (29) While a modern novelist, such as Henry James in The Golden Bowl, will enrich and unify a novel by the deliberate use of such symbols, critics of Jane Eyre are generally quick to point out that this technique need not be, and in Charlotte Brontë's case was not, deliberate, planned, or conscious. "Is it, one might ask, the total artistry of the structure, the whole organization so firm that it welds even the limpest materials together, holds even coincidence and miracle firmly in place? Hardly. The structure of Jane Eyre is nearly artless." (30) "But Charlotte Brontë was not an Elizabethan; nor was she a highly self-conscious and deliberate symbolist novelist like Joyce or Conrad." (31) "Can one not generalize on the nature of all these aspects of Charlotte Brontë's art to the extent of saying that it is largely an unconscious art?" (32)

The potential contradiction in this concept of "unwilled art" (33) does not disturb or impede these critics, for there is plenty of Romantic and Platonic criticism that can see meaningful and coherent use of imagery and verbal patterns as the unconscious manifestation of the intensely "poetic" sensibility. With regard to larger structural manipulations, overall form and unity, and the use of carefully controlled point of view, "unconscious art" becomes a less tenable concept. Turning to Charlotte Brontë's own statements about her methods of composition and to the critical methods and presuppositions of her day, one finds that both sound so utterly "unmodern" as to disarm, if not inhibit, modern criticism. The tacit presumption that Jamesean (to use a convenient label) artistry requires Jamesean self-consciousness and even Jamesean articulateness often limits the use of Jamesean analysis.

This is not always the case however. Much recent criticism of Emily Brontë's

Wuthering Heights avoids the problem and is not disturbed to find her doing by
accident or unconsciously what Conrad, say, was pleased to achieve on purpose.
(34) And by limiting the concept of "Unity" to the thematic unity of philosophical
discourse, this sort of "Unity" may be demonstrated in Charlotte Brontë's work.
(35) The presentation through exempla of all the various "heads" of a central
thesis, such as, "what options are open to a girl like Caroline Helstone and where
will each lead her?", becomes then the unifying plan. This would relate the
novels to the tradition of the argumentative sermon, and to its debased form,
the Evangelical didactic fiction of the "mad Methodist Magazines" (36) - two
modes with which Miss Brontë was very familiar. On the other hand we have
her insisting: "Nor can I write a book for its moral", (37) and, "I am no
teacher - to look on me in that light is to mistake me - to teach is not my
vocation - what I am, it is useless to say - those whom it concerns feel and
find it out." (38)

Modern critics might take heart however from some evidences of Miss Brontë's
consciousness of the possible effects of various narrative points of view. Writing
to her publisher in March of 1852, she asks: "Is the first number of 'Bleak House'
generally admired? I liked the Chancery part, but when it passes into the autobiographic form, and the young woman who announces that she is not 'bright'
begins her history, it seems to me too often weak and twaddling; an amiable
nature is caricatured, not faithfully rendered, in Miss Esther Summerson." (39)
In November 1851, Miss Brontë wrote to James Taylor, in India on business for
her publishers. She is here responding to his apology for an "ill-written" letter. ". . . It appeared to me throughout highly interesting. It is observable
that the very same information which we have previously collected, perhaps
with rather languid attention, from printed books, when placed before us in
a familiar manuscript, and comprising the actual experience of a person with
whom we are acquainted, acquires a new and vital interest: when we know the
narrator we seem to realise the tale." (40)

Suggestive as these remarks of Miss Brontë may be of her sensitivity to the
management of the first person, there is a timidity, perhaps a naïveté, in them
that one might not expect from an acclaimed novelist of thirty-five years of
age. An interesting contrast to them is furnished by John Fowles, who takes
twelve columns in Harper's to describe the progress of his technical manipulations in a novel whose composition is still under way. He writes a memorandum
to himself: "You are not the 'I' who breaks into the illusion, but the 'I' who is
a part of it", which he then amplifies for us: "In other words, the 'I' who will
make first-person commentaries here and there in my story, and on one occasion will even attempt to enter it, will not necessarily be my real 'I' in 1967;
but much more just another character, though in a different category from the
purely fictional ones." (41) Does this, in essence, indicate more sophistication
than Charlotte Brontë's deliberate distancing of herself from the first-person
narrator of Villette?- "But I am not leniently disposed towards Miss Frost
(i.e. Lucy Snowe); from the beginning I never meant to appoint her lines in
pleasant places." (42) Is Fowles's interest in technical problems much more
spirited than that indicated by Harriet Martineau's description of the genesis
of Jane Eyre? -

"Jane Eyre" was naturally and universally supposed to be Charlotte herself;
but she always denied it, calmly, cheerfully, and with the obvious sincerity
which characterised all she said. She declared that there was no more ground
for the assertion than this: She once told her sisters that they were wrong -
even morally wrong - in making their heroines beautiful, as a matter of
course. They replied that it was impossible to make a heroine interesting
on other terms. Her answer was, "I will prove to you that you are wrong.
I will show you a heroine as small and as plain as myself who shall be as
interesting as any of yours. Hence, 'Jane Eyre,' " said she in telling the
anecdote, "but she is not myself, any further than that." (43)

(One might want to temper one's admiration of this last by comparing it with Walter Scott's Introduction (1831) to The Fortunes of Nigel (1822): "Having, in the tale of the Heart of Midlothian, succeeded in some degree in awakening an interest in behalf of one devoid of those accomplishments which belong to a heroine almost by right, I was next tempted to choose a hero upon the same unpromising plan.") (44)

But the most striking suggestion of Charlotte Brontë's concern for technical matters, and of her conscious planning of her work, is to be found in her "Scheme for a May Tale", an outline appearing inside the front cover of a school exercise-book. It is dated May 1843. Miss Brontë was almost twenty-seven, and teaching at the Pensionnat Heger, Brussels.

Time	- from 30-50 years ago
Country	- England
Scene	- Rural
Rank	- Middle
Person	- First
Subject	- Certain remarkable occurrences
Sex of Writer	- At discretion
No of Characters	- Limited
Plot	- Domestic - the romantic not excluded
Opening	- Cheerful or Gloomy
Occurrences	- 1st Reverses of Fortune - 2nd New Arrival 3rd Loss of Relations 4th Crosses in the Affections 5. Going abroad Return 6th
Characters	- Hero - Heroine - Family of d^o - Rival or Rivalness (sic) - Villain N.B. Moderation to be observed here - Friends Avoid Richardsonian Multiplication
P.S.	- As much compression - as little explanation as may be.
Mem(orandum?)	- To be set about with proper spirit - To be carried on with the same - To be concluded idem
Observe	- No grumbling allowed.

Inside the back cover of the same exercise-book were written some more notes:

Uncle	- R.C. Priest - Atonement
Eliza	- some food (fool?) - like Mr. R - Georgiana
School	- L(ov?)e not for 1st person - 2nd character
Sympathy	- Keep 1st person for Spectator - Narrator Commentator (45)

This on the eve of her twenty-seventh birthday! Miss Brontë carefully sets herself a task and reminds herself of the need to persevere in it without "grumbling", as a twelve-year old might draw up New Year's resolutions to brush her hair regularly or to improve her posture. And how "prissy" is the idea of the outline itself, with its complacent specifications, its ordering up of "certain remarkable occurrences". There is, in short, such a large infusion of childishness in this "Scheme for a May Tale", that one might undervalue the intelligence that made the reference to "Richardsonian Multiplication", and that linked "Sympathy" with what seems to be a decision to maintain the first-person mode while avoiding the autobiographic form.

This discussion of the "Scheme for a May Tale", speculative as it is, presents the possibility at least, that with Charlotte Brontë we are dealing with a most uneven, unusual, idiosyncratic mind, hesitant and inefficient to be sure in 1843, but attending to the then arcane "Art of Fiction" in remarkable if not prophetic ways. And this admittedly speculative reading is largely sustained by examination of Charlotte Brontë's juvenile fiction, particularly the later stories of the 1830's. (46) Here we find obvious imitation of Scott, Byron, Radcliffe, Richardson, perhaps Balzac, (47) as earlier we saw imitation of various features of Blackwood's Magazine. Most striking, of course, in these tales is the content: the fantastic and extravagant Angria and Verdopolis, and the overheated Byronism of the Duke of Zamorna. But the tales are also strewn with experiments - and failures, in narrative techniques. They do not seem to have been revised or adequately planned, for time and again, the first-person narrator finds himself up against that limitation of the first person symbolized by the need to report an action that takes place behind doors barred to him. Charlotte Brontë's ways out of this dilemma are inventive, if childish, and the very variety of solutions tried is evidence of a mind dissatisfied with repetition of old solutions. The simplest solution to the barred door is to enter, unseen, through some other unspecified entrance. (48) Another is merely to preface knowledge that should be unavailable to the narrator, in this case Zamorna's state of mind, with, "I suppose." (49) Or to be able to report on another's state of mind, Miss Brontë has him soliloquize, a practice she justifies in advance by: "According to books, men in general soliloquize when they are by themselves, and so did Hartford." (50) An economical and unobtrusive solution is merely to say, "I heard afterwards." (51) Three pages later, Miss Brontë shifts to the continuous journal technique of Richardson; the narrator has got a look at the journal and reproduces part of it for us. Since the journal is contemporary with the particular part of the story that the narrator has difficulty in learning at first hand, not a retrospect of the entire story, the narrator is able to evade the usual first-person limitations without entirely breaking the valuable illusion that he is "in" the story, learning as he goes along, not outside and omniscient. (52) The execution of this maneuver leaves much to be desired but its concept would probably have delighted James or Percy Lubbock.

Alongside the persistent narrative awkwardness and the makeshift but often ingenious responses to narrative difficulties, there is also a confident use of authorial intrusion which works as a sort of punctuation, as a relief from the excitement of a dramatic scene, and as a reminder of the maturity, the suavity of the narrator: "It may now be as well to connect the broken thread of my rambling narrative before I proceed further." (53) There is also a free use of shifts into present tense for added drama, and from first to third person, both often done with a deft touch that is unobtrusive and successful.

Surely Charlotte Brontë's oddest experiment in setting the narrative framework is found in The Spell, An Extravaganza (1834). Like many of the Angrian tales it is narrated by Lord Charles A. F. Wellesley, brother of Arthur Wellesley, Marquis of Douro, Duke of Zamorna. A hint of jealousy but something of natural affection is seen in Charles's constant chiding of Zamorna.

The Spell begins with a preface, signed by Charles, which further characterizes him, and tells us that this story has a hidden ulterior motive.

> The Duke of Zamorna should not have excluded me from Wellesley House, for the following pages have been the result of that exclusion. Does he think I can patiently bear to be wholly separated from my sister-in-law, a lady whom I love and honour more than any other in Verdopolis? . . . In this book I have tampered with heart-strings. Perhaps a casual spectator may think that he is highly flattered and so forth, the tale, part of it at least being told by his wife (through her letters), but to him the whole affair will be unendurable. There are passages of truth here which will make him gnash his teeth with grating agony. I am not at liberty to point out what those passages are, but he will discover them. . . .

All this is declared in my present work rather by implication than assertion.

The reader will find here no lengthened passage which elaborately sets forth his outrageous peculiarities. He must gather it from the hints interwoven with the whole surface and progress of the story. When he has finished, let him shut the book, and dismissing from his mind every fictitious circumstance let him choose such only as have self-evident marks of reality about them, then after due consideration let him deliver his opinion. Is the Duke of Zamorna sane or insane? (54)

Whether a domestic upset at Haworth Parsonage is the motive behind the story or not, it shows a deliberate use of fiction for other ends than the simple reporting of real, or even feigned, events, and an assumption, on the part of the narrator, of a wide range of tone. The simple separation of the author from the first-person narrator, which seems an article of Miss Brontë's faith, is here complicated to an extent that brings to mind the oblique and experimental techniques of Gide's Counterfeiters, of John Barth and John Fowles.

4

Of course The Spell is not otherwise to be mentioned in the company of such accomplishments. It is unpublishable juvenilia that seems in large part immature for a young woman of seventeen. Yet it is the most striking suggestion among those surveyed here of Charlotte Brontë's enduring interest in narrative techniques, in the separation and characterization of the narrator, in, in short, the potential uses of the controlled point of view. These suggestions, taken along with the facts that Charlotte Brontë's mature novels were immediately acclaimed in her own day, and that the power and appeal of at least Jane Eyre and Villette have not faded, may lead one to suspect that some of the power of the novels may be related to their narrative technique - for, "clearly, the aesthetic effect of a work of art does not reside in what is commonly called its content". (55) But, with the exception of those studies of "unwilled" verbal and image patterning, and of what we may call "argumentative" unity, both as described above, "content" has been the focus of most estimates of Charlotte Brontë's work. And not always the pure "content" of the novels, but that "enriched" by what James called "the romantic tradition of the Brontës", that "muddle", that accretion, perhaps now insoluble, of sentiments which, however well founded they may be, oversimplify the complexity of life, and thereby diminish it. This is not limited to our maudlin, "our wonderful public", as James called them. A widely admired critic gives us these findings: "Jane Eyre, Villette, The Professor, the best parts of Shirley, are not exercises of the mind, but cries of the heart; not a deliberate self-diagnosis, but an involuntary self-revelation. . . . She was a very naïve writer, her faults have the naked crudeness of a child's faults . . . . She was incapable of seeing things in ironical proportion. . . . She was a genius. . . . It is the key to the problem of (her) achievement." (56) Similar pronouncements are not far to seek: "The mechanical mysteries of her art had no charm for Currer Bell." (57) "The author (of Jane Eyre) pays not too much but too little attention to the more conscious and more mechanical aspects of her art." (58) "If it were not for the unity of tone, Jane Eyre would be incoherent, for as a construction it is artless." (59)

Conclusions such as these, one is forced to suspect, owe a good deal to "the romantic tradition of the Brontës", and it is this tradition also, working in more subtle ways, that one senses behind most of those studies that do touch on Charlotte Brontë's technical achievements. For there are a number of studies that note and explicate evidence of craftsmanship in the novels - but it is generally craft of a rather simple order that is brought to our attention, craft of the isolated instance rather than of the overall structure. And while tonal unity, thematic balance, and the use of contrasted characters in Jane Eyre are well presented, the larger narrative techniques of this and the other novels are most often decried, and their faults at last related to biographical data.

5

In 1958 Robert B. Heilman published his "Charlotte Brontë's 'New' Gothic", (60) a valuable contribution to Brontë studies, and on two counts. In the course of his argument that shows Charlotte Brontë's transformation of the Gothic mode, Heilman goes through the novels, ticking off her use of sexual imagery, her creation of characters of "urgent sexuality", her depiction of confrontations and tensions with marked sexual overtones. That these aspects of the novels had been overlooked heretofore is additional evidence of the triumph of "the romantic tradition of the Brontës" in inhibiting popular and even critical response.

But Heilman has a larger aim, and one almost equally neglected: the definition of Charlotte Brontë's placement in, and contribution to, that large abstraction, the English Novel. It has always been apparent that Jane Eyre in particular, despite its large infusion of Gothic setting and Gothic melodrama, is not a Gothic novel at all, but a new thing. Heilman characterizes the transformation incisively: "Charlotte goes on to make a . . . radical revision of the mode: in Jane Eyre and in the other novels, . . . that discovery of passion, that rehabilitation of the extra-rational, which is the historical office of Gothic, is no longer oriented in marvelous circumstances but moves deeply into the lesser-known realities of human life. This change I describe as the change from 'old Gothic' to 'New Gothic.' " (61) Though in the line of descent from Richardson, the Brontës are seen to react variously to the tradition - they adopt its conventions, undercut them ("anti-Gothic"), and transform them.

Heilman contents himself with showing how this is so, leaving it to others to attempt the historical generalizations: "As Thackeray was the first English writer to make the novel the vehicle of a conscious criticism of life, so she (Charlotte Brontë) is the first to make it the vehicle of personal revelation. She is our first subjective novelist, the ancestor of Proust and Mr. James Joyce and all the rest of the historians of the private consciousness." (62) And here is an interesting variation on the theme: "The influence she exercised on the development of the English novel was more profound than is often acknowledged; it is Villette, more than any work of Thackeray or George Eliot, that we must recognize as the pioneer of an extension of the province and function of the novelist's art only completely worked into the tradition of the English novel by Meredith and Henry James." (63) But Herbert Read does not rest here. We turn the page to learn that Charlotte and Emily Brontë "are the least influenced and most original geniuses in the whole history of the English novel". And one finds the same assertion elsewhere: "There never was author of highest rank so uninfluenced by, because there never was one so unconscious of, literary models." (64) Virginia Woolf does not deny the Brontës their reading, but, likening Charlotte Brontë to Thomas Hardy, denies the influence of their literary culture on their literary productions: "They learn little from other writers, and what they adopt they cannot assimilate. . . . Charlotte Brontë, at least, owed nothing to the reading of many books." (65)

A collation of these opinions, and except for Mr. Leavis' sacrifice of the Brontës to the cause of his "Great Tradition", (66) they may be said to represent a fair consensus of those who have addressed themselves to the subject, (67) a collation then, gives a most unusual phenomenon of literary history: a prodigy, exerting great influence, itself uninfluenced. No one argues with Dr. Johnson when he credits Dryden with the single-handed renovation of English poetry - "he found it brick and left it marble" - but no one quite believes him either. And so it is, one ventures to say, with all great innovation: modern investigations discover the fertile soil from which it sprang, the contemporary parallel development, the cause, the source. Carlyle's notion of "Hero-Worship" may be inspirational, but it is questionable history.

Justification can be found for those who "the romantic tradition" has provided with a heroine for whom books were unavailable, or who had not time nor inclination for such a mundane occupation; but what of those who acknowledge the evidence of Miss Brontë's wide but irregular literary culture, and yet deny, out of hand, its influence on her work? An investigation, a demonstration, is due.

6

Despite the great accumulation on the Brontë bookshelf, the basic task of the literary critic-scholar-historian remains largely undone. He must, firstly, seek to discover the secret springs of the abiding aesthetic power of Charlotte Brontë's novels. Yes they are all variations of "the Cinderella theme", perhaps they are analyses of "the sense of inferiority", (68) but literary criticism must not so relinquish its part in "the main intellectual concern of the last three hundred years". This has been, as Basil Willey puts it, "to give a 'philosophical' account of matters which had formerly been explained 'unscientifically', 'popularly', or 'figuratively'". (69)

A "philosophical" account of a novel, the present writer holds, is most approachable, through study of its narrative techniques. And such an account must not neglect the assignment, if not of value - that most illusive of all determinations, at least of place, place in that part of human history that is the history of the English novel. What, to descend to the immediate case, were the relations between Charlotte Brontë and the literary culture of her day? To what shaping pressure did she make what responses? Wherein lies the uniqueness of response, the existence of which, though incompletely defined, is acknowledged by the continued attention we pay to her work?

NOTES:

(1) E.M. Delafield (pseud.), ed., The Brontës, Their Lives Recorded by Their Contemporaries (London, 1935), 13.
(2) The Three Brontës (Boston and New York, 1912), x.
(3) Godfrey Fox Bradby, The Brontës and Other Essays (Oxford, 1932).
(4) Quoted by Mark Schorer, in "Jane Eyre", The World We Imagine, Selected Essays (New York, 1968), 82.
(5) The Sources of "Jane Eyre" (Cambridge, 1940), and The Sources of "Wuthering Heights" (Cambridge, 1937).
(6) Sources of "Jane Eyre", 41, her italics.
(7) Sources of "Jane Eyre", 37, my italics.
(8) Charlotte Brontë, A Psychological Study (New York, (1929). This is a book often named - for its subtitle one suspects, but rarely examined critically. It is the acknowledged basis of Rebecca West's "Charlotte Brontë" in The Great Victorians, ed. H.J. and Hugh Massingham (New York, 1932), 47-58, and is treated with undue respect in Richard Chase's celebrated article, "The Brontës, or, Myth Domesticated", in Forms of Modern Fiction, ed. William Van O'Connor (Minneapolis, 1948), 102-119. Chase uses the support of Langbridge as well as errors of fact as to the contemporary reception of Jane Eyre (102) and the character of Patrick Brontë (103-104), to further his thesis that "Rochester's injuries are, I should think, a symbolic castration" (108).
(9) Victims of the Creative Spirit, A Contribution to the Psychology of the Brontës from the Jungian Point of View, The Guild of Pastoral Psychology Lecture No. 68 ((London), 1951).
(10) Such are, Martin S. Day, "Central Concepts of Jane Eyre", Personalist, XLI (1960), 495-508, R.E. Hughes, "Jane Eyre: The Unbaptized Dionysos",

NCF, XVIII (1964), 347-364, and Wayne Burns, "Critical Relevance of Freudianism", Western Review, XX (1956), 301-314.
(11) Shelley's phrase (Prometheus Unbound, II, iii, 193) now has a useful ironic ambiguity.
(12) So reads the title page of the first edition (1847).
(13) The Letters and Private Papers of W.M. Thackeray, ed. Gordon N. Ray, 4 vols. (Cambridge, Mass., 1945-46), II, 318-319.
(14) This review is reprinted in The Life and Letters of Sydney Dobell, ed. E.J., 2 vols. (London, 1878), I, 163-186.
(15) This is the title of one of the better works in this genre, by Ernest Raymond (London, 1948).
(16) Two early offenders are Mary Robinson Duclaux, Emily Brontë, A Memoir, English Women of Letters Series (London, 1883), and F.A. Leyland, The Brontë Family with Special Reference to Patrick Branwell Brontë (London, 1886).
(17) Letters, III, 11.
(18) Documents in this dispute are printed in Letters, IV, 297-314.
(19) Lawrence and Elisabeth Hanson, The Four Brontës, 4th ed. ((Hamden, Conn.:) Archon Books, 1967), vii, 374.
(20) Anne Brontë (London, 1959); Branwell Brontë (London, 1961); Charlotte Brontë, The Evolution of Genius (London, 1967).
(21) Letters, IV, 291.
(22) Robert Bernard Martin, Charlotte Brontë's Novels: The Accents of Persuasion (New York, 1966) is a full-length study based on this theme.
(23) Fannie E. Ratchford, The Brontës' Web of Childhood (New York, 1941).
(24) See Herbert E. Wroot, Sources of the Brontë Novels: Persons and Places, BST, VIII (1935), for some 200 pages of such sources.
(25) As a famous instance, Charlotte told Mrs. Gaskell that "many traits in Shirley's character were taken" from her sister Emily. Life of Charlotte Brontë, Everyman ed. (London, 1960), Ch. XII, 184.
(26) Charles Burkhart, "Another Key Word for Jane Eyre", NCF, XVI (1961), 177-179, and for the preceding phrase in the text.
(27) "Charlotte Brontë, Reason, and the Moon", NCF, XIV (1960), 283-302.
(28) The World We Imagine, 80-96.
(29) "Fire and Eyre: Charlotte Brontë's War of Earthly Elements", Language of Fiction (New York, 1966), 114-143, esp. 120-121. Eric Solomon, "Jane Eyre: Fire and Water", CE, XXV (1963), 215-217, finds these images more coherently arranged than does Lodge.
(30) Schorer, 88.
(31) Lodge, 121.
(32) Burkhart, 177.
(33) Burkhart, 178.
(34) Philip Drew, "Charlotte Brontë as a Critic of Wuthering Heights", NCF, XVIII (1964), 365-381, describes and corrects some of the excesses of this criticism, exp. p. 372.
(35) Jacob Korg, "The Problem of Unity in Shirley", NCF, XII (1957), 125-136. W.A. Craik, The Brontë Novels (London, 1968), agrees, and sees something of the same sort of unity in Jane Eyre also, pp. 70-157, passim.
(36) The phrase appears in Shirley, Ch. XXII. Miss Branwell brought along a complete set of the Methodist Magazine when she married Rev. Patrick Brontë, and it was later available to their children (Gérin, Charlotte Brontë, 35).
(37) Letters, IV, 14.
(38) Letters, III, 42.
(39) Letters, III, 322.
(40) Letters, III, 288-289.
(41) "Notes on Writing a Novel", CCXXXVII (July, 1968), 88-97.
(42) Letters, IV, 16.
(43) Letters, IV, 16.
(44) Caledonian Ed. (Boston and New York, 1913), ix. Charlotte reversed Scott

by first producing her plain hero, William Crimsworth of <u>The Professor</u>, then her plain heroine.
(45) Gérin, <u>Charlotte Brontë</u>, 317, provides a transcript from the ms. in the Brontë Parsonage Museum. My text follows hers, adding my own emendations.
(46) The recently published fragment (1834) of juvenile fiction by Charlotte's near contemporary George Eliot, shows, on the other hand, merely inept imitation of the techniques of Scott. See Gordon S. Haight, <u>George Eliot, A Biography</u> (New York and Oxford, 1968), 554-560 for this.
(47) A suggestion by Laura Hinkley, <u>The Brontës</u>: Charlotte and Emily (New York, 1945), 25; but Charlotte denied in 1853, ever having read Balzac (<u>Letters</u>, IV, 38).
(48) <u>The Spell: An Extravaganza</u>, ed. George Edwin MacLean (London, 1931), 6-7.
(49) <u>Legends of Angria</u>, ed. Fannie E. Ratchford and W.C. DeVane (New Haven, 1933), 204.
(50) <u>Legends of Angria</u>, 168.
(51) <u>The Spell</u>, 74.
(52) <u>The Spell</u>, 77 ff.
(53) <u>Legends of Angria</u>, 70, a clear imitation of Scott.
(54) <u>The Spell</u>, 3-4.
(55) René Wellek and Austin Warren, <u>Theory of Literature</u>, 2nd ed. (New York, 1960), 128.
(56) David Cecil, <u>Victorian Novelists</u> (New York, 1958), 103, 105, 117, 113 (slightly rearranged).
(57) Henry H. Bonnell, <u>Charlotte Brontë</u>, <u>George Eliot</u>, <u>Jane Austen</u> (New York, 1902), 43.
(58) Bruce McCullough, "The Subjective Novel: <u>Jane Eyre</u>", <u>Representative English Novelists</u> (New York and London, 1946), 178.
(59) Walter Allen, <u>The English Novel</u> (New York, 1954), 190.
(60) <u>From Jane Austen to Joseph Conrad</u>, ed. Robert C. Rathburn and Martin Steinmann, Jr. (Minneapolis, 1958), 118-132.
(61) <u>From Jane Austen to Joseph Conrad</u>, 123.
(62) Cecil, 102. McCullough's essay makes the same point.
(63) Herbert Read, "Charlotte and Emily Brontë", reprinted in <u>The Critical Performance</u>, ed. Stanley Edgar Hyman (New York: Vintage Books, 1956), 61-78, see 72-73. First pub., <u>Yale Rev.</u>, XIV, n.s. (1925), 720-738.
(64) Bonnell, 11.
(65) "<u>Jane Eyre</u> and <u>Wuthering Heights</u>", <u>The Common Reader</u>, First Series (New York: Harvest Books, 1967), 162, Craik, 252, presents a similar conclusion.
(66) F.R. Leavis, <u>The Great Tradition</u> (London, 1948), 37-38. Compounding the depreciation, Leavis adds Jane Austen and D.H. Lawrence to the Tradition immediately before his "Note: 'The Brontës'".
(67) There are exceptions, of which Robert A. Colby, "<u>Villette</u> and the Life of the Mind", <u>PMLA</u>, LXXV (1960), 410-419, most merits mention.
(68) Rebecca West, "Charlotte Brontë", in <u>The Great Victorians</u>, 47, 49.
(69) <u>The Seventeenth Century Background</u> (Garden City: Anchor Books, 1953), 11.

II

Literary Culture

1

"Cease that chatter, blockhead! and do my bidding." It is the eighteenth chapter of <u>Jane Eyre</u>. In Rochester's absence, an old gypsy woman has introduced herself at Thornfield Hall, now inhabited by an elegant party of house guests. The Lady Ingram has objected to her daughter Blanche's desire to have her fortune told by the gypsy in a private interview. Blanche is increasingly insistent, and appears to have silenced opposition when Sam, a servant, interposes: "But she looks such a tinkler". (1) "Cease that chatter, blockhead! and do my bidding", is the reply, and all discussion of the matter ends (I, 249). All discussion in the novel that is, for Blanche's speech has often acted as a red flag to readers, shocking them, as it were, out of the novel and into speculation about the origin of the incongruity they feel. We have, before this point, learned a good deal about Blanche Ingram, although not enough to be sure of her attitude toward Rochester. "The noble bust, the sloping shoulders, the graceful neck, the dark eyes and black ringlets were all there: - but her face? Her face was like her mother's; a youthful unfurrowed likeness: the same low brow, the same high features, the same pride. . . . I cannot tell whether Miss Ingram was a genius, but she was self-conscious - remarkably self-conscious indeed" (XVII; I, 221). And later, Jane asserts that she is not jealous of Blanche's rapport with Rochester:

> Miss Ingram was a mark beneath jealousy: she was too inferior to excite the feeling. Pardon the seeming paradox: I mean what I say. She was very showy, but she was not genuine: she had a fine person, many brilliant attainments; but her mind was poor, her heart barren by nature: nothing bloomed spontaneously on that soil; no unforced natural fruit delighted by its freshness. She was not good; she was not original: <u>she used to repeat sounding phrases from books</u>: she never offered, nor had, an opinion of her own. She advocated a <u>high</u> tone of sentiment; but she did not know the sensations of sympathy and pity; tenderness and truth were not in her. (XVIII; I, 239, my italics)

When Blanche comes to the forefront of the action, Jane keeps up the characterization of her by ironic and depricating epithets. Yet this has often been felt insufficient preparation or explanation for the stilted dialogue of the Ingrams, of which the quoted outburst is the culmination.

Lady Eastlake's (Miss Rigby) famous review of <u>Jane Eyre</u>, atypical as it was, and probably designed as a deliberate counterattack on the novel's "jacobinical spirit" (2) and on the large number of earlier and commendatory reviews, based its insistence, in part, that Currer Bell was a man, and a coarse one at that, on his "total ignorance of the habits of society". (3) That Miss Ingram's wardrobe was so untrue to life in such society seemed "incontrovertible" evidence of the masculine hand. But Lady Eastlake finds her speech so important an indication too that she reprints a large block of the passage in question. (4)

More attention has been given, more need for explanation felt, by later readers than by the first ones, for Lady Eastlake's attention to the scene is not at all typical, while in the present century it has presented something of a critical crux. We have the not unusual theory that Miss Brontë had a singular "absence of wit", and "lack of experience". (5) She could not portray characters other than those of her own sphere realistically. Ernest A. Baker notices "blunder and absurdities in the picturing of a society to which Charlotte Brontë was a complete stranger", but he adds a psychological explanation of it as well: "Strong feeling provokes her (Jane or Charlotte, who are here equated) to exaggerate unconsciously those traits which have annoyed her or otherwise affected her vision; hence the worldly people at the big house become the caricatures of humanity which they actually seemed to the hostile eyes of the governess." (6)

Thirty years later Robert Bernard Martin proposed this ingenious explanation:

> The much-criticized accounts of "society" when the Ingrams and their party invade Thornfield perhaps owe less to Miss Brontë's lack of experience in such company than they do to the deliberate intention of making the account of their doings seem the reporting of Jane's maturity remembering her jejune reactions to a society that despises and excludes her. Miss Brontë's own humiliations as a governess have been objectified and exorcized. Blanche Ingram's immortal words of reproof to the footman . . . quite properly tell us more of the young Jane's stereotyped and immature reaction to "haughty beauty" than they do of the character and speech habits of the relatively unimportant Blanche. (7)

And to end this catalogue, the words of David Cecil, with which this writer is pleased, for once, in part, to agree: "Lady Ingram is not original: she is extremely conventional, the conventional silly grande dame of third-rate farce. Charlotte Brontë, unacquainted with such a character herself, has just copied it from the crude type which she found in the commonplace fiction of the time. And her lack of technical skill has made her copy even cruder than its model". (8) One might, however, give Miss Brontë the benefit of the doubt here and call it deliberate parody rather than inept imitation, but all it needs now is for some lucky scholar to find the very words of Blanche Ingram in some probably long-forgotten novel. This would provide a parallel case to Miss Brontë's exact but unannounced quotation from Lady Eastlake's review in Shirley (XXII; II, 66). It is put in the mouth of a Miss Hardmen, who is "a very strong-minded" aristocrat and the clear object of the narrator's scorn.

2

The foregoing excursion has sought to demonstrate the commonplace that historical perspective can be indispensable. As Gordon Ray has said of "the great English novelists" of the nineteenth century, "We shall never understand their work properly unless scholars and critics, whose labors keep the past alive, come to know in detail the setting out of which the books of these masters emerged." (9) Such knowledge is, however, not easily achieved. Since the lifetime of Charlotte Brontë, a lot of literature has gone over the dam; out of print, out of libraries, out, in some cases apparently, of existence. What is missing presents a relatively negligible problem compared with what remains - for those early English Victorians, and their continental and American brethren, display, in Carlyle's phrase, a "stupendous copiousness. . . . Thomas Parr (or 'Old Parr', who is said to have lived from 1483 to 1635) might begin reading in his long-clothes, and stop in his last hundred and fiftieth year without having ended". (10)

The study of Charlotte Brontë's literary culture has a special problem to face in addition to the massiveness of the contemporary materials. Until the publication of Jane Eyre and the ensuing correspondence with her publishers and with others in the literary world, there is precious little to tell us what part of the materials flowing from the presses reached her, and what of this was important to her. Miss Brontë's chief, almost her only correspondent who kept her letters during these years was Ellen Nussey, a friend and classmate from the days at Miss Margaret Wooler's school at Roe Head. While Miss Brontë acknowledges, at times with desperate self-accusation, her friend's superiority in faith and moral courage, unquestionably her intellectual and literary capabilities and interests were not such as to draw from Miss Brontë anything more than passing and superficial comments on literature.

Milestones in Miss Brontë's early literary life, her submission of part of a story to Wordsworth, (11) the completion of a particularly ambitious story, (12) both occur within days of letters to Ellen Nussey in which no reference to these events is made at all. The subject of literature is not absent from the Charlotte Brontë-Ellen Nussey correspondence, but it is to be remembered that the literary opinions expressed therein, on Miss Brontë's part continue this reticence. The letters must be treated cum grano salis for what they contain, but what they exclude should not be taken as evidence of the limits of Miss Brontë's familiarity with books. The well-known reading list, for instance, which she provided for Ellen in 1834 - "For fiction - read Scott alone; all novels after his are worthless" (13) - is, in part, tailored to Charlotte Brontë's idea of Ellen's interests, capabilities, and, perhaps, moral standards. Its significance for us is that it tells us what we might otherwise know less certainly: Charlotte Brontë, at eighteen, had read, or read of, a goodly number of contemporary novels. Yet even this should be qualified by the fact that such fiction was not come by easily at Haworth Parsonage or at Roe Head School. The library of the Keighley Mechanics' Institute, just a four-mile walk from the parsonage, and one of Miss Brontë's major sources of books, had not acquired even by 1841, much contemporary fiction. (14) Its catalogue of that year includes six works by Bulwer, of which three are novels, the latest being Eugene Aram (1832), eleven titles of James Fenimore Cooper, and twenty-six titles of Sir Walter Scott's fiction, with an additional eighteen volumes of his history and biography. Emily Brontë's diary paper dated 26 June 1837, describes Branwell reading Eugene Aram to his sister Charlotte. (15) Only through less direct evidence can we assume familiarity with other books at Keighley. Other fiction there included Maria Edgeworth's Tales, (16) Don Quixote, Gulliver's Travels, and two of Smollett's novels along with "Penny" journals and magazines, a good deal of children's fiction, and some miscellaneous and unrecognized titles with no author's name given in the catalogue. With this sort of library, although it did not exhaust Miss Brontë's resources, it became for her almost a matter of self-defense, of protection of one's literary self-esteem, to, in a moment of weakness prefer the available Scott to all his "worthless" and unavailable successors. In fact, of the twenty authors, in Poetry, History, and Biography, that she recommended to her friend at this time, fifteen were on the shelves at Keighley in 1841. That the following titles in the Keighley library do not appear in the correspondence is in no way evidence that Miss Brontë did not know them, and so a few may be listed as possible contributors to her literary culture:

Bacon's Novum Organum
Blair's Lectures on Rhetoric, 2 volumes
Burton's Anatomy of Melancholy
Locke, On the Understanding
Montesquieu, Spirit of Laws
Paley's Moral Philosophy
Seneca's Morals
Watts's Logic, or the Right Use of Reason
Gibbon's Roman Empire
Reynold's (Sir Joshua) Works
Smith's Wealth of Nations
Trollope's Domestic Manners of the Americans
Lyell's Geology

Addison's Guardian
Cicero's Orations
Coleridge's Table Talk
Howard's Beauties of Literature, 40 volumes
Manual of Phrenology
Laws of Ecclesiastical Politic

In addition to Keighley, there was at a four-mile walk in the other direction, the library of the Heaton family at Ponden House at which the Brontë children had borrowing privileges. (17) Here were available a good deal of older poetry, standard works in French history and literature, much Elizabethan drama, Voltaire's Henriade, which Miss Brontë translated in 1830, (18) and travel books including those of Chateaubriand, Parry, and Mungo Park. (19) There were no novels.

Actual ownership of books in the Brontë household was slight. In addition to his own works, (20) poems, essays and sermons on political and ecclesiastical topics, and even a didactic moral novel, the Rev. Mr. Brontë owned, among other books, his Bible and Concordance, Homer, Horace, a well-annotated copy of Graham's Modern Domestic Medicine (1824), Dryden's Virgil, the Poems of Ossian, and Pilgrim's Progress. (21) Charlotte Brontë's early books included copies of Scott, Lindley Murray's English Grammar and other school texts, Aesop's Fables, (22) the Arabian Nights, The Imitation of Christ, (23) and The Doctrine of the Passions Explained and Improved, (24) by Isaac Watts. One eventual result of this early literary culture is that references to, quotations or echoes of, classical and Biblical learning, Richardson, Scott, Swift, Thomson's Seasons, Milton, Dryden, Pope, Dr. Johnson, Henry Brooke's Fool of Quality, perhaps Shakespeare, (25) perhaps Miss Radcliffe, (26) are to be found in Jane Eyre.

While its effects cannot be as neatly pinpointed, early exposure to eighteenth-century prose left its mark on Miss Brontë's later style, generally when it is at its worst. Her fondness for sententia and personification of abstractions can be seen in her correspondence with literary people, as well as intermittently in the novels. The appeals to "Reason", "Conscience", "Nature", the use of latinate multisyllables, and unnecessary periodicity, owe much to early reading.

In addition to standard eighteenth-century literary prose works, the Keighley library held for example, prose of Isaac Watts, the noted writer of hymns (1674-1748). His On the Improvement of the Mind and Education of Youth on the shelves at Keighley was a title apt to interest the earnest young Charlotte, either as student or would-be teacher. Watts combines the principles of Locke with a gently expressed but austere Calvinism, and the result is often something that recalls aspects of Jane Eyre and Lucy Snowe. Watts is fearful of amateur theatricals, and adamant against "midnight assemblies, play-houses, gaming-tables, and masquerades". (27) Such typical Protestant rigor, imbued early by Charlotte Brontë from reading as well from her Aunt and from the teachers at Cowan Bridge, (28) is seen, either adhered to or trespassed with excitement, in the novels. Here is a characteristic passage:

> Children should be instructed in the art of self-government. They should be taught as far as possible, to govern their thoughts, to use their wills, to be determined by the light of their understandings, and not by headstrong and foolish humours; they should learn to keep the lower powers of nature under the command of their reason: they should be instructed to regulate their senses, their imagination, their appetites, and their passions. (29)

This is to become a central motif of the novels, particularly of Jane Eyre, in which such precepts are tested. Lucy Snowe in Villette tests the limits of the following:

Let children be taught early, that the little things for which they are zealous, for which they grieve or rejoice so impetuously, are not worthy of these affections of their souls. . . . Inform them what a happiness it is to have few desires and few aversions, for this will preserve them from a multitude of sorrows, and keep their temper always serene and calm. Persuade them never to raise their hopes very high of things in this world and then they will never meet with great disappointments. (30)

3

Another category of literature to which Charlotte Brontë was exposed - probably early and to a considerable extent - was that of France. In addition to the French classics at Ponden House, and French school texts, there was modern French fiction. A letter to Ellen Nussey of August, 1840 contains this intriguing paragraph: "I have got another bale of French books from Gomersal - containing upwards of 40 volumes - I have read about half - they are like the rest clever wicked sophistical and immoral - the best of it is they give one a thorough idea of France and Paris - and are the best substitute for French conversation I have ever met with." (31) Gomersal was the home of their friends Mary and Martha Taylor whose father - Joshua - had commercial interests in France and Brussels, and who traveled there frequently. What this "bale" of books contained is not known directly, nor do we have clear information about other such shipments. There are no other references to French books until Miss Brontë is herself in Belgium, and working with Constantin Heger to improve her skill in French composition, by imitation of de la Vigne's poetry, Guizot, Bossuet, and Victor Hugo. (32) Heger's guidance went beyond simple matters of grammar and verb forms. His notations on her <u>devoirs</u> deal with principles of literary composition: "When you are writing, place your argument first in cool, precise language; but when you have thrown the reins on the neck of your imagination, do not pull her up to reason." (33) A most interesting <u>devoir</u> is "Le Nid", dated 30 April 184(2?), (34) just two months after Charlotte and Emily Brontë arrived in Brussels. As might be expected, the interest lies in Heger's comments on the little essay. On the fourth side, in the remaining space and over his signature, he writes his "<u>Conseil</u>". I translate rather freely, bracketing restorations of the not clearly decipherable:

How very much importance you must give to your details as you unfold your subject! You must sacrifice, without pity, everything that does not contribute to clarity, to verisimilitude, and to the effect (<u>l'effet</u>). You should vigorously exclude everything which (detracts from your principal idea), so that the impression you give is highly colored (<u>colorée</u>) and vivid. (Faith? Joy?) is a good thing in its place, but producing the half-tint (<u>demi-teinte</u>), is not what gives your style, nor what gives painting, unity, perspective, and effect.
Read Lamartine's fourteenth Harmonie: As to reaching the heights (<u>l'infini</u>), we will arrange to do that together, by paying attention to the details.

It is difficult to believe that this advice was occasioned simply by "Le Nid". The speculation that Miss Brontë showed him at this time some of her Angrian extravagances, perhaps some early poetry, is somewhat strengthened.
Alphonse de Lamartine's <u>Harmonies Poétiques et Religieuses</u> (1830) were widely acclaimed from the first, and ran to a fifth edition in less than three months. (35) An earlier work, <u>Le Dernier Chant du Pèlerinage d'Harold</u> (1825) had been a tribute to Byron, dead the year before, a hero at Missolonghi. But the <u>Harmonies</u> find in the Byronic situation, that cycle of infinite aspiration and profound dejection, a solemn religious consolation. In the fourteenth <u>Harmonie</u>, "L'infini dans les cieux", the poet examines the skies and is over-

whelmed by his own sense of smallness and mortality: "Oh! que tes cieux sont grands! et que l'esprit de l'homme / Plie et tombe de haut, mon Dieu! quand il te nomme!" (ll. 145-146). His attention turns to the insects below him on the grass, as insignificant to him as he to God. But God cares for "cet insecte invisible, / Rampant dans les sillons" (ll. 125-126), and so the poet reasons: "Il est donc aussi grand d'être homme que soleil!" (l. 200). He ends with exclamations of praise and a biblical echo:

> Que cette humilité qui devant lui m'abaisse
> Soit un sublime hommage, et non une tristesse;
> Et que sa volonté, trop haute pour nos yeux,
> Soit faite sur la terre ainsi que dans les cieux.
> (ll. 213-216)

Such consolation was the avowed purpose of the <u>Harmonies</u>, (36) and the source of their early acclaim. Perhaps this played a part in Heger's recommendation. Religious melancholy was not unknown to Charlotte Brontë. Otherwise the poem is well constructed, its movements of thought clearly signaled and straightforward, and with nothing indefensibly digressive.

But the importance of the poem to Heger as to Miss Brontë and to us, was certainly its astonishing opening. Here "l'infini", the most extravagant visual effects, is achieved by realistic methods, by exquisite and single-minded attention to observed details. It is well worth quoting:

> C'est une nuit d'été, nuit dont les vastes ailes
> Font jaillir dans l'azur des milliers d'étincelles;
> Qui, ravivant le ciel comme un miroir terni
> Permet à l'oeil charmé d'en sonder l'infini;
> Nuit où le firmament, dépouillé de nuages,
> De ce livre de feu rouvre toutes les pages:
> Sur le dernier sommet des monts, d'où le regard,
> Dans un double horizon se répand au hasard,
> Je m'assieds en silence, et laisse ma penseé
> Flotter comme une mer où la lune est bercée.
>
> L'harmonieux éther, dans ses vagues d'azur,
> Enveloppe les monts d'un fluide plus pur;
> Leurs contours qu'il éteint, leurs cimes qu'il efface,
> Semblent nager dans l'air et trembler dans l'espace,
> Comme on voit jusqu'au fond d'une mer en repos
> L'ombre de son rivage onduler sous les flots.
> Sous ce jour sans rayon, plus serein qu'une aurore,
> A l'oeil contemplatif la terre semble éclore;
> Elle déroule au loin ses horizons divers
> Où se joua la main qui sculpta l'univers.
> Là, semblable à la vague, une colline ondule;
> Là le coteau poursuit le coteau qui recule,
> Et le vallon, voilé de verdoyants rideaux,
> Se creuse comme un lit pour l'ombre et pour les eaux;
> Ici s'étend la plaine, où, comme sur la grève,
> La vague des épis s'abaisse et se relève;
> Là, pareil au serpent dont les noeuds sont rompus,
> Le fleuve, renouant ses flots interrompus,
> Trace à son cours d'argent des méandres sans nombre,
> Se perd sous la colline et reparaît dans l'ombre;
> Comme un nuage noir, les profondes forêts,
> D'une tache grisâtre ombragent les guérets,
> Et plus loin, où la plage en croissant se reploie,

> Où le regard confus dans les vapeurs se noie,
> Un golfe de la mer, d'îles entrecoupé,
> Des blanc reflets du ciel par la lune frappé,
> Comme un vaste miroir brisé par la poussière,
> Réfléchit dans l'obscur des fragments de lumière.

As a recent editor says, the fantastic remains firmly anchored to the real. (37)

Heger seems to have prescribed wisely for his pupil's tendency to undisciplined "Imagination", and more generally been of help in directing her to think of literature as a thing carefully designed and constructed, not merely as an effusion of personal emotion. His guidance in this regard was most probably the most important, if not the only critical help the young authoress received, and its effect seems to have been great. Not that the Angrian narratives had not been already moving clearly toward realism in the 1830's, but after Heger's tutelage our best knowledge is that Miss Brontë occupied herself with at first abortive attempts to write naturalistic fiction and with poetry - poetry which frequently takes off from a realistic or even domestic base to a visionary or supernatural climax for which psychological motivation has been prepared. It is an attempt at controlling the use and the effect of the highly imaginative, an attempt infrequent in the early juvenilia.

Charlotte Brontë's diary fragment of late 1839, the so-called "Farewell to Angria", shows the grip the Angrian cycle had on her, and the void its absence would create despite her deep desire "to quit for a while that burning clime where we have sojourned too long".

> I have now written a great many books and for a long time I have dwelt upon the same characters and scenes and subjects. . . . My readers have been habituated to one set of features, which they have seen now in profile, now in full face, now in outline, and again in finished painting, . . . but we must change, for the eye is tired of the picture so oft recurring and now so familiar.
>
> Yet do not urge me too fast, reader; it is no easy theme to dismiss from my imagination the images which have filled it so long. . . . When I depart from these I feel almost as if I stood on the threshold of a home and were bidding farewell to its inmates. When I strive to conjure up new images I feel as if I had got into a distant country where every face was unknown and the character of all the population an enigma which it would take much study to comprehend and much talent to expound. (38)

It is not too much to say that what Charlotte Brontë learned and experienced in Brussels provided not only much of the material to replace that of the Angrian cycle, but something too of the knowledge of literature as "craft" which made the artistic use of this material possible.

In addition to assigning and correcting her <u>devoirs</u>, Heger lent Miss Brontë books and spoke with her, presumably about them, while she reciprocated by giving English lessons to him. (39) What books were given we discover in her letter to him of October, 1844: "Je viens de faire relier tous les livres que vous m'avez donnée quand j'étais à Bruxelles; j'ai un plaisir à les considérer - cela fait tout un petite bibliothèque - Il y a d'abord les ouvrages complet de Bernadin St. Pierre - Les Pensées de Pascal - un livre de poësie, deux livres allemands - et (ce qui vaut tout le reste) deux discours de Monsieur le Professeur Heger - pronouncés à la distribution des Prix de l'Athénée royal." (40) The bound set of St. Pierre turns up again, along with a set of Racine, in the possession of Louis Moore, in the twenty-seventh chapter of <u>Shirley</u>, where we also find references to La Fontaine, Corneille, and Bossuet. Miss Brontë's reticence in literary matters is nowhere clearer shown than in the absence of references to these authors, clearly important to her, in all her letters, not only those to Ellen Nussey. Lamartine alone is mentioned, (41) but only in reference to his idealistic political ideas.

The abiding influence however of Lamartine, and of Bernardin de St. Pierre, whose Harmonies de la Nature were a major influence on him, (42) is clearly seen in Miss Brontë's novels. Let us bear in mind the opening of "L'infini dans les cieux", quoted above, and this from one of St. Pierre's many scientifically oriented observations of the colors of the sky:

> C'est aux vapeurs aquatics de l'air qui décomposent les rayons du soleil, que l'aurore doit ses magnifiques couleurs. Ces couleurs célestes se manifestent d'abord à l'horizon par la couleur blanche, qui est celle de la lumière pure. On lui a donné le nom d'aube, du mot latin alba, qui signifie blanche. Cette blancheur, en s'élevant au-dessus de l'horizon, se décompose en différentes nuances de jaune qui parviennent au jaune doré, qui est en général la couleur des rayons du soleil dans notre atmosphère. Ce jaune doré, relevé d'un peu de vermillon, forme la couleur de l'aurore proprement dite, et s'élève ensuite, par différentes teintes de rouges, jusqu'au carmin au zenith: de là, descendant par les nuances du pourpre et du violet, il arrive au bleu vers le couchant, et enfin du bleu au noir au bleu où la nuit étend encore ses voiles. Toutes les teintes imaginables sont composées de ces cinq couleurs primitives. (43)

Here is one of many examples of what Charlotte Brontë does with such materials:

> I leaned over a parapeted wall; there was space below me, depth I could not fathom, but hearing an endless dash of waves, I believed it to be the sea; sea spread to the horizons; sea of changeful green and intense blue: all was soft in the distance; all vapour-veiled. A spark of gold glistened on the line between water and air, floated up, approached, enlarged, changed; the object hung mid-way between heaven and earth, under the arch of the rainbow; the soft but dusk clouds diffused behind. It hovered as on wings; pearly, fleecy, gleaming air streamed like raiment round it; light, tinted with carnation, coloured what seemed face and limbs; a large star shone with still lustre on an angel's forehead; an upraised arm and hand, glancing like a ray, pointed to the bow overhead, and a voice in my heart whispered -
>   "Hope smiles on Effort!" (XIX; p. 188)

This is a dream of William Crimsworth in The Professor, its motivation clearly being an exhilarating meeting he had just had with his beloved Frances. The visionary figure in this sort of setting, common in the poems and in dreams in other novels, particularly Jane Eyre, is not derived from the French poets, but one can suggest Miss Brontë's familiarity with the Bible, especially Revelations, her knowledge of Scottish, Evangelical, and Elizabethan supernaturalism, and perhaps her interest in the paintings of John Martin, (44) as influencing, but of course not determining factors.

The French poets' influence, with an example of Miss Brontë's peculiar idiosyncrasy, the excessive use of alliteration, can be found here in Jane Eyre: "Where the sun had gone down in simple state - pure of the pomp of clouds - spread a solemn purple, burning with the light of red jewel and furnace flame at one point, on one hill-peak, and extending high and wide, soft and still softer, over half heaven. The east had its own charm of fine, deep blue, and its own modest gem, a rising and solitary star: soon it would boast the moon; but she was yet beneath the horizon" (XXIII; II, 10). In Villette we find this: "In an instant we were out of doors; the cool, calm night revived me somewhat. It was moonless, but the reflex from the many glowing windows lit the court brightly, and even the alleys - dimly. Heaven was cloudless, and grand with the quiver of its living fires. How soft are the nights of the continent! How bland, balmy, safe! No sea-fog; no chilling damp: mistless as noon, and fresh as morning" (XIV; I, 171-172). Here the sensitive notation of night is used as a revealing psychological insight, and as a symbolic contrast to the attic in which Lucy has been memorizing her part for that evening's performance, and to the English night.

Note the word "reflex", an "alien" and, in this sense "rare" word to the Oxford English Dictionary, which cites for it another appearance in Villette. Miss Brontë reveals its origin in this passage from Shirley: "A calm day had settled into a crystalline evening; the world wore a North Pole colouring: all its lights and tints looked like the 'reflets' * of white, or violet, or pale green gems. The hills wore a lilac-blue; the setting sun had purple in its red; the sky was ice, all silvered azure; when the stars rose, they were of white crystal - not gold; gray, or cerulean, or faint emerald hues - cool, pure, and transparent - tinged the mass of the landscape" (XXXII; II, 272). The asterisk on "reflets" directs us to Miss Brontë's footnote, one that survived her deletion of footnotes in the second edition: "Find me an English word as good, reader, and I will gladly dispense with the French word. Reflections won't do." We recall the climax of the passage from Lamartine: "Des blancs reflets du ciel par la lune frappé", and do not wonder at the unforgettable associations it continued to have for Miss Brontë.

4

It is unlikely that Heger's recommended reading included the novels of Balzac or George Sand, but whether as early as those bales of French books from Gomersal, or after the final departure from Brussels, Miss Brontë did read these authors. (45) By 1846 she felt she knew enough French fiction to allow Crimsworth, in The Professor, to say this:

> I was no pope - I could not boast infallibility: in short, if I stayed, the probability was that, in three months' time, a practical modern French novel would be in full process of concoction under the roof of the unsuspecting Pelet. Now, modern French novels are not to my taste, either practically or theoretically. Limited as had yet been my experience of life, I had once had the opportunity of contemplating, near at hand, an example of the results produced by a course of interesting and romantic domestic treachery. No golden halo of fiction was about this example, I saw it bare and real, and it was very loathsome. (XX; 197)

Another reference to French novels is found in Shirley. Mr. Sympson confronts the independent Miss Keeldar with this evidence of her moral weakness: "You read French. Your mind is poisoned with French novels. You have imbibed French principles" (XXXI; II, 254). Sympson's stance is clearly meant to reflect his Philistinism, thus indicating Charlotte Brontë's increased esteem for French novels, perhaps the result of increased familiarity, since at least the letter to Ellen Nussey about them. She wrote to Heger in 1845, assuring him that "I read all the French books I can get, and learn daily a portion by heart. . . I love French for your sake with all my heart and soul." (46) And regularly, at least in 1845, Miss Brontë was receiving French newspapers from Ellen Nussey. (47)

There was something daring, in the 1840's about such an avowal of appreciation of French letters, for a critical argument was raging over the mass importation and sale of novels often thought degraded and degrading. While a shop in the Burlington Arcade, catering to the rage for French novels, sold nothing else, (48) critics campaigned against them. As early as 1833, the rage and the reaction was evidenced in a review of George Sand's just published Lélia:

> This is the book of the season - of the month - of the day; but, as we have not,

in truth, cast its nativity, we had better not offer any prophetic anticipations as to the duration of its fame: enough, then that it is the book of the hour - the fashionable novelty - the romance the most sought after in the reading rooms, and the most talked of in the literary saloons, of Paris. . . . We cannot look upon it but as an "unreal mockery" - a bold, brazen paradox, born, fostered, and nourished, in the very hot-bed of scepticism, in the whirl and turbulence of Parisian politics, manners, and questionable morality. . . . We shall not again dip our pen in this mire of blood and dirt, over which, by a strange perversity of feeling, the talent of the writer, and that writer a woman! has contrived to throw a lurid, fearful, and unhallowed light. (49)

In the 1840's, Thackeray and others attacked, parodied, and disdained Sand and other contemporary French novelists, on both moral and aesthetic grounds. (50) Thackeray finds Balzac "not fit for the salon", (51) to which The Athenaeum adds this: "Without hazardous prophecy or prognostic, this Balzac library seems to us, as a sign of the times, infinitely more discouraging than the ravings of Sue's benevolence or the evangelical Pantheism of George Sand." (52) And French fiction of less stature than these, full of "sadism and coarseness" was being imported and translated for the less literary reader. (53)

The widespread critical attention paid to the French novels is no more than an especially clear instance of the growing interest in the moral affect of novels and novel-reading. Production of novels in England, responding to the demands of new readers, and more dedicated ones, increased about four-fold in the thirty years after 1820, (54) and to the production of some one hundred new novels in 1850 must be added periodical fiction and the mass reprinting of earlier works. Bentley's Standard Novels produced cheap editions, in the forties, of Mrs. Gore, Theodore Hook, J.F. Cooper, and lesser writers. (55) The Railway Library, in 1848, added another channel of distribution to the expanding private circulating libraries, (56) and novel-reading was for large numbers of people an obsession and their chief delight.

While Scott and his imitators remained the most widely sold and read - Scott's novels, poems, and the biography by John Gibson Lockhart, accounted for the sale of nearly 150,000 sets between 1829 and 1851 (57) - their sway was under heavy attack in the better periodicals. The prime exhibition in the downgrading of Scott was probably Carlyle's famous article, ostensibly on Lockhart's biography, in the London and Westminster Review in 1837, and Thackeray made it one of his prime concerns to deprecate and parody a wide range of fashionable fiction.

Implicit in such criticism is the faith that the novel need not be merely a frivolous entertainment, and that novel-writing could and should be more than a mercenary art. As the morally unimpeachable Scott receded from the forefront of fashionable and intellectual interest, many types of fiction, most owing him some debt, sought to fill the void. Critics, then and now, classify the output by their leading characteristics, and we have historical novels, "Silver-Fork" or "fashionable" novels, (58) "Condition-of-England" novels, "Newgate" novels, (59) and, reflecting the great popularity of female authors, the "she-novel". (60)

The characterization is generally by subject matter as is the typical criticism of individual works. Verisimilitude, accuracy of details and dialogue, in a word, "realism", is the criteria by which critics, Thackeray prominent among them, judge. It is a moral criteria fully as much as an aesthetic one - for the "Newgate" novel which misrepresents and glorifies vice and the vicious, the "Silver-Fork" novel which falsifies the life of the rich and panders to snobbery - have deleterious moral effects. Some criticism makes moral "uplift" the stated and primary desideratum, this being a common Evangelical position as novels gained acceptance in those quarters. There was, of course, as always, the criticism of special pleading - High Tory, Benthamite, etc., at which we may laugh with Thackeray, while bearing in mind that it is part of the widespread, earnest, energetic, and many-faceted overall attempt to discover the place of the Novel in literature and the life of England. Here is Thackeray:

> This is a favorite method with many critics - viz. to find fault with a book for what it does not give, as thus - "Lady Smigsmag's new novel is amusing, but lamentably deficient in geological information." "Dr. Swishtail's Elucidations of the Digamma show much sound scholarship, but infer a total absence of humour." And "Mr. Lever's tales are trashy and worthless, for his facts are not borne (sic) out by any authority, and he gives us no information upon the political state of Ireland. Oh! our country; our green and beloved, our beautiful and oppressed. . . ." (61)

5

How much of the foregoing was the aspiring novelist of Haworth Parsonage aware of? Although some criticism of fiction appeared in Bulwer's England and the English, a book in the Keighley Library, and in other volumes, it is the periodical press that largely disseminates it. London, a city in the first half of the 1840's, of almost two million souls, was turning out 227 different monthly journals, 38 quarterly publications, well over 20 million copies of weekly publications every year, not to mention the daily press or the important contributions from Edinburgh. (62) How much of this material, how much of the best of it, found its way to Haworth (population 6,303), (63) and into Charlotte Brontë's hands?

Blackwood's Edinburgh Magazine was an important part of the early life of the Brontë children, and back issues as well as current numbers were on hand at the parsonage. (64) Blackwood's is imitated in miniature facsimiles called "Blackwood's Young Men's Magazine", written and edited by Charlotte and Branwell in the late twenties. It is to Blackwood's that Branwell presented himself as a candidate for literary fame in 1835 and 1837, although by then a change had come to the reading habits of the family. Miss Brontë, from Roe Head, writes to her brother in 1831: "I am extremely glad that aunt has consented to take in 'Fraser's Magazine', for though I know from your description of its general contents it will be rather uninteresting when compared with 'Blackwood', still it will be better than remaining the whole year without being able to obtain a sight of any periodical publication whatever; and such would assuredly be our case, as in the little wild, moorland village where we reside, there would be no possibility of borrowing or obtaining a work of that description from a circulating library." (65) Evidently the company of more cosmopolitan schoolmates is responsible for this uncharacteristic and overstated description of the isolation of Haworth.

The reading of Fraser's Magazine for Town and Country and nothing else, in the thirties and early forties, would have made Miss Brontë very much au courant with regard to literary affairs. A continuing feature was the "Gallery of Literary Characters", short and often flippant one-page literary biographies, which it is surprising to learn was an innovation in English journalism. (66) A companion feature, "Fraser's Maids of Honour", dealt with woman writers, but this courtesy did not prevent forthrightness such as the following: "Nothing can compensate in the novel for want of experience. And therefore is it, that the attempt of ladies generally to write of 'many-figured life', is so utterly cold, incapable, and ridiculous." (67) Charlotte Brontë's reiterated statements, in the later letters, that she could and would only write from her experience, limited as it was, was in keeping with this common critical precept.

Thackeray was a regular though anonymous contributor to Fraser's as critic and as author. In 1838 his "Yellowplush Correspondence" is running, in 1844 Barry Lyndon begins. Between them Catherine and A Shabby Genteel Story appeared. Carlyle's Sartor Resartus made its first appearance in Fraser's (November, 1833 to August, 1834). And despite the typical critic's lament over the large number of novels sent him for review, a broad spectrum of fiction is reviewed, quoted at length, and its plot and characters described. Articles of thirty or more two-column pages, treating six to twelve novels, are frequent. Mercenary motives of contemporary novelists, critics, and publishers, immoral tendencies, sensationalism, and sentimentalism, are severely castigated. But on this wealth of material in Fraser's Charlotte Brontë makes no comment. Surely she read some of it, perhaps she read most of it - her literary references in the correspondence after Jane Eyre's publication surely reflect more than the results of the day-to-day reading of those years - but no more than this can be stated with any confidence.

It is tempting to speculate on her seeing Barry Lyndon, for this, like Thackeray's Henry Esmond, is technically of great interest, and may profitably be related to The Professor, Jane Eyre, and Villette, as Vanity Fair may be related to Shirley. If, a few months after her return from Belgium, Fraser's was on hand, Miss Brontë would surely have been interested in Titmarsh's impressions of Brussels in it:

In the Park is a little theatre, a café somewhat ruinous, a little palace for the little king of this little kingdom, some smart public buildings (with S. P. Q. B. emblazoned on them, at which pompous inscription one cannot help laughing), and other rows of houses somewhat ressembling a little Rue de Rivoli. Whether from my own natural greatness and magnanimity, or from that handsome share of national conceit that every Englishman possesses, my impressions of the city are certainly anything but respectful. It has an absurd kind of Lilliput look with it. There are soldiers, just as in Paris, better dressed, and doing a vast deal of drumming and bustle; and yet, somehow, far from being frightened at them, I feel inclined to laugh in their faces. (68)

If "Villette" is a deprecatory reference to the "great capital of the great kingdom of Labassecour", (69) the conception may owe something to Thackeray's diminution and his Swiftian reference.

At the close of 1846, Charlotte Brontë had this advice for Ellen Nussey: "I can fancy that you have not much in common with those you see at Oundle . . . regard all their ways in the light of fresh experience for you - if you see any honey amongst them, gather it, and never mind their snobbishness (see 'Punch')."(70) The editors of the Shakespeare Head "Letters" annotate the mention of Punch by reference to a paper there which elucidates the reference to "honey". More to our purpose is the fact that what was, much revised, to become The Book of Snobs, had been running in Punch since February 28 of that year. It was Thackeray's first widely-recognized piece, (71) and Miss Brontë's use of the new word "snobbishness", (72) in her letter strengthens the reasonable assumption that she too had seen it.

Chapter sixteen of "The Snobs of England, by One of Themselves", treats of literary snobs. If Charlotte Brontë had remained a literary innocent until now, her innocence would not survive this:

If anybody wants to know how intimately authors are connected with the fashionable world, they have but to read the genteel novels. What refinement and delicacy pervades the works of MRS. BARNABY! What a delightful good company do you meet with in MRS. ARMYTAGE! She seldom introduces you to anybody under a Marquis! I don't know anything more delicious than the pictures of genteel life in Ten Thousand a Year, except perhaps the Young Duke, and Coningsby. There's a modest grace about them, and an air of easy high fashion, which only belongs to blood, my dear Sir - to true blood.

And what linguists many of our writers are! LADY BULWER, LADY LONDONDERRY, SIR EDWARD himself - they write the French language with a luxurious elegance and ease, which sets them far above their continental rivals, of whom no one (except PAUL DE KOCK), knows a word of English.

And what Britton can read without enjoyment the works of JAMES, so admirable for terseness; and the playful humour and dazzling off-hand lightness of AINSWORTH? Among other humorists, one might glance at a JERROLD, the chivalrous advocate of Toryism and Church and State; at a BECKETT, with a lightsome pen, but a savage earnestness of purpose; a JEAMES, whose pure style, and wit unmingled with buffoonery, was relished by a congenial public.

Speaking of critics, perhaps there never was a review that has done so much for literature as the admirable Quarterly. It has its prejudices, to be sure, as which of us have not? It goes out of its way to abuse a great man, or lays mercilessly on to such pretenders as KEATS and TENNYSON; but on the other hand, it is the friend of all young authors, and has marked and nurtured all the rising talent of the country. It is loved by everybody. There, again, is Blackwood's Magazine - conspicuous for modest elegance and amiable satire; that review never passes the bounds of politeness in a joke. It is the arbiter of manners; and, while gently exposing the foibles of Londoners (for whom the beaux esprits of Edinburgh entertain a justifiable contempt), it is never coarse in its fun. The fiery enthusiasm of the Athenaeum is well known; and the bitter wit of the too difficult Literary Gazette. The Examiner is perhaps too timid, and the Spectator too boisterous in its praise - but who can carp at these minor faults? No, no; the critics of England and the authors of England are unrivalled as a body; and hence it becomes impossible for us to find fault with them. (73)

The assurance with which Miss Brontë refers Ellen to Punch suggests that the political and literary allusions of that extraordinary "London Charivari" were generally understood by them. While predominantly politically oriented in those years, Punch did not miss the chances for fun that the literary situation afforded. Allusions to Dickens indicate his preëminent place in contemporary fiction. Sairey Gamp and Betsey Prig are given commemoration in a wonderful full-page drawing. (74) Oliver Twist's famous "More please" scene gets full-page illustration with the figures labeled with the names of political personalities, and a comic parallel is drawn. (75) A sketch of Pecksniff appears over the report that Dickens is going to "apply to the Court of Chancery for an injunction to prevent Sir Robert Peel continuing any longer to personate, in his capacity of Premier, the character of Mr. Pecksniff, as delineated in Martin Chuzzlewit, that character being copyright." (76) Dickens is warned that he has no case: Peel has been playing Pecksniff so long that he antedates all Dickens' work - he "is the original Pecksniff". Could our two readers of Punch, one of whom at least had long been interested in politics and particularly in Peel's career, (77) have seen this fun and not read their Dickens? Yet if Charlotte Brontë knew Chuzzlewit and Oliver Twist no direct record of that fact survives.

6

The last important documents we have, on the question of the limits of Miss Brontë's early literary culture, are her letters to Aylott and Jones, publishers of the 1846 volume of poetry. She seems in them to be aware of the importance of getting review copies to the right journals quickly. She knows that advertising can influence the appearance and verdict of reviews. She plans to spend more for additional advertising if early reviews are favorable, yet is realistic enough to know that, "If, on the other hand they should pass unnoticed or be condemned, I consider it would be quite useless to advertise as there is nothing either in the title of the work or the names of the authors to attract attention from a single individual." (78) She seems to know, in short, a good deal about the devious machinations of the London literary market place, (79) and lays out, in these respects, a reasonable if conservative program.

Review copies, a total of two Pounds of advertising, and her hopes, she directs initially to eight magazines and two newspapers. Four publications are given preference, by their prime position in her letter above a long separating dash. These are <u>Colburn's New Monthly</u>, <u>Bentley's Miscellany</u>, <u>Hood's Magazine</u>, and <u>Jerrold's Shilling Magazine</u>, (80) four periodicals that one would assume from this that she knew. The <u>New Monthly</u> ran travel pieces, many by Mrs. Trollope, and serial fiction of a miscellaneous but generally masculine order. "Confessions of a Keyhole", a reminder that this old form was still popular, and "Reminiscences of a Medical Student", are typical titles. (81) Books were reviewed mainly in "Literature of the Month", which ran from ten to fourteen pages, of which no more than a third dealt with poetry, and that typically older or by established current writers. Yet very brief notices, three or four on one page, of new and unknown poets, generally of the "Album" variety, do appear and are done with surprising receptivity.

Rough as much of the magazine was, the <u>New Monthly</u> could say this of Dickens' <u>A Christmas Carol</u>: "This Christmas Carol - it is not only the best that was ever carolled, but it will better all others for the time to come - nay, it will better Christmas itself". (82) The <u>New Monthly</u> gives considerable space, as do <u>Hood's</u> and <u>Jerrold's</u>, to Disraeli's novels: <u>Sybil</u>, the publishing sensation of 1845, following the successful <u>Coningsby</u> of 1844. If Miss Brontë read at all in literary periodicals, we must disbelieve her protestation to Ellen Nussey in 1845: "I know of no new books - unless it be <u>The Chimes</u>, by Dickens, which I have not read". (83)

<u>Bentley's Miscellany</u> specialized in serial fiction of the "Newgate" and adventure types. It had however carried Dickens' "Mudfog" papers (1837-38) and <u>Oliver Twist</u> (1837-39), Dickens himself being an editor from 1836 to 1840. It published some poetry, but preferred travel sketches, personal anecdotes, and "curiosities". Its literary interest is mainly with older rather than contemporary writers, and its tone is well characterized by the continuing feature, "Literary Retrospects by a Middle Aged Man". (84) A rather strange magazine from which to expect a favorable notice of the Bells' poetry. And much the same can be said of <u>Hood's Magazine and Comic Miscellany</u>. "Sensations of Sixteen, by a Very Old Man", and "The Modern Othello, A Tale Founded on Facts", are typical titles of its serial fiction, but it did present considerable poetry, including some by Browning in 1844.

<u>Douglas Jerrold's Shilling Magazine</u> was Miss Brontë's best choice in her initial selection. "Newgate", and what one might call "Novelty" fiction are the staple items, but good space is allotted to reviews of current books, such as Emerson's <u>Essays</u>, a biography of Jean Paul Richter, and novels by such as G.P.R. James and Fredricka Bremer. (85) Poetry was published here and regularly reviewed. <u>Jerrold's</u> and the <u>New Monthly</u> might well have chosen to notice the Bells' poems, and to do so briefly and favorably. The other two journals however remain enigmatic selections. It may be that having heard of these magazines, perhaps as respectable but less awesome institutions than the leading journals, Miss Brontë simply took a blind chance. Her careful disbursement of copies and advertising funds militates against such a belief in what would have been an essentially haphazard selection. The balance is, for this writer at least, tipped by a request she made to Aylott and Jones for a copy of one - and only one - of the ten magazines she eventually selected, this "in case it should contain a notice of the work". (86) The other nine, one gathers, she could procure locally.

Any familiarity at all with the four magazines in question would provide, if nothing else previously had done so, a forceful introduction to the dominating mass of low-grade fiction of the forties. The respectability that the Waverley novels are so often said to have given to the novel is hardly in evidence in all but the best fiction and criticism of the period. Jane Austen's work was not widely known - Miss Brontë did not then know Pride and Prejudice (87) and there is no reason to believe she knew any of Austen - Thackeray's masterpieces were yet unwritten, and his Catherine and Barry Lyndon, seen in Fraser's and perhaps only in part by a relatively inexperienced reader of contemporary novels, might well not have been distinguishable from the very sort of fiction they were designed to counteract. Despite the adoration Dickens gained with Pickwick and the Christmas books, his reputation was not uniformly high. Aside from the frequent complaints that he wrote too fast, and that he romanticized the low and overworked the pathetic, his very popularity militated against serious acceptance in important quarters. (88) If Francis Jeffrey wept over Little Nell, Dickens was treated with coolness, at times with contempt, by those arbiters The Edinburgh Review, Blackwood's, and, with exceptions, Fraser's. (89) Comparing Scott, then, with the hordes of his followers, imperfectly known, Miss Brontë might well say in 1844 what she said a decade earlier: "For fiction - read Scott alone; all novels after his are worthless."

The final complication in our examination of Charlotte Brontë and the contemporary literary press, is that the Keighley library catalogue for 1841 shows twenty-two periodicals on hand. Only one listing is dated: "Monthly Teacher, for 1829." But alongside the Temperance Star and Printing Machine, were copies, full runs for all the listings tell us, of the Literary Gazette, Westminster Review, and Quarterly Review. None of Miss Brontë's first four selected recipients of the Poems however, were on hand here.

We should also recall here that the reading of one "three-decker" novel often provided information about many others, through publishers' advertisements bound into them. The first edition of Jane Eyre, for instance, carried, at the end of the first volume, a thirty-two page dated catalogue of the wares of Smith, Elder, and Company. The novels of G.P.R. James, Leigh Hunt's Selections from the English Poets, the anonymous first two volumes of Modern Painters, and works of science, history, theology, and travel, are announced here, with excerpts from favorable reviews. Shilling prints of "Eminent Authors" are offered for sale. Carlyle, Dickens, Wordsworth, Tennyson, Browning - Smith, Elder knew well who the age's immortals were.

7

The preceding pages have sought to discover and illustrate what I have called Charlotte Brontë's "literary culture", in the years before the publication of Jane Eyre. From that point on, Miss Brontë has books and magazines thrust upon her, particularly by her friends at Smith, Elder. She has literary friends and correspondents. She has, for the first time, a relatively full purse, which allows travel and the purchase of whatever literary materials she cares to see. But by this time also, two of her four novels have been written, and a third, Villette, has its roots deep in the earlier period. More generally, one can say that her essential literary culture had, for the most part, already been formed.

The extent of Miss Brontë's reading in standard and older authors has been suggested, as has her exposure to some modern French literature and to the guidance of Constantin Heger. Less immediately clear, yet of at least equal importance is the extent of her knowledge of the theory and practice of contemporary English fiction. The absence of comment before 1847, on these matters, misleading as I believe it to be, is nonetheless strikingly complete. That specific data on Miss Brontë's early reading of particular works of contemporary fiction is lacking does not mean that she did none, nor does the impracticality of traditional studies in literary filiation require us to treat her novels in a historical vacuum. As I have been at pains to demonstrate, contemporary fiction and critical response to it was no esoteric or specialist interest, but an issue of public concern. The novel was not only on its way to becoming the universal literary form for the mass markets, but was already widely held to be, at least potentially, a serious artistic and intellectual pursuit. Fiction and criticism of fiction was available in large quantity from innumerable sources. It was ubiquitous and unavoidable. Any efforts made to find it would be productive. This fiction, however, was preponderantly of low grade, and not infrequently meretricious - either artistically, morally, or commercially - and the better critics knew this and said it. Thackeray was merely the genius among the group of writers of the day who devoted themselves to amelioration of the low estate of fiction.

Another genius, Carlyle, came to despise modern fiction and had this to say, in 1847, to a young man who asked him for advice about joining the profession of literature:

> By quitting reality again, and taking in to some popular department of literary rope-dancing, a person of real toughness and assiduity, not ashamed to feel himself a slave, but able even to think himself free and a king in rope-dancing well paid, contrives, with moderate talent otherwise, if he be really tough and assiduous, to gain sometimes considerable wages; in other cases dies of heartbreak, drinking, and starvation. That really is his economic position, so far as I have seen it. But for a man really intent to do a man's work in literature in these times, I should say that even with the highest talent he might have need to be fed oftentimes like Elijah, by the ravens. (90)

Charlotte Brontë is on record as not liking the style of Carlyle, (91) but she shared with him an intense disdain for the meretricious before her eyes, and an intense faith in the better future in her mind's eye. Both imbibed stringent Protestant zeal early and were exposed to the exercise of Evangelical rhetoric. Probably something of Carlyle's work was known to her, for Jane Eyre, writing her autobiography ten years after her marriage to Rochester, after praising "the golden age of modern literature", the age of Scott, goes on to this close approximation of Carlyle's manner:

> Alas! the readers of our era are less favoured. But, Courage! I will not pause either to accuse or repine. I know poetry is not dead, nor genius lost; nor has Mammon gained power over either, to bind or slay: they will both assert their existence, their presence, their liberty and strength one day. Powerful angels, safe in Heaven! they smile when sordid souls triumph, and feeble ones weep over their destruction. Poetry destroyed? Genius banished? No! Mediocrity, no: do not let envy prompt you to the thought. No; they not only live, but reign, and redeem: and without their divine influence spread everywhere you would be in hell - the hell of your own meanness (XXXII, II, 174)

In a calmer mood, Miss Brontë, in a preface to The Professor, prepared after the publication of Shirley, comes closer to direct reference to modern fiction. Where high life and high adventure, indiscriminately and dishonestly glamorized are the prevailing norms, Miss Brontë, looking back to the composition of The Professor, remembers herself thinking this way:

> I said to myself that my hero should work his way through life as I had seen real living men work theirs - that he should never get a shilling he had not earned - that no sudden turns should lift him in a moment to wealth and high station; that whatever small competency he might gain, should be won by the sweat of his brow; that, before he could find so much as an arbour to sit down in, he should master at least half the ascent of "the Hill of Difficulty"; that he should not even marry a beautiful girl or a lady of rank. As Adam's son

he should share Adam's doom, and drain throughout life a mixed and moderate cup of enjoyment.

If the author of Waverley proudly introduced the third canto of Marmion with this:

> Like April morning clouds, that pass,
> With varying shadow, o'er the grass,
> And imitate, on field and furrow,
> Life's chequer'd scene of joy and sorrow;
> . . . .
> Thus various, my romantic theme
> Flits, winds, or sinks, a morning dream.
> Yet pleas'd, our eye pursues the trace
> Of Light and Shade's inconstant race;
> Pleas'd, views the rivulet afar,
> Weaving its maze irregular;
> And pleas'd, we listen as the breeze
> Heaves its wild sigh through Autumn trees:
> Then, wild as cloud, or stream, or gale,
> Flow on, flow unconfin'd, my Tale! (92)

the author of The Professor would slip in behind William Crimsworth to say this. "Novelists should never allow themselves to weary of the study of real life. If they observed this duty conscientiously, they would give us fewer pictures chequered with vivid contrast of light and shade; they would seldom elevate their heroes and heroines to the heights of rapture - still seldomer sink them to the depths of despair" (XIX; 166). They would, in short, tell the truth, and not mislead provincial young ladies. Lucy Snowe, recalling her discovery of Madame Beck's perfidy, speaks of her loss of childish innocence in these terms: "I shall never forget that first lesson, nor all the undercurrent of life and character it opened up to me. Then first did I begin rightly to see the wide difference that lies between the novelist's and poet's ideal 'jeune fille', and the said 'jeune fille' as she really is" (VIII; I, 96).

A summary statement of Charlotte Brontë's intentions as novelist appears in an early letter written to W.S. Williams. She tells him that "the standard heroes and heroines of novels are personages in whom I could never from childhood upwards take an interest, believe to be natural, or wish to imitate. Were I obliged to copy these characters I would simply not write at all. Were I obliged to copy any former novelist, even the greatest, Scott, in anything, I would not write at all. Unless I have something of my own to say, and a way of my own to say it in, I have no business to publish." (93)

Her business, as she saw it, however, was to publish, and to do so because she had something of her own to say, and, as she puts it, most remarkably, "a way of my own to say it". These two come together as a revolt against the traditional and the contemporary "romance". Isolated as she was from the great centers of England's literary life, and restricted as were her financial, social, and cultural resources, Miss Brontë, as a prolific writer, and as a reader, could feel herself in close touch with that great world. In this sense, literature was the most "real" part of her life, for it was her link with the world beyond Haworth. Her novels are, in large measure, and often explicitly, demonstrations, through both form and content, of her opposition to "romance", an opposition made all the more passionate by her strong desire to put behind her that "burning clime" of her own Angrian tales. Her opposition to "romance" in fiction was inseparable from her opposition to "romance" in life. "Romance", as crystallized in her Angria, was a projection of herself that she both feared and cherished.

Her early reading, as her early writing, exercised a fascination over her that is apparent in her style and allusions, and not far to seek for those who compare the Angrian tales with the later novels. Images from the Arabian Nights, and from Revelations, from Byron and from Cowper, are part of all she wrote. The rhetoric and the precepts of the Bible and of the French romantics, of Isaac Watts and Wordsworth, became her rhetoric and her precepts. The conflict signaled by these pairings was paralleled by the conflict between "realism" and "romance" which was being fought out in the periodical press, and in her own ambivalence toward the Angrian "Imagination". It is a conflict about literature and about life; it is never resolved. It is what her novels can be said to be "about".

Miss Brontë's insistent refusal to "copy" other writers exhibits a naïve and impossible "romanticism". Novels are made, like anything else, out of what has come before, and Charlotte Brontë's novels are no exception. Mannerisms, commonplace figures, echoes and devices from Richardson, Fielding, Thackeray, in fact from the common stock of a century of novelists, are readily discovered in her work. Like Charlotte Brontë, George Sand and Walter Scott were both arch-romantics who felt themselves distinctly superior to the excesses of both the Gothic novelists and their contemporary descendants. To both, though in different ways, fiction was a serious medium for serious purposes, and Miss Brontë, as we shall see, drank deep at their streams.

NOTES:

(1) "Tinkler" is propably here a variant of "tinker", an itinerant gypsy, often a metal-worker (OED).
(2) Kathleen Tillotson, Novels of the Eighteen-Forties (London, 1961), 58-59. Also see Inga-Stina Ewbank, Their Proper Sphere (Cambridge, Mass., 1966), 31-33, 60.
(3) "Vanity Fair, Jane Eyre, and the Governesses' Benevolent Institution Report for 1847", Quarterly Review, LXXXIV (Dec., 1848), 175-176.
(4) "Vanity Fair...", 169. As it happened the Ingrams' views on the care of the governess class are not wholly unlike those expressed by Lady Eastlake in this article. That, plus Jane's victory and clear moral superiority over Blanche Ingram, it is not too much to say, rankled. Despite the presentation of "incontrovertible" evidence of masculine authorship, Lady Eastlake hedges her bet in the famous closing: "for if we ascribe the book to a woman at all, we have no alternative but to ascribe it to one who has, for some sufficient reason, long forfeited the society of her own sex." And even the insistence on Currer Bell's ignorance of the "habits of society", is tempered by this, early in that part of the article that deals with Jane Eyre: "The moment Jane Eyre sets these graceful creatures (the Ingram circle) conversing, she falls into mistakes which display not so much a total ignorance of the habits of society, as a vulgarity of mind inherent in itself. They talked together by her account like parvenus trying to show off. They discuss the subject of Governesses before her very face, in what Jane affects to consider the exact tone of fashionable contempt" (p. 168). This may be translated to mean: Currer Bell is presenting her complaint about the employers of governesses, i.e., the upper class, by deliberately satirizing their speech, manners, and dress, in an exaggerated and untrue manner, derived from current fashions - probably literary fashions, the "Silver-Fork" novels, and parodies of them.
(5) Henry H. Bonnell, Charlotte Brontë, George Eliot, Jane Austen (New York, 1902), 105, 108.
(6) The History of the English Novel, 10 vols. (London, 1924-39), VIII, 36, 44. This is helped somewhat by the fact that Anne Brontë worked as governess for an "Ingham" family (Gérin, Charlotte Brontë (London, 1967), 40) and described their unkind treatment to Charlotte (Letters, I, 175).
(7) Charlotte Brontë's Novels (New York, 1966), 60.

(8) Victorian Novelists (New York, 1958), 114.
(9) Bibliographical Resources for the Study of Nineteenth Century English Fiction (Los Angeles, 1964), 16.
(10) "Diderot", in Works, ed. H.D. Traill, The Centenary Edition, 30 vols. (London, 1898-1901), XXVIII, 178. This ed. hereinafter cited as Works.
(11) Letters, I, 211-212; I, 209.
(12) Fannie E. Ratchford, The Brontës' Web of Childhood (New York, 1941), 269, and Letters, I , 109-110.
(13) Letters, I, 122.
(14) Clifford Whone, "Where the Brontës Borrowed Books", BST, XI (1950), 344-358.
(15) Gérin, 116-117.
(16) A possible source for the name of Miss Temple in Jane Eyre is a character so named in the tale of "Mademoiselle Panache".
(17) Gérin, 24. Miss Gérin (Mrs. John Lock) has been good enough, in reply to my query, to provide a break-down, by subject, of the library, which was sold at auction in 1899. It contained a good deal of "practical" material - Agriculture, Brewing, Medicine, etc. The largest category was Poetry, containing 482 titles dating from 1610-1854. Drama was represented by 57 titles, ranging from 1653-1800. Unspecified Magazines (1748-1857) ran to 58 titles. There were no novels in the library.
(18) E.L. Duthie, "Charlotte Brontë's Translation: The First Canto of Voltaire's Henriade", BST, XIII (1959), 347-351.
(19) Gérin, Branwell Brontë, 31, 43-44.
(20) See Brontëana, Collected Works and Life of Rev. Patrick Brontë, ed. J. Horsfall Turner (Bingley, 1898).
(21) John Lock, A Man of Sorrows (London, 1965), 486, 95, for the last three titles.
(22) Mrs. Gaskell, Life of Charlotte Brontë, Everyman ed. (London, 1960), ch. II, 35.
(23) Letters, I, 7, 76.
(24) Catalogue of the Bonnell Collection in the Brontë Parsonage Museum (Haworth: Brontë Society, 1932).
(25) Martin, 85, shows echoes of King Lear.
(26) See Tillotson, 149, and Robert A. Colby, "Villette and the Life of the Mind", PMLA, LXXV (1960), 419.
(27) On the Improvement of the Mind (London: Scott and Webster, 1751), 371.
(28) Gérin, Charlotte Brontë, 11-13, gives examples of the didactic children's fiction used at the Cowan Bridge School, some of it by the Rev. Carus Wilson. Portions of his work are also accessible in Ruth Blackburn, ed. The Brontë Sisters, Selected Source Materials (Boston, 1964), 9-11.
(29) Watts, On the Mind, 333-334.
(30) On the Mind, 339.
(31) Letters, I, 215.
(32) Gaskell, ch. XI, 151-153, 154, 157, 158.
(33) Gaskell, ch. XI, 158.
(34) This ms is in the Berg Collection of The New York Public Library.
(35) Henri Maugis, ed., Harmonies Poétiques et Religieuses, Classique Larousse (Paris, 1934), 7. References to the poem are made in the text to this ed.
(36) See "Avertissement", Harmonies, 2 vols. (Paris: Charles Gosselin, 1836), I, 3-4.
(37) Maugis, 11.
(38) Ratchford, 149.
(39) Letters, I, 293-294.
(40) Letters, II, 18.
(41) Letters, II, 198, 201.
(42) Maugis, 8. Also see Jonathan N. Ware, "Bernardin de Saint-Pierre and

Charlotte Brontë", MLN, XL (1925), 381-382.
(43) Harmonies de la Nature, 3 vols. (Paris, 1815), II, 4-6.
(44) Gérin, Charlotte Brontë, 43-51.
(45) Letters, III, 172-173; IV, 44.
(46) Letters, II, 69.
(47) Letters, II, 28.
(48) Tillotson, 7.
(49) Athenaeum, VI (1833), 646-647.
(50) For Thackeray: "Madame Sand and the New Apocalypse", Paris Sketch Book (1840), Centenary Biographical Ed., "Works" (London, 1910-11), XXII, 230-231, and "On Some French Fashionable Novels", Fraser's, 1843, Works, XXII, 95-115. See also Blackwood's, "The French Novels of 1849", LXVI (1849), 607-619, and a review of Consuelo, Athenaeum, XVI (1843), 766-767.
(51) "Jérôme Paturot", reprinted from Fraser's, 1843, in Critical Papers in Literature by W.M. Thackeray, ed. Harry Furniss (London, 1911), 234.
(52) Review of Le Cousin Pons, XX (1847), 809.
(53) Louis James, Fiction for the Working Man, 1830-1850 (London, 1963), 138.
(54) George H. Ford, Dickens and his Readers (Princeton, 1955), 27.
(55) John W. Dodds, The Age of Paradox (New York, 1952), 361.
(56) Dodds, 361.
(57) Dodds, 473.
(58) See Matthew Whiting Rosa, The Silver-Fork School (New York, 1936). Carlyle, in Sartor Resartus, "The Dandiacal Body", has this to say: "Loving my own life and senses as I do, no power shall induce me, as a private individual, to open another Fashionable Novel" (Works, I, 221).
(59) See Keith Hollingsworth, The Newgate Novel (Detroit, 1963).
(60) Miriam M.H. Thrall, Rebellious Fraser's (New York, 1934), 112.
(61) "A Box of Novels", Fraser's, XXIX (1844), 156.
(62) Dodds, 111-113. Figures used all refer to 1841-45.
(63) Letters, I, 53, gives the census figure for 1841.
(64) Gérin, Charlotte Brontë, 24 ff.
(65) Letters, I, 88.
(66) Thrall, 19.
(67) Quoted in Thrall, 111.
(68) "Little Travels and Road-Side Sketches, by Titmarsh: From Richmond in Surrey to Brussels in Belgium", Fraser's, XXIX (May, 1844), 524-525.
(69) "Villette" is colloquial for "small town; "Labasse cour" may be "poultry yard" or "farm yard". See Georgia S. Dunbar, "Proper Names in Villette", NCF, XV (1960), 77-80.
(70) Letters, II, 119. Italics in original.
(71) Gordon N. Ray, Thackeray, The Uses of Adversity, 1811-1846 (New York, 1955), 373, 493.
(72) The OED's earliest citation is Thackeray's "Snob Papers" of 1846. The word appears, in small capitals, in Punch, XI (1846), 125.
(73) Punch, XI (1846), no. 258 for June 19, 271. Thackeray's small capitals are represented in my text by capitals.
(74) Punch, VII (1844), 49.
(75) Punch, VI (1844), 141.
(76) Punch, VII (1844), 25.
(77) For Charlotte's interest in Peel, see Letters, I, 91, 119, 124, 126.
(78) Letters, II, 93, 94.
(79) See Leslie A. Marchand, The Athenaeum (Chapel Hill, 1941), esp. "The Fight Against Puffery", 98-165.
(80) Letters, II, 93.
(81) LXX (1844).
(82) LXX (1844), 148-149.
(83) Letters, II, 27.
(84) Running through XVIII (July-Dec., 1845).

(85) All these appearing in 1845.
(86) Letters, II, 111.
(87) Letters, II, 179.
(88) See Ford, Dickens and his Readers, exp. 3-54.
(89) Ford, 57.
(90) Quoted by Froude, Thomas Carlyle, A History of his Life in London, 1834-1881, 2 vols. (London, 1884), I, 409-410.
(91) Letters, II, 326.
(92) Poetical Works, ed. J. Logie Robertson (London, 1944), 112b.
(93) Letters, II, 255.

III

George Sand and Walter Scott

1

Charlotte Brontë's correspondence provides the following references to George Sand. In 1848, responding to the literary advice of G.H. Lewes, Miss Brontë said:

> Now I can understand admiration of George Sand; for though I never saw any of her works which I admired throughout (even "Consuelo", which is the best, or the best that I have read, appears to me to couple strange extravagance with wondrous excellence), yet she has a grasp of mind which, if I cannot fully comprehend, I can very deeply respect: she is sagacious and profound; Miss Austen is only shrewd and observant. . . . What I call - what I will bend to, as a great artist, then - cannot be destitute of the divine gift. But by poetry, I am sure, you understand something different to what I do, as you do by "sentiment". It is poetry, as I comprehend the word, which elevates that masculine George Sand, and makes out of something coarse something godlike. (1)

Two years later, again to Lewes, she voices these opinions:

> Truly - I like George Sand better. Fantastic, fanatical, unpractical enthusiast as she often is - far from truthful as are many of her views of Life - misled as she is apt to be by her feelings - George Sand has a better nature than M. de Balzac - her brain is larger - her heart warmer than his. The "Lettres d'un Voyageur" are full of the writer's self, and I never felt so strongly as in the perusal of this work - that most of her very faults spring from the excess of her good qualities; it is this excess which has often hurried her into difficulty, which has prepared for her enduring regret. But - I believe - her mind is of that order which disastrous experience teaches without weakening or too much disheartening, and in that case - the longer she lives the better she will grow. A hopeful point in all her writings is the scarcity of false French sentiment - I wish I could say its absence - but the weed flourishes here and there in the "Lettres".(2)

George Sand published Indiana and Lélia in 1832 and 1833, the Lettres d'un Voyageur in 1834-36, Mauprat in 1837, and brought out novels regularly in the 1840's. Consuelo (1842-43) was followed by its sequel La Comtesse de Rudolstadt in 1843-45. How much of and how early Charlotte Brontë knew Sand's writings is a matter of guesswork. Perhaps they made part of the bales of French books she received from Mr. Taylor of Gomersal. Her remarks to Lewes prove no more than her knowledge, before 1848, of Consuelo and other but unspecified works of Sand. It is tempting to speculate that Miss Brontë felt some personal sympathy for the Frenchwoman, for the confessional Lettres d'un Voyageur are full of the sort of anguish that is depicted as her own by Miss Brontë's biographers. Here is George Sand in 1836: "Oh! non, je n'étais pas fait pour être poète; j'étais fait pour aimer! C'est le malheur de ma destinée, c'est la haine d'autrui qui m'ont fait voyageur et artiste. Moi, je voulais vivre de la vie humaine; j'avais un coeur, on me l'a arraché violemment de la poitrine. On ne m'a laissé qu'une tête, une tête pleine de bruit et de douleur, d'affreux souvenirs, d'images de deuil, de scènes d'outrages." (3) One can only guess at the effect such a public display of intimate emotions made on Miss Brontë.

On the other hand much of what Charlotte Brontë could have known of George Sand's work is dedicated to the proposition that love conquers all - expecially and specifically conquers the sacrament or convention of marriage. At the climax of <u>La Comtesse de Rudolstadt</u>, Wanda, the oracle, proclaims Consuelo's divorce from Albert de Rudolstadt simply on the grounds that Consuelo does not love him but rather one who is known only by the alias of Liverani, a name assumed by all the members of the occult revolutionary group, The Invisibles. Liverani stands with Consuelo before Wanda who says to the assembled membership, "Vous voyez bien, par qui elle est amenée ici; vous voyez bien que celui de nos enfants dont elle tient la main, est l'homme qu'elle aime et à qui elle doit appartenir, en vertu du droit imprescriptible de l'amour dans le mariage." (4)

The emancipation from conventional ideas of the marital bond is emphasized by the fact that Albert, whose passion for Consuelo is monumental, who pined away to a trance that all so took for death that they buried him, is the only son of Wanda herself. Jane Eyre faces a parallel situation, and though her decision is painful it is sure - no extenuating circumstances, nothing whatever, should break the yoke which exists between Rochester and his wife. This clearcut oppostion of priorities is however more superficial than it looks. Jane does indeed flee Thornfield, but, hearing Rochester's telepathic call for her, and not in the least aware that death has severed his marital bond, she rushes back to him. What she would have done had Bertha Mason Rochester survived the fire is a question we should not ask and cannot answer. And Wanda's decision too is hedged, as it were, by the fact that she knows, as does the suspicious reader, that Albert and Liverani are one and the same. Consuelo had sworn to remain faithful to Albert, and had been tormented by her new feelings for Liverani and by her suspicion that miraculously Albert was still alive - or alive again. Her marriage to Albert was chaste, for she married him on his death-bed; in this case it is a chair to which he retires for the final days of life. All this works to make either the return of Albert, or a marriage with Liverani, as morally "correct" as the most scrupulous could desire - and this while the declamation of revolutionary moral principles proceeds apace. The meaning of <u>Consuelo</u> and its sequel, like that of Miss Brontë's novels, transcends its explicit moral formulations. None of these books argues a position as effectively as it presents a conflict.

We have seen how Charlotte Brontë, in her novels, deprecates commonplace fiction. Yet although stock "Gothic" trappings are undercut, or used for new purposes, lapses from "realism" into "Gothic" mystery and landscape provide a good part of the immediate appeal of <u>Jane Eyre</u> and <u>Villette</u> and of the mechanisms by which the novels' other ends are achieved. The same ambivalence toward the conventional in fiction is seen in Sand:

> Si l'ingénieuse et féconde Anne Radcliffe se fût trouvée à la place du candide et maladroit narrateur, de cette trèsvéridique histoire, elle n'eût pas laissé échapper une si bonne occasion de vous promener, madame la lectrice, à travers les corridors, les trappes, les escaliers en spirale, les ténèbres et les souterrains pendant une demi-douzaine de beaux et attachants volumes, pour vous révéler, seulement au septième, tous les arcanes de son oeuvre savante. Mais la lectrice esprit fort que nous avons chargé de divertir ne prendrait peut-être pas aussi bien, au temps où nous sommes, l'innocent stratagème du romancier. (5)

Despite this complacent self-congratulation, <u>Consuelo</u>, not to mention its more fantastic sequel, is teeming with "Gothic" trappings that make <u>The Mysteries of Udolpho</u> and <u>The Castle of Otranto</u> seem unimaginative. Complex systems of underground caverns, inexplicable voices, the strongest suggestion that we have to do with long-dead souls uneasy in new incarnations, Gothic castles and churches nestled in lonely forests, and a good supply of mouldering skeletons - all, and more, are here.

The crucial difference between Rudolstadt and Udolpho is that while the latter is peopled with villains and incites to fear, the former is filled with Percy Bysshe Shelley in the moods of "Queen Mab", "Alastor", and "Prometheus", and inculcates a visionary idealism grounded in human love. Consuelo moves from the false lover, Anzoleto, the infatuation of her innocent childhood, to the almost divine union, at the end of almost half a million words, with Albert. (Miss Brontë manages a similar plot movement more economically in Villette.) The focal point of it all is Consuelo's love. The accelerated heart-beat and the other physiological reactions to fear, are also indices - in fiction at least - of the passion of love, and this convergence is Sand's central enabling metaphor. There are no villains in the caverns under Rudolstadt or in the crypts of The Invisibles. The terrors of the settings are "objective correlatives" for the emotions generated by approaching the sacred mysteries of love and of life. George Sand almost says it outright: "Les mystères, les circonstances romanesques attisent le feu de l'amour." (6) Jane Eyre's use of Gothic terror is similarly related to its heroine's emotional and spiritual life, and in Villette the relationship between fear and love is both used and investigated.

George Sand, as literary critic, sees that the "Gothic" mode is absurd, childish, and, in contemporary hands, an instrument for meretricious pandering to base motives. George Sand, as artist, knows that the "Gothic" is a form, a convention, that shapes, controls, and paradoxically, liberates. The dichotomy is also true of Charlotte Brontë and even of Walter Scott, who, like George Sand, displays the emblem of his ambivalence by his failure to decide, for good and all, how to refer to his own books: they are "Novels", "Romances", or "Tales", as the mood directs.

Different as the novels of Charlotte Brontë are from those of George Sand, they both bear this similar relationship to the "Gothic" tradition. The Black Nun in Villette is discovered to be a sham and a prank, but not before it has contributed to Lucy Snowe's terror. The lovers' telepathy in Jane Eyre, and dreams and omens in both these novels, despite their grounding in psychological analysis, retain some residual supernaturalism. On a larger scale, Consuelo is strewn with the supernatural, with unexplained mysteries, many of which are given natural explanations in La Comtesse de Rudolstadt. But even with the sequel, much remains unexplained and unearthly. Description of the residual super-naturalism in Sand's book will strike a familiar chord for the reader of Charlotte Brontë. While these provide the most obvious evidence of Sand's influence on Miss Brontë, what is of greater significance is the less definable influence of the novels' overall patterns.

Related to the manipulation of the "Gothic" mode is Sand's manipulation of the conventions of what we may call the "romance of courtship". Consuelo, when we first meet her is poor, of common Spanish stock, dark, simple, and plain. Shortly she will be an orphan. Much is made of her appearance. She takes it for granted that she is not only plain, as the narrator tells us, but ugly (laide). Anzoleto must ask her how she looks, beautiful or ugly, for it never occurs to him to define her looks. Such is the power of innocence. As time passes, references to her plainness diminish, but she retains the humility and reticence of the unfavored, and this throws her isolated acts of boldness and initiative into high relief. Consuelo is also the finest singer of operatic and religious music in the world - no one denies it, or even suggests that her superior has ever lived. Her foil is Corilla, a magnificent beauty and a star of the opera, whose shallowness only the cognoscenti can spot. In true romantic fashion, Corilla's moral blemishes overwhelm her taste and technique as a singer. Consuelo is forever studying her musical scores, though not training her angelic voice, and her performance is a clear symbol of her personal and moral greatness.

Corilla is a wanton, a coward, and a cheat. She abandons her own child at its birth. Yet she is aware of her failings, often friendly to Consuelo, and on one occasion, grateful and gracious to her. She has an admirable vigor, strength, a healthy élan, all which Consuelo rightly envies. She is, to us, a conventional character, and her function is also conventional - one thinks of Rosamond Lydgate and Dorothea Brooke as a similar opposition. But Sand's pairing is also a reaction to the conventions of romance in which the opposition is total, consistent, and irredeemable. This earlier convention is used in the Jane Eyre-Blanche Ingram pairing. More like Sand's manipulation of conventions is the pairing of Lucy Snowe with Ginevra Fanshawe.

Sand likens the early idyl of Consuelo and Anzeleto, on the streets of Venice, to the pastoral idyl of the innocent lovers in Bernardin de St. Pierre's Paul et Virginie. (7) But Anzeleto, playing Paul, is not innocent but, very soon, corrupt. Love, for Consuelo, is neither an idyl nor fated to be an impossibility - the two chaste relationships in St. Pierre - but her achievement of love will be an arduous trial. In like manner Lucy Snowe briefly lives an idyl, figured as floating on a boat in calm water. A storm arises and precipitates her desperate struggles toward love and beyond innocence. This requires a plot movement in two acts, so to speak, the idyl of innocence serving as prelude. This is true to varying degrees in all Miss Brontë's novels, and it is true of Consuelo.

We move on to more concrete evidences of Sand's influence. Mystic telepathy between Consuelo and Albert occurs frequently and inexplicably. In moments of crisis Albert calls to the distant Consuelo, and she hears and answers. Much of the time Consuelo believes Albert to be dead and she therefore ponders the possibility that, though dead, he can hover near and communicate with her. (Students of Wuthering Heights take note.) On the estate of the Rudolstadts lie the remains of an old oak tree. The tree, says Albert, had been the gibbet for some twenty losers in an old religious war, and as Albert confuses not only his own identity but also the century in which he is living, he describes the shattering of the tree by lightening as a supernatural omen of revenge on the assassins. (8) Superstition clings to the remnants of the tree; no one wants to disturb them, and so it continues as a prominent and ominous part of the décor at Rudolstadt. It persists into La Comtesse de Rudolstadt, and arrives at last in the garden of Mr. Rochester where it is again destroyed by lightning.

George Sand, like Charlotte Brontë, has a liking for the word "pressentiments". Both writers are interested in the possible solace of loneliness. (9) Sand writes intimately and at length of Albert's mental anguish, of his "terreurs de la nuit". (10) It is all very like Miss Brontë's descriptions of "hypochondria". There is a strange discussion, in the secret crypts of The Invisibles, in which the significance of the ancient alchemical myth of Hiram is debated. Consuelo has meditated on it and gives this analysis: "Hiram, c'est l'intelligence froide et l'habileté gouvernementale des antiques sociétés; elles reposent sur l'inégalité des conditions, sur le régime des castes." (11) The interpretation is not confirmed or denied by the high priest, who only says that it proves the nobility of Consuelo's heart. It is however a possible explanation of the name and oddity of Hiram Yorke in Shirley.

There are some narrative habits and devices common to George Sand and Charlotte Brontë, which I have not found in Scott, Thackeray, or indeed in any English novel Miss Brontë could have read. Probably wider reading would turn up complicating instances but the following would remain supporting evidence of Sand's influence. Consuelo opens in action and dialogue, without any authorial introduction, framing, or preface. Exposition comes later. Like the opening of Jane Eyre this is unusual for the period. Direct authorial appeals to the reader are a staple of earlier nineteenth-century fiction, but Sand's incessant references to the "lecteur" are as rare as Miss Brontë's "Reader". The previously noted footnote in Shirley, defending the use of a foreign word, has a parallel in Consuelo: "(Pardon, cher lecteur, ceci se dit en italien, et le comte ne faisait point un néologisme.)." (12)

A most effective, and unusual narrative technique in Jane Eyre is the shift from past to present tense at moments of crisis, or as the scene is being set for a new series of actions. Edgar Shannon finds at least seven instances of this in Jane Eyre. (13) I find three in Consuelo. (14) Like the dropping out, in dialogue scenes, of the "he said" and "she said", also common to Sand and Miss Brontë, these switches to present tense function to make the story more dramatic, in fact more "present". The inescapable fact that the action, all of it, is over and that the narrator knows all about it, is hereby obscured. Especially when this occurs at a moment of crisis, the reader's attention being held by the plot, the technique is admirably effective.

It seems sure that Miss Brontë learned from and borrowed from Consuelo at least among George Sand's novels, yet as we have seen, her stated intention was strenuously opposed to copying "any former novelist". (15) Sand's personal reputation, her heterodox pronouncements on love and law, and the severe rebukes she suffered at the hands of Thackeray and other respected critics, together with Miss Brontë's declaration of artistic independence make it absurd to suppose that she would have been pleased to be thought the Frenchwoman's disciple. Indeed, it is not impossible that the explicit moral choice of Jane Eyre is a deliberate repudiation of George Sand's blasphemies.

There are of course important aspects of Sand's work which Miss Brontë does not follow. The use of authenticated historical personages, incidents, and settings, an unforgettable part of Consuelo, most probably influenced by Scott's example, is but faintly traceable in Miss Brontë's novels. But the juvenile writing achieves the same effect, without historical knowledge or research, by a displacement of geography which functions as does historical displacement. The Angrian fiction teems with royalty, but the mature novels show only the royal family of Labassecour, in Villette. Unlike Scott's Elizabeth in Kenilworth, and Sand's Frédéric in Consuelo, Charlotte Brontë's King is extraordinary only for the signs of hypochondria Lucy Snowe detects in him.

In the simplest terms, Consuelo is held together by the centrality of its heroine, but to say the same of The Professor, Jane Eyre, or Villette, is to miss the radical differences in technique and form between the two novelists. The passionate force with which Sand takes up the first-person mode for her commentary has tonal resemblances with some parts of Jane Eyre and Villette, but as far as the overall narrative techniques and their effects are concerned, the works are quite disparate. The attempt to characterize the narrator, something notable as early as the Angrian narratives, is completely absent from Consuelo, and probably as a result of this, Consuelo and La Comtesse de Rudolstadt are sprawling and shapeless compared to Miss Brontë at her best. "Avoid Richardsonian Multiplication", Miss Brontë reminded herself in 1843, and about that same time she also managed to avoid the influence of George Sand's prolixity.

The relationship of George Sand to Charlotte Brontë is then a complex one - all such relationships are. What Miss Brontë's intentions were at that critical moment when she touched pen to paper is beyond conjecture, indeed beyond notation, but unquestionably the reading of George Sand made her work other than it would have been if the sway of other influences, particularly that of Walter Scott, had not been so challenged.

It would be wise here to remind ourselves that more than strictly literary influences are at work in the crucial moments of literary conception and execution. The characterization of the narrator, which seems to draw attention to the author while in fact it masks him, would be a most attractive technique for one who was personally both passionately assertive and remarkably diffident. The special relationship between Sir Walter Scott and "The Author of Waverley", and in turn the relationship of the latter with Peter Pattieson and Jedediah Cleishbotham, I believe, furnished an example of some importance to Charlotte Brontë. If George Sand provided an example of "poetry" in fiction for her, Walter Scott, to whom we now turn provided some means for its expression.

2

"One night, about the time when the cold sleet and stormy fogs of November are succeeded by the snowstorms and high, piercing night winds of confirmed winter, (the Brontë children) were all sitting round the warm blazing kitchenfire", at a loss for something to do. (16) Charlotte, not quite thirteen years old, asks what each of them would do with an island of their own. The question intrigues the children who then "chose who should be the chief men in our islands". Charlotte selects "the Duke of Wellington and two sons, (and) Christopher North & Co., and Mr. Abernathy". (17) Emily Jane chooses Walter Scott, his son-in-law John Gibson Lockhart, and his grandson Johnny Lockhart. One result of the great celebrity of Scott in the British Isles and at Haworth Parsonage, can be seen in Charlotte's tiny illustrated story of July, 1829, "The Keep of the Bridge". (18) Here is the "Ivanhoe" landscape, emphasizing the deserted and decaying Gothic building, very much in the manner of the background which surrounds Scott in Sir Henry Raeburn's famous portrait of 1808. Both scene and story are bristling with magicians and fairies. After an expository opening, the tale adopts the first person view of Gambia, of African or Angrian derivation, who, as the dungeon's door mysteriously shuts behind him, shows us that Miss Brontë understood even then the uses of the "Gothic" machinery. "I thought how dreadful it would be to die in such a place", he says.

Twenty years later, despite her maturity and her broad knowledge of literature, and despite G.H. Lewes' attempt to convince her of the superiority of Fielding and Jane Austen, Scott is still, to her eyes, indisputably "the greatest" (19) of the novelists. Something of this judgment, we may be sure, is due to extra-literary factors. Scott's works were bought and read in those years at an unprecedented rate, and Scott the man was to many a towering hero. His admirers could feel they knew him, as they could not know, say, Wellington, because Scott's very words, in rows of volumes, were at hand on their shelves, or, as in Miss Brontë's case, on the shelves of the local library.

After Scott's death they could know him still better, particularly through Lockhart's exhaustive biography (1837-38). (20) Of special interest to Charlotte Brontë would have been Scott's early addiction to "romances of knight-errantry - the Castle of Otranto, Spenser, Ariosto, and Boiardo", and his pleasure, as a boy, in making up his own "interminable" stories modeled after these. (21) The General Preface to <u>Waverley</u> describes this pastime as a "childish mystery" between himself and one special friend: "As we observed a strict secrecy on the subject of this intercourse, it acquired all the character of a concealed pleasure; and we used to select, for the scenes of our indulgence, long walks. . . ." (22) <u>Waverley</u> itself is, in part, the story of a young man whose love of romance distorts his view of reality and leads him into most dangerous political and emotional adventures.

The parallel between Scott's early story-telling and Charlotte Brontë's strong and ambivalent feelings with regard to her own Angrian tales is most striking, as is the fact that the Preface quoted above, and the earliest juvenile narratives are both dated 1829. (23) Scott might well have seemed to Miss Brontë a fellow thrall to the charms of romance, but one whose great success offered a model to be emulated. It is, in fact, surprising that with all the speculative biographies of Charlotte Brontë no one has portrayed her life as one controlled by the idea of emulating Scott. Without doing so here, it is interesting to note some instances, which, in any event, probably contributed to her interest and admiration.

Scott's wife was an Englishwoman of French birth, and with a trace of a French accent. Her name was Charlotte. (24) Her early letters, which were printed by Lockhart, show her to have been charming. Scott himself said the following of her shortly before their marriage: "I may give you a hint that there is no <u>romance</u> in her composition - and that though born in France, she has the sentiments and manners of an Englishwoman, and does not like to be thought otherwise." (25)

Scott's personal friends and acquaintances included the known literary heroes of Miss Brontë's youth: Southey, Wordsworth, Byron, Hogg, and Mungo Park. (26) The novelist "Monk" Lewis was also a friend. (27) Wellington himself, the great hero of the Brontë family and of so much of the juvenile writing, was not above noticing Scott. In Lockhart's biography Miss Brontë might well have been excited to find this: "The Duke of Wellington, to whom (Scott) was first presented by Sir John Malcolm, treated him then, and ever afterwards, with a kindness and confidence, which, I have often heard him say, he considered as 'the highest distinction of his life.' " (28)

Coincidentally, Scott and Miss Brontë suffered similar family tragedies. Scott's brother Daniel had disappointed expectations by his behavior in the West Indies. Dishonored, he returned home to Scotland where "his health, shattered by dissolute indulgence, and probably the intolerable load of shame, gave way altogether, and he died as yet a young man". (29) Scott's severe view of the matter was matched by Miss Brontë's scorn of her own disgraced brother Branwell, until his death brought sentiments of forgiveness. Scott's literary career too, the movement from verse to prose, has its parallel in Miss Brontë's career, and it appears more than coincidental, to this writer at least, that the first chapter of Miss Brontë's first novel bears the same title as the first chapter of Scott's first novel, "Introductory".

3

Soon after Scott undertook to edit the poetry of John Dryden, Wordsworth gave him this advice: "A correct text is the first object of an editor - then such notes as explain difficult or obscure passages; and lastly, which is much less important, notes pointing out authors to whom the poet has been indebted, not in the fiddling way of phrase here and phrase there - (which is detestable as a general practice) - but where he has had essential obligations either as to matter or manner." (30) "Detestable" as the practice generally is, I have now to point out some phrases, here and there, which indicate Miss Brontë's obligations to Scott. Many of these have not been remarked heretofore, and they should serve, by their cumulative weight, to lead us to, and to support, the probability of larger and more significant debts.

Shirley Keeldar's unusual name, we have been told, (31) derives from the verses at the head of chapter three of Scott's The Black Dwarf, which title itself recalls that of the Angrian tale, "The Green Dwarf". To this we can add the fact that de Hamal, a secondary character in Villette may derive his name from a de Hamel who appears very briefly in the first chapter of Old Mortality. We note also the fact of the appearance in The Professor and Kenilworth of characters named respectively Hunsden and Hunsdon. (32) Diana "Die" Vernon of Rob Roy is similar in character and in name to Diana "Die" Rivers of Jane Eyre, (33) and it is also interesting to note that the six unmarried young women whom Miss Ratchford traces through Miss Brontë's juvenilia to their appearances as Seacombes in The Professor and Sykes's in Shirley (34) appear as well in chapter two of Waverley. A good deal of the persistence into the mature fiction, so well displayed by Miss Ratchford, of Angrian characters, themes, and techniques, could of course be due to the influence of Scott at both stages of Miss Brontë's work.

W.A. Craik, who elsewhere notes some "unconscious" similarities in tone and technique between Scott and Miss Brontë, suggests that Dr. John Graham Bretton's name may owe something to John Grahame of Claverhouse in Old Mortality. (35) One can also see resemblances between the character of Lucy Snowe of Villette and Lucy Ashton of The Bride of Lammermoor. This last novel is particularly interesting from our present standpoint. To one fresh from a reading of Miss Brontë's novels and letters, The Bride seems to bombard him with echoes. There is a particularly close approximation of the scenery of Angria. There are disdainful references to the "lionizing" of authors who visit London. Lucy calls Ravenswood "Master", Lady Ashton is quite like Villette's Madame Beck. Discussions of "hypochondria" and of the problems of loneliness occur here, as does the last-minute interruption of a wedding ceremony. Here, as in other novels, Scott's use of the word "éclaircissement", reminds us of Miss Brontë's memorable uses of the word, and the use of the word "tinkler" instead of the more common "tinker", and Scott's repeated allusions to the biblical story of Sisera also catch the eye. The Latin phrase "lucus a non lucendo" which is used, to move on from The Bride, in Kenilworth, is one of Miss Brontë's very rare excursions into Latin. The unusual use of the word "propensities" in The Professor has forerunners in both The Black Dwarf and The Heart of Midlothian. Miss Brontë imperfectly remembers Milton's "some natural tears they dropp'd", (36) and we find the phrase used to like effect in Guy Mannering - and almost identically misquoted. Guy Mannering also precedes Miss Brontë in the comic use of "a novel" to mean a love affair. (37) Another comic metaphor, that of "sailing" to describe the progress of a grand lady, is notably common to both authors. (38)

Instances of these sorts could be given it seems endlessly. Some of course are less impressive than others - but read Scott after Charlotte Brontë and you will sense the relationship of which these specific cases are merely the handiest indices. To say that it is like the sensation one gets reading a novel he has forgotten that he had read before may communicate something of this odd sensation so much seems somehow so familiar. Curiously, reading Charlotte Brontë after Scott does not give the same effect. This may be partly because Scott much more often permits the reader's attention to wander, and partly because Miss Brontë did not copy Scott, rather she absorbed him, or, even more passively, was born into a traditon of fiction which was for her as for her generation largely the tradition of Scott.

A somewhat larger example of Scott's influence has to do with the plot of The Professor. Chapter eleven of Guy Mannering announces the omission of almost seventeen years in the narration of the story. Mannering's astrological forecasts and the fate of Henry Bartram, abducted at the age of five and missing since, will now be followed. Before this however, the task of exposition with regard to Mannering's life during these seventeen years, remains to be done - indeed of all his life, for he had been introduced at first rather mysteriously. Scott's procedure is simplicity itself: he gives us Mannering's letter to his old school chum Arthur Mervyn - a new character in the book and one who will appear again only as a convenient correspondent. Mannering's letter includes the following:

And now, why will you still upbraid me with my melancholy, Mervyn? Do you think, after the lapse of twenty-five years, battles, wounds, imprisonment, misfortunes of every description, I can be still the same lively, unbroken Guy Mannering who climbed Skiddaw with you, or shot grouse upon Crossfell? . . . . Let me recall to you - but the task must be brief - the odd and wayward fates of my youth, and the misfortunes of my manhood.

The former, you will say, had nothing very appalling. All was not for the best; but all was tolerable. My father, the eldest son of an ancient but reduced family, left me with little, save the name of the head of the house, to the protection of his more fortunate brothers. They were so fond of me that they almost quarrelled about me. My uncle, the bishop, would have had me in orders, and offered me a living; my uncle, the merchant, would have put me into a counting-house, and proposed to give me a share in the thriving concern of Mannering and Marshall, in Lombard Street. So, between these two stools, or rather these two soft, easy, well-stuffed chairs of divinity and commerce, my unfortunate person slipped down, and pitched upon a dragoon saddle. Again the bishop wished me to marry the niece and heiress of the Dean of Lincoln; and my uncle, the alderman, proposed to me the only daughter of old Sloethorn, the great wine-merchant, rich enough to play at span-counter with moidores and make thread-papers of bank-notes. (39)

The Professor opens with a letter of remarkably similar tone, from William Crimsworth to his old school chum Charles. It also functions to provide exposition of Crimsworth's past life, and to describe his then future plans and hopes. Charles himself has no other role in the novel. Like Mannering, Crimsworth's branch of his family was happier in its past position than in its present prospects. He also is offered a career in the church by his uncle, an offer contingent on an arranged and distasteful marriage. His alternative is "trade", for his brother thrives at it. Both heroes will spurn these vocations and seek their fortunes outside of England.

Crimsworth's situation also has similarities of emotion with Morton's in Old Mortality. Crimsworth's self-analysis includes this: "As I grew up, and heard by degrees of the persevering hostility, the hatred till death evinced by them against my father - of the sufferings of my mother - of all the wrongs, in short, of our house - then did I conceive shame of the dependence in which I lived, and form a resolution" (ch. I, p. 4). Here are parts of an outburst by Morton:

"Can I be a man and a Scotchman, and look with indifference on that persecution which has made wise men mad? Was not the cause of freedom, civil and religious, that for which my father fought; and shall I do well to remain inactive . . . ?
. . . . I am weary of seeing nothing but violence and fury around me - now assuming the mask of lawful authority, now taking that of religious zeal. I am sick of my country, of myself, of my dependent situation, of my repressed feelings . . . . ."

"But I am no slave", he said aloud, and drawing himself up to his full stature, - "no slave in one respect surely. I can change my abode, my father's sword is mine, and Europe lies open before me." (40)

For Scott's distant past Miss Brontë substitutes the nearly present. For his public and political themes, she substitutes the private and personal emphasis - unlike Scott's two heroes, Crimsworth's search for a wife is an integral part of his achievement of maturity and self-respect - but the line of descent from Scott's heroes is clear. Crimsworth and other characters in Miss Brontë's novels are subjected to, and sustain, a much more searching psychological analysis than do Scott's characters, but, as far as the basic plot goes, Professor Crimsworth's pen is the domestic equivalent of Morton's sword.

This movement toward the domestic and the contemporary, despite the ardor with which Miss Brontë announces it and defends it, is hardly her innovation. Rather it is a part of the overall movement toward domestic realism which is a major trend of the 1840's, as witness Dickens, Thackeray, and Mrs. Gaskell. This trend is largely a reaction against Scott and more strenuously against the excesses of his followers. Such reactions are more clear-cut in theory than in practice, for Scott provided lessons in the art of fiction which his detractors did not scruple to profit by.

4

Charlotte Brontë's correspondence shows no clearly expressed detraction of Scott, but her novels themselves are instances of dissent from aspects of his work, and the fact that the Ingrams of Jane Eyre read and remember Scott's novels is hardly a compliment to him. (41) On the other hand, the severely anti-romantic intentions behind The Professor backfired, and resulted in the often sensational Jane Eyre. After this novel's success, Miss Brontë was decided on making her next book different again, and was considering the avoidance in it of what G.H. Lewes called "melodrama". (42) Shirley represents less than perfect adherence to these intentions, but the general avoidance of melodrama here is also the occasion for Miss Brontë's acceptance of another aspect of Scott.

Charlotte Brontë's outspoken admiration of Thackeray and the double set of heroines Shirley has in common with Vanity Fair make the latter seem a likely influence. Thackeray's panoramic scope and his explicit moral purpose also bear on Shirley, but without denying the influence of Vanity Fair, we can look with profit as well to Walter Scott.

It was in 1849 that Eugène Forçade saw in Shirley an illustrated investigation of marriage - its importance considered from the points of view of a wide range of women in differing relation to it. (43) Over a hundred years later, Jacob Korg found much the same thing, although he understands the theme under investigation to be larger, i.e. the "romantic and 'commonsense' views of love and life". (44) Recollection of Shirley confirms these judgments. Such criticism, convenient and helpful as it is, runs the danger, however of confounding this unifying theme, this part of the novel, with the novel itself. With this caveat in mind, let us turn to Scott's Heart of Midlothian for another example of thematic unity, one closer to Shirley than is Vanity Fair.

For our present purposes, this novel's crucial situation is the imprisonment of three characters in the Edinburgh jail which bears the ironic name, "The Heart of Midlothian". In the first chapter of the book, this name is the subject of a competiton of wit: "The metropolitan country may, in that case, be said to have a sad heart." ". . . and a close heart, and a hard heart", ". . . and a wicked heart, and a poor heart". "and yet it may be called in some sort a strong heart, and a high heart". (45) Scott's use of the prison's name for the title of his novel points to the importance of the idea of justice to this story - for this idea is at the "heart" of Scotland, Edinburgh, and the novel.

Effie Deans has been wrongly accused of infanticide, under a statute which requires a verdict of guilty when a specific combination of circumstances which indicate opportunity and possible motive can be shown. Also in the jail is Jim Ratcliffe, a hardened criminal, but not an ignorant nor a cruel one. The third important prisoner is James Porteous, Captain-Lieutenant of the City-Guard. His death sentence has been respited for six weeks, to the great anger of those who fear his eventual pardon. Porteus, acknowledged by his superiors to be a callous and violent man, is nonetheless of great value to them in the preservation of the public safety and order. His crime was a too enthusiastic attention to duty. Presiding at a public execution, Porteous cruelly mistreated his prisoner, and thus inflamed a mob already sympathetic to the prisoner. After the man was hanged, the crowd voiced its disapproval; some threw stones while some moved to prepare the body for burial. Porteous let this become the signal for reprisals which soon left six or seven dead and many wounded. The jury found him culpable and the Lords passed sentence of death. "The Heart of Midlothian" then contains three prisoners, exemplifying varying degrees of guilt and of menace to the public welfare.

George Robertson, who is Effie Deans' lover, and the father of her illegitimate child, is also a much-indebted friend of the man so unfeelingly executed by Porteous. He takes advantage of the popular outrage against his reprieve and leads an assault on the prison. Porteous is taken out and hanged, but Effie and Ratcliffe both refuse the chance of escape. Ratcliffe is soon offered a pardon, and a job with the City-Guard, if he will assist in the search for Robertson. He agrees, but learning of Effie's relationship to the outlaw, protects him. Effie cannot be convicted if she can show that she shared the secret of her pregnancy, but she will not endanger Robertson by naming him. Her half-sister Jeanie is then faced with the moral dilemma: a lie will save her sister's life and harm no one. To Jeanie, however, truth is sacred; there are no extenuating circumstances.

Various minor characters provide additional illustration of the variety of complication to which the simple idea of retributive justice is, in practice, subject. As with the theme of marriage in Shirley, the legal, ideal, religious, popular, moral, and pragmatic aspects of the theme are brought to bear on it. None of the characters exists as illustration merely, nor even primarily; each has his relationship to the others and to the whole without reference to the novel's thematic unity. Nor does Scott provide an explicit commentary on this level of the story. But as in Shirley, the thematic unity deepens the meaning and tone of the book.

Scott's plotting is managed - that part of it that I have sketched - with great skill. Nothing seems too pat or disturbingly coincidental. This is so partly because the intricate relationships between characters are revealed in exposition, as "givens", not in a forward-moving chronological narrative in which the author's responsibility for the story is more obvious. Jane Eyre "feels" less strewn with coincidence than its plot outline shows it to be, for similar reasons.

Scott alternates his narration from scenes in the present to exposition of the past, and among the various threads of the story. The several threads are kept rather strictly separate, although Effie's story, for instance, provides vague hints about Robertson's, hints which later prove significant. Great plot interest is generated by this technique. In each thread, present action has its own inherent interest, while it increases interest when it touches lightly on other, only half-known, threads. Exposition of background, given generally after the presentation of the pertinent action, comes with the force of revelation of the partly inexplicable. The big dramatic scenes of the novel, Jeanie Deans in the witness box and before the Queen, are almost matched in excitement by those high points of the narrative in which Scott connects his various plot threads. The connection of the heretofore disparate provides an aesthetic pleasure in the narrative technique alone, without reference to content. Fielding's Tom Jones employs similar structures, but with differing effect. In Scott there is a continuing gratification of aroused interest, and the improbable is welcomed because interest in explanation has been so enticed.

This technique requires a good deal of what John Lester, writing of Thackeray, calls "redoubling", (46) backward movements in an otherwise chronological narrative. It tends, as in both Vanity Fair and Shirley, to make presentation of action less important while increasing the sense of panorama and of timelessness. While Shirley provides Miss Brontë's clearest example of both thematic unity and redoubling, these elements are important in the other novels too. Jane Eyre contains a thematic sub-structure based on various attitudes to religion, and Villette is "about" love and justice. Autobiographical presentation itself, in Miss Brontë's hands, is itself a continuous redoubling.

In addition to the example of narrative management, Scott provides a continuous stream of comments and precepts on such matters:

> Like the digressive poet Aristo, I find myself under the necessity of connecting the branches of my story, by taking up the adventures of another of the characters, and bringing them down to the point at which we have left those of Jeanie Deans. It is not, perhaps, the most artificial way of telling a story, but it has the advantage of sparing the necessity of resuming what a knitter (if stocking-looms have left such a person in the land) might call our "dropped stitches"; a labour in which the author generally toils much, without getting credit for his pains. (47)

The necessity Scott mentions does not occur in quite the same way in autobiographical narratives, such as Jane Eyre and Villette. The value of the method, as illustrated by Scott, may have been felt by Miss Brontë as she planned the redoubling autobiographical structure of those novels.

Here is Scott on the value of using summary narrative, in a special case, in preference to dramatic presentation: "At the risk of being somewhat heavy, as explanations usually prove, we must here endeavour to combine into a distinct narrative information which the invalid communicated in a manner too circumstantial, and too much broken by passion, to admit of our giving his precise words." (48) In this case Scott finds explanation more important than the chance to depict "passion". So Thackeray often, and so Charlotte Brontë's emphasis on explanatory introspection.

Scott's practice probably counted on a more effective level, for Miss Brontë - indeed for the Misses Brontë, than did the wealth of comment on it which appears in the Waverley Novels. The comments though are extremely specific, and, cumulatively present him as one highly conscious of detailed technical matters. That the Novel has its own "poetics", that its composition required planning and deliberation as to methods, that "poetry" and sentiment could exist through and alongside coldly conscious technical designs - herein lay much of the value of Scott's comments on novel-writing.

"It is fortunate for tale-tellers that they are not tied down like theatrical writers to the unities of time and place, but may conduct their personages to Athens and Thebes at their pleasure, and bring them back at their convenience." (49) To one whose reading was heavily pre-Romantic, Scott provided an authoritative sanction on such matters.

"In classical literature, Waverley had made the usual progress, and read the usual authors; and the French had afforded him an almost exhaustless collection of memoirs, scarcely more faithful than romances, and of romances so well-written as hardly to be distinguished from memoirs." (50) Jane Eyre was to make another of these.

The narrative method of The Heart of Midlothian requires the author to continually withhold vital information from his readers, while avoiding the danger of abusing their patience by taking too blatant advantage of his position. This danger is ever-present in the autobiographical mode, and in Miss Brontë's case, it is generally well skirted. Scott taught that the practice was the novelist's indisputable prerogative: "The quarrel which ensued between Edward and the Chieftain is, I hope, still in the remembrance of the reader. These circumstances will serve to explain such points of our narrative as, according to the custom of story-tellers, we deemed it fit to leave unexplained, for the purpose of exciting the reader's curiosity." (51)

"The passion for realism - as George Eliot defines it, 'the faithful representing of commonplace things' - led the Victorians to strive in all the arts for meticulous imitation of original models", and as Professor Haight goes on to demonstrate, the novelists shared this passion in their modeling of characters on real people. (52) Charlotte Brontë is something of an exception, for she repeatedly claimed to have done otherwise: "You are not to suppose any of the characters in 'Shirley' intended as literal portraits. It would not suit the rules of art, nor my own feelings, to write in that style. We only suffer reality to suggest, never to dictate. The heroines are abstractions, and the heroes also. Qualities I have seen, loved, and admired, are here and there put in as decorative gems, to be preserved in that setting." (53) Despite the characters in her novels that are, in some cases admittedly portraits from life, (54) Miss Brontë generally is faithful to her theory, and in this sides with Scott. He defends his work in this regard, often, with words such as these: "Yet the province of the romance writer being artificial, there is more required from him than a mere compliance with the simplicity of reality; just as we demand from the scientific gardener that he shall arrange, in curious knots and artificial parterres, the flowers which 'nature boon' distributes freely on hill and dale." (55)

On the other hand, Scott, like Miss Brontë is not afraid of trying a new theory: "The novel which follows is upon a plan different from any other that the Author has ever written, although it is perhaps the most legitimate which relates to this kind of light literature. It is intended, in a word - <u>celebrare domestica facta</u>, - to give an imitation of the shifting manners of our own time, and paint scenes, the original of which are daily passing round us, so that a minute's observation may compare the copies with the originals." (56)

These last quotations, like many other that appear in Scott's Prefaces written for new editions, make him seem a precursor of the Henry James of the Prefaces to his New York Edition. Before Scott gets off on his antiquarian hobbyhorse, he usually, like James, tells us the germ of the novel and evaluates the technical decisions reached before, and sometimes during, composition. Exposure to this early "Art of the Novel", and to such models of rather simple but well-made narratives as <u>Kenilworth</u> and <u>The Heart of Midlothian</u> provided probably the most important background from which Charlotte Brontë's novels emerged.

5

Charlotte Brontë's debt to Scott, and the admiration she expressed for him should not mislead us. As early as 1833, Miss Brontë gives evidence of feeling a good deal less than awe at Scott's achievement. She writes to Ellen Nussey, as per their agreement to correspond once a month. She is in an unusual mood - almost peremptorily business-like, and with an ill-disguised superiority to her friend. Something of Miss Brontë's disdain is also directed at Scott:

> I am glad you like 'Kenilworth'; it is certainly a splendid production, more resembling a Romance than a Novel, and in my opinion one of the most interesting works that ever emanated from the great Sir Walter's pen. I was exceedingly amused at the characteristic and naïve manner in which you expressed your detestation of Varney's character, so much so, indeed, that I could not forbear laughing aloud when I perused that part of your letter; he is certainly the personification of consummate villainy, and in the delineation of his dark and profoundly artful mind, Scott exhibits a wonderful knowledge of human nature, as well as surprising skill in embodying his perceptions so as to enable others to become participators in that knowledge. (57)

There is a suggestion in this that "Romance" is a derogatory label, and that Miss Brontë, unlike her naïve friend, does not find the portrait of Varney sufficiently life-like to provide that illusion of his real existence that elicited Ellen's reaction.

If Miss Brontë preferred "Novels" to "Romances", and used these words consistently to discriminate clear differences, she was well ahead of the literary criticism of 1833. Scott had defined the terms by reference to subject-matter, the Romance deriving its interest from "marvelous and uncommon incidents", while the Novel dealt with "the ordinary train of human events, and the modern state of society". (58) He called <u>Kenilworth</u> a "romance" and referred to himself in it as "a poor romance-writer", and a "tale-teller". (59) Despite the self-deprecation of these epithets, Scott elsewhere wrote that the "temper, conduct, and happiness" of the young reader "may be materially injured", not as in <u>Waverley</u> and <u>The Bride of Lammermoor</u>, by "romances of chivalry", <u>but by novels.</u> (60) His argument is that romances are harmless because no one believes them to be true, but novels, under the pretense of being true, and therefore illustrative of moral truths applicable to real life, are often, in fact, "romantic", and therefore insidiously misleading. The confusion, or at least the ambivalence toward the possibilities of fiction, is typical of the first half of the nineteenth century, and indeed, Henry James, well into the second half of the century, discovered with a shock that his own <u>The American</u> was in fact, and despite his intentions, "arch-romance". (61)

Scott himself contains any number of deprecating references to romances, including his own, and in this exhibits more than modesty. If Scott could feel his work to be morally and artistically superior to some of his predecessors, he could not entirely emancipate himself from suspicions that had long attached to the genre and to its practitioners. Miss Brontë's reaction to the larger tradition of fiction is in turn complicated by Scott's reaction to it, and by her reaction to Scott. Her own later literary criticism largely retreats from these complications. She can refer to "mere novel readers", and to Jane Eyre as "a mere domestic novel", (62) but generally her critical method is to refer to books as if they were persons. Eighteenth-century critical concepts appear when closer analysis is essayed, such as in her discussions of "Nature and Truth" in Art, (63) and of Thackeray's "exact keeping". (64) Her appreciation of the structural design of Mrs. Gaskell's North and South is a rare exception to this, (65) for her criticism is most often based on the metaphor that makes it possible to say of a book: "I find in it no real blood or life; it is painted and cold." (66) This assumption yields such results as the finding in the work of Eliza Lynn, "Lytton Bulwer in petticoats - an overwhelming vision", (67) but it makes less for serious criticism than for an escape from it.

By confounding an author and his work, the work itself, as a construct for objective examination, ceases to exist. Miss Brontë is most typical of her age in this, for formal concepts of fiction were then in their infancy while the moral considerations of the genre, and the sense of personal responsibility, (68) were in the ascendent. Miss Brontë's response to Sand and Scott had a large personal component. Her reaction to Sand's books moves quickly and automatically from "they are", to "she is", and it is this second predication that gets her almost exclusive attention. It was just this method which Miss Brontë found detestable when she was its subject. (69) Much like Scott, she hid herself behind the mask of a pseudonymous editor of a third party's memoirs, but unlike Scott, she exploited the mask for important personal and literary ends. For Scott the mask seems to have been partly an amusing game, partly a convenient and soon habitual way to begin. Confounding Currer Bell with Jane Eyre was not only impertinent, it represented a misreading of the novel. Confounding Scott with "The Author of Waverley", or both with the original narrators whom Scott edits and paraphrases, was utterly harmless.

We turn at this point to Charlotte Brontë's novels themselves. Our preceding investigations, it is hoped, have armed us with an awareness of the literary culture out of which Charlotte Brontë's work arose, and of the literary intentions and influences that affected it. Indebted as Miss Brontë was to her reading, striking as are the manifold connections with earlier writers and conventions, her novels are important to us as much for their relationship to the future as to the past.

NOTES:

(1) Letters, II, 180.
(2) Letters, III, 172-173.
(3) Lettres d'un Voyageur, ed. Pierre Salomon, Libraire Larousse (Paris, 1936), 72, letter 19.
(4) La Comtesse de Rudolstadt, ed. Calmann-Lévy, 2 vols. (Paris, 1879), II, 213.
(5) Consuelo, ed. Calmann-Lévy, 3 vols. (Paris, 1878), I, 297. See also I, 295, II, 349, for deprecating references to novels.
(6) Rudolstadt, II, 44.
(7) Consuelo, I, 23.
(8) Consuelo, I, 195.
(9) Consuelo, III, 10-11, with which cf. Lucy Snowe's case.
(10) Consuelo, II, 88-89.

(11) Rudolstadt, II, 188-189.
(12) Consuelo, I, 49.
(13) Edgar F. Shannon, "The Present Tense in Jane Eyre", NCF, X (1955), 141-145.
(14) Consuelo, II, 12-13; II, 62; II, 74.
(15) Letters, II, 255. And see II, 150, for "I hope I shall not find I have been an unconscious imitator."
(16) Charlotte's Preface to the "Tales of the Islanders". The ms in the Berg Collection shows a date of 12 March 1829. Extracts are published in Miscellaneous and Unpublished Writings of Charlotte and Patrick Branwell Brontë, ed. T.J. Wise and J.A. Symington, 2 vols. (Oxford, 1936-38), II, 467-468.
(17) John Abernethy, F.R.S. (1764-1831), an eminent surgeon at St. Bartholomew's, London, and author of The Constitutional Origin and Treatment of Local Diseases.
(18) Berg Collection.
(19) Letters, II, 255, and see also II, 179.
(20) Miss Brontë makes no reference to this work although her letters show her to be interested in biography, esp. on near contemporaries. Whone, "Where the Brontës Borrowed Books, The Keighely Mechanics' Institute", BST, X (1950), 349, lists only some unspecified "Life of Sir Walter Scott" on this library's shelves. Even if she didn't see Lockhart - and surely she would have wanted to, we can assume some familiarity with his life. Such information was everywhere.
(21) John Gibson Lockhart, Memoirs of the Life of Sir Walter Scott, 7 vols. (Edinburgh, 1837-38), I, 121.
(22) Waverley, Caledonian Edition, 50 vols. (Boston and New York, 1912-14), I, xvi. This ed. is that cited in future as Works.
(23) Fannie Ratchford, The Brontës' Web of Childhood (New York, 1941), xiv.
(24) Lockhart, I, 266.
(25) Lockhart, I, 273.
(26) Lockhart, I, 402 ff., 408; II, 298; III, 336 ff.
(27) Lockhart, II, 10.
(28) Lockhart, III, 368-369.
(29) Lockhart, II, 255.
(30) Lockhart, II, 81.
(31) Lew Girdler, "Charlotte Brontë's Shirley and Scott's The Black Dwarf", MLN, LXXI (1956), 87.
(32) He figures most in Kenilworth, ch. XXXIV.
(33) W.A. Craik, The Brontë Novels (London, 1968), 145.
(34) Ratchford, 85.
(35) Craik, 130, 184n.
(36) Paradise Lost, XII, 645. Charlotte puts the phrase in quotation marks but gives "sheds" for "dropp'd" in Jane Eyre, ch. XVII; I, 214. Scott also says "sheds", in Guy Mannering, ch. XIX; Works, III, 172.
(37) The Professor, ch. XX, 197, and Guy Mannering, ch. XVIII; Works, III, 159.
(38) Jane Eyre, ch. XX; I, 267, and Old Mortality, ch. IX; Works, IX, 121.
(39) Mannering, ch. XI; Works, III, 113-115.
(40) Old Mortality, ch. VI; Works, IX, 70-71.
(41) Jane Eyre, ch. XVII; I, 230.
(42) Letters, II, 215-216, 152-153, 179.
(43) "Le Roman Contemporain en Angleterre", Revue des Deux Mondes, XXV (1849), 719 ff.
(44) "The Problem of Unity in Shirley", NCF, XII (1957), 125-136, quoting 134. Korg refers to and quotes Forçade.
(45) Heart of Midlothian, ch. I; Works, XI, 12.
(46) John A. Lester, Jr., "Thackeray's Narrative Technique", PMLA, LXIX (1954), 392-409. While Lester helpfully counts Thackeray's "redoublings", and characterizes their functions, our look at Scott makes us question his concluding

paragraph in which Thackeray is credited with more innovation of the technique than seems his due.
(47) Heart of Midlothian, ch. XVI; Works, XI, 228.
(48) Heart of Midlothian, ch. XXXIII; Works, XII, 116.
(49) Old Mortality, ch. XXXVII; Works, X, 184.
(50) Waverley, ch. III; Works, I, 23, my italics.
(51) Waverley, ch. LXV; Works, II, 252.
(52) Gordon S. Haight, "George Eliot's Originals", in From Jane Austen to Joseph Conrad, ed. Rathburn and Steinmann (Minneapolis, 1958), 177.
(53) Letters, III, 37, to Ellen Nussey, italics in original.
(54) Letters, II, 150, 173-174, 313.
(55) Introduction (1830) to The Monastery; Works, XVII, xxvii-xxviii.
(56) Introduction (1832) to St. Ronan's Well; Works, XXXI, ix.
(57) Letters, I, 108-109.
(58) Quoted from Miriam Allott, ed., Novelists on the Novel (New York, 1959), 49.
(59) Kenilworth, Introduction and ch. I; Works, XXI, ix, x, 1.
(60) Quarterly Review, 1809, excerpted by Allott, 49-50.
(61) "I had been plotting arch-romance without knowing it, just as I began to write it that December day without recognising it and just as I all serenely and blissfully pursued the process from month to month and from place to place", Preface to The American, in The Art of the Novel, ed. R.P. Blackmur (New York, 1934), 25.
(62) Letters, III, 35; II, 151.
(63) Letters, III, 83.
(64) Letters, III, 314.
(65) Letters, IV, 153.
(66) Letters, IV, 51.
(67) Letters, II, 288.
(68) Letters, IV, 76-77, for Miss Brontë's wrestling with the problem of the novelist's moral responsibilities.
(69) Letters, III, 11-12, IV, 16-18, 52-53, 182, et al.

IV

The Professor

1

" 'God deals with poets as we do with nightingales, hanging a dark cloth round the cage until they sing the right tune.' " So did the anonymous reviewer in The Athenaeum quote Jean Paul to conclude an appraisal of Charlotte Brontë's newly published The Professor. His findings are essentially the same as those of the few critics of our own day who have written at any length about the book. It gives the impression, he says, of "pain and incompleteness". "Unity or arrangement there is none", (1) is his simpler version of more sophisticated modern views: "The Professor is a single-track novel . . . masquerading as a more complex unity, and with raw edges broken off from Angrian stories. The relation between the Crimsworth brothers raises interest but leads nowhere. . . . The early chapters also introduce a further false lead . . . in Yorke Hunsden, a sharply etched character with a misleading semblance of function; . . . The fault of the novel is that the real story occupies barely half its space; the rest is an awkward prologue." (2)

The Athenaeum's critic, like his successors, is interested in the novel's relationship to Miss Brontë's other novels, but although Mrs. Gaskell's Life of Charlotte Brontë was available to him, he does not comment on autobiographical parallels. While modern critics do this, (3) they find the novel "pale and colorless", (4) if not "bloodless" and "frigid". (5) The Athenaeum was hardly a leader in the movement toward prudery, but its reviewer saw in The Professor "the same rough, bald, coarse truthfulness of expression, the same compressed style, offence of dialogue, preference for forbidden topics, (6) and pre-Raphaelitish contempt for grace" that had distinguished Miss Brontë's other novels. Evidently there was something here that later readers have usually missed.

Enumeration of The Professor's flaws we have and to spare. The best, and the least prone to blame unfairly, is probably that by W.A. Craik. (7) Loose ends, and uneasiness with the mechanical limitations of the first-person mode, and the transparently obvious use of characters and scenes merely to move along a staggering plot, are here admirably described. Less well supported are the statements that Crimsworth himself does not develop during the course of the book, that the plain heroine is an innovation, and that Crimsworth's judgments are meant to be "accurate and just", that he is in other words a "reliable narrator".

The central fact, and problem, of the novel is indeed Crimsworth. Odd he is surely, even ludicrous, perhaps even "unbelievable", by the canons of realism. (8) The weight of a century of sentimental and speculative biography makes nothing easier than to see Crimsworth's oddness as the accidental and regrettable result of Miss Brontë's isolation from male society and of the ignorance which this caused. The Professor then is a tactical error, an attempt to portray a man Miss Brontë could not have known nearly well enough to reproduce convincingly. But Charlotte Brontë was not so unused to masculine society that she could produce nothing better than the ludicrous and absurd William Crimsworth. Even if she did badly misunderstand her father and brother, the local curates, and the young men of the Nussey and Taylor households, surely her reading, even of Scott alone, would have provided enough of a corrective.

Before investigating The Professor's "coarse truthfulness" and the oddity of its protagonist, a word about the text is in order. The only manuscript we possess is a fair copy in Miss Brontë's hand dated 27 June 1846 on its last page, and shows mostly minor emendations of an unspecified but presumably later date. On at least two occasions after Miss Brontë's success with Jane Eyre, she proposed to W.S. Williams that the novel, which had been previously turned down by a succession of publishers, might now be publishable. (9) Revisions might well have been made while such a possibility was being entertained, but they need not have been limited to those times. Nor are revisions necessarily limited to minor interlinear word changes. The first twelve pages of the manuscript, for instance, are on a paper whose difference from the remainder the passage of time has made clear by the darker color of their present condition. (10) The revisions that appear in the manuscript are in Miss Brontë's hand, and in that of her husband, the Rev. Arthur Bell Nicholls, who edited the text for posthumous publication. It is sometimes impossible to tell to whom we are indebted for particular emendations. Evidently Nicholls objected to even the typesetters' seeing passages his wife had already deleted, but which remained legible under her light excising strokes. His vigorous scoring-out is done over hers, but in some cases he may be deleting what she meant to let stand.

According to M.M. Brammer's comparison of the manuscript with the first edition, the one on which all good subsequent editions are based, the printer did a credible job with a manuscript whose punctuation and capitalization was so highly idiosyncratic that they required regularization. But there remains a gap between the nuance intended and that which printed texts provide. While my analysis of the novel does not at all depend on readings from the manuscript, my quotations, in the interests of accuracy, will be from it.

2

Perhaps the easiest way into The Professor is through its obvious structural design. The action breaks, chronologically and geographically, into three sections: the Yorkshire town of X----, Brussels, and back to Yorkshire, to the home of William Crimsworth, his wife and child, thirty miles from X----. With the exception of Crimsworth himself, who, as narrator figures in the actions of all three sections of the book, only one character, Yorke Hunsden, does so. The relationship between Crimsworth and Hunsden, often a tempestuous one, is portrayed in the three segments of the book, and as Hunsden himself only figures in the novel in so far as he interacts with Crimsworth, his function seems to be as a barometer or touchstone for successive evaluations, by the reader, of Crimsworth.

Between sections one and three, Crimsworth achieves financial independence and a successful marriage. Hunsden, who has neither striven for nor accomplished any such feats, remains what he has been: a remarkable combination of the kind, intelligent, helpful, friend to Crimsworth, and the severely cynical, brutally, unfeelingly analytic foil to him. We have every reason to believe that Hunsden's acting as Crimsworth's foil and goad is not only his habitual and most comfortable role, but one in which he sees he can best help Crimsworth. No matter how callous Crimsworth tells us Hunsden is toward him, Hunsden's guidance and support do, in fact, contribute largely to Crimsworth's success.

In the closing scene of the Crimsworths' domestic comfort and happiness, we learn that Hunsden and Crimsworth are now neighbors and most friendly ones, visiting each other with high frequency and pleasure:

> When Hunsden is staying alone at the Wood, (which seldom happens), he generally finds his way two or three times a week to Daisy Lane. He has a philanthropic motive for coming to smoke his cigar in our Porch on summer evenings; he says he does it to kill the earwigs amongst the roses, with which insects but for his benevolent fumigations, he intimates we should certainly

be over-run. On wet days too, we are almost sure to see him; according to him, it gets on time to work me into lunacy by treading on my mental corns, or to force from Mrs. Crimsworth, revelations of the dragon within her, by insulting the memory of Hofer and Tell. (XXV, 274) (11)

Crimsworth here appreciates, or at least is happy to tolerate, Hunsden's joke about his cigar smoking, and there is no suggestion that Hunsden's insults and treading of corns, seriously displease. When we compare this reaction to earlier ones, it is apparent that the Crimsworth of Daisy Lane is much changed from the charmless and humorless man he was earlier in the novel.

Crimsworth's first meeting with Hunsden occurs at Edward Crimsworth's home in X----. Hunsden comes upon William gazing at a picture of his mother, and, very much in character, Hunsden phrases his compliment this way: " 'Humph! there's some sense in that face' " (III,20). Crimsworth is embarrassed. "A shy noodle", he calls himself, for Hunsden is a wealthy manufacturer, himself "only a clerk". Crimsworth is conscious of his acute sensitivity to such distinctions, and this increases the awkwardness of his response to Hunsden's friendliness. Unquestionably Hunsden has Miss Brontë's approbation for his further comment on the portrait of Crimsworth's mother: "Pretty! no - how can it be pretty with sunk eyes and hollow cheeks? but it is peculiar; it seems to think. You could have a talk with that woman, if she were alive, on other subjects than dress, visiting and compliments" (III,22). Hunsden also makes clear here his suspicions of "Patrician descent" and privilege, his conviction that Crimsworth is not made for a "tradesman", phrenological evidence explaining a part of this belief.

Their second encounter occurs after Crimsworth knows just how little sympathy and advancement he can expect at the hands of his brother and employer. Meeting on the street, Hunsden overcomes Crimsworth's self-conscious reserve far enough for the clerk to accept his hospitality. The neatness of Hunsden's room, the titles on his shelves, the avoidance of strong spirits in the refreshments proffered, all "suit" Crimsworth, as they would suit Miss Brontë. But when Hunsden harangues him on the subject of the tyranny he undergoes at his brother's hands, speculates rhetorically on the motives behind such submission, and assures Crimsworth that "you'll never be a tradesman", Crimsworth wonders "at the perversion into which prejudice had twisted his judgment of my character" (IV, 34-35). Nevertheless Hunsden had struck home. Crimsworth leaves abruptly and torments himself with the seemingly hopeless situation in which his brother's coldness has placed him, and which Hunsden had reminded him of: "All that night did I ask myself these questions and all that night fiercely demanded of my soul an answer. I got no sleep, my head burned, my feet froze; at last the factory-bells rang, and I sprang from my bed with other slaves" (IV, 36). Hunsden has started to bring Crimsworth to the realization that, however painful, is a necessary forerunner of productive action. And Crimsworth, outside of Hunsden's presence, can see that his dislike of Hunsden is not wholly fair to him: "He is a talented, and original-minded man, . . . your self-respect defies you to like him; he has always seen you to disadvantage" (V, 38). It is these last conditions that Hunsden is in fact moving to change.

Yet another indication that Hunsden largely represents the voice of wisdom and charity in the novel is that Edward Crimsworth, the hard-hearted brother, calls Hunsden a "treacherous villain" (V, 41). It is his villainy that directly precipitates William's revolt, for Hunsden had been publicly reviling Edward for his cruelty to William, and Edward, incensed by this, had turned wildly on William. We are surely to assume that this is part of Hunsden's attempt to liberate William from his brother's bondage. His actions will support no other motive, and later he tells William this directly. But now he insists that he acted from a disinterested hatred of injustice (VI, 47).

William is dismissed from Edward's employ, returns to his rooms in X---- after a calming walk, and finds Hunsden ensconced in his sitting-room. He has cleaned the hearth and lit a fire, accurately anticipating Crimsworth who recently "shuddered at the prospect of a grate full of sparkless cinders" (VI, 44). But if Hunsden has been instrumental in freeing Crimsworth from dependence on his brother, avowal of gratitude for this will intensify Grimsworth's sense of dependence on Hunsden. Crimsworth therefore repulses Hunsden, who in turn twists the knife, trying to force, not gratitude, but understanding and initiative out of Crimsworth. Hunsden defends his actions which led to Crimsworth's dismissal: surely William has other relatives, he says, who can provide a new career. He is toying with William, who "bites" completely, and is almost pleased to refute Hunsden on this point. Gently, Hunsden leads him on toward the declaration of independence: "I must follow my own devices." His aim accomplished, by indirection, the only way it could be done, "Hunsden yawned. 'Well,' said he, 'in all this, I see but one thing clearly - that is, that the whole affair is no business of mine.' He stretched himself and again yawned. 'I wonder what time it is,' he went on; 'I have an appointment for seven o'clock' " (VI, 49-50).

Having indicated his lack of interest in Crimsworth's future, Hunsden deftly leads his unsuspecting companion to consider alternatives: travel, Europe, Brussels would be nice and inexpensive to get to, and on the spot Hunsden furnishes him with a letter of introduction to that rare being, a friend in Brussels who "generally has two or three respectable places depending upon his recommendation" (VI, 51). Crimsworth accepts the plan, and Hunsden exits, "laughing to himself", as well he might.

Crimsworth settles in Brussels and pursues his vocational and amatory adventures. Hunsden's friend Mr. Brown names available places as "clerk and shopman" which Crimsworth rejects in favor of a new idea: teaching. Not until Crimsworth is deeply enmeshed in his pursuit of Frances Henri does Hunsden obtrude himself on him again. Hunsden soon arrives. He is met by Crimsworth's attempts to maintain his dignity by refusing to accede to Hunsden's brusque informality. Hunsden will not change his tack, and, in the ensuing silence, takes up a book off Crimsworth's shelf. " 'You did not ask for it, and you shall not have it,' " says Crimsworth taking the book from him (XXII, 211). As with other such responses which seem juvenile, if not ridiculous, we must bear in mind the tensions under which Crimsworth is operating. These tensions, of which more later, can, in part, be deduced from what Crimsworth tells us has been happening to him, but his own interpretation of them, his own analysis of the state of his psyche, is often unreliable. Whether this is sufficiently clear to the reader or not, this unreliability is as it should be, for tensions which can motivate such grotesque behavior are not normally available to the sufferer for explication. But if Miss Brontë is psychologically accurate in this, she runs the risk of obscurity. If Crimsworth is not a reliable analyst, he cannot, in his role as narrator, tell us so directly. Hunsden's insights into the case are clouded by the extravagances of his own personality which make him vividly real, but at a cost. A sympathetic reading, one in which we hold onto the hypothesis, as long as possible, that it is a good novel, that Crimsworth's oddness is functional, can lead to more complete appreciation and more just evaluation of the wrongs the author has in fact perpetrated.

In the interview under consideration, Crimsworth withstands Hunsden's rough teasing and probing analysis of the state of his affections, because: "Cutting as these words might have been under some circumstances - they drew no blood now - My life was changed; my experience had been varied since I left X----, but Hunsden could not know this; he had seen me only in the character of Mr. Crimsworth's clerk; a dependent amongst wealthy strangers, meeting disdain with a hard front. . . . A sweeter secret nestled deeper in my heart; one full of tenderness and as full of strength; it took the sting out of Hunsden's sarcasm; it kept me unbent by shame, and unstirred by wrath" (XXII, 215-216). In other words, Hunsden knows nothing of Frances Henri and cannot wound Crimsworth in this newly sensitive place. He brings however news of changes at Crimsworth

Hall.

As we have seen, the portrait of Crimsworth's mother is important to him, and Hunsden knows this very well. He has, in fact, at an auction at the Hall, bought the painting and shipped it to William, but he is up to his old tricks again: "What pictures?" he responds to William's inquiry, "Crimsworth had no special collection that I know of - he did not profess to be an amateur." Reminded of the portrait he says: "Why as a matter of course it would be sold among the other things. If you had been rich - you might have bought it. . . . I never inquired who purchased anything" (XXII, 218). The next day the portrait arrives with a note from Hunsden, pointing out the increase in Crimsworth's obligations to him. Crimsworth, furious now ("You have paid yourself in taunts."), is nevertheless happy to have the picture. If Hunsden had brought it himself, or announced its coming, William might well have refused to accept it.

The next encounter with Hunsden, and the last in Brussels, occurs after Crimsworth has secured a new teaching position and the promise of Frances Henri's hand. His independence, his dignity, has never been so well buttressed, but he can no longer keep his secret love of Frances from Hunsden. Crimsworth tries to exert his independence and to excite Hunsden's aggravation, by telling him only that his intended is a "lace-mender". Hunsden has no wish to interfere: " 'Good night, William,' he said, in a really soft voice, while his face looked benevolently compassionate. 'Good night, lad; I wish you and your future wife much prosperity, and I hope she will satisfy your fastidious soul.' " William simply does not believe that Hunsden feels anything but pitying disdain for him, for here is his response to the above: "I had much ado to refrain from laughing as I beheld the magnanimous pity of his mien" (XXIV, 246).

Note here how Miss Brontë attempts to use her unreliable narrator to present reliable material. Crimsworth's physical description of Hunsden's voice and face is accurate, and uncolored by the distorted view he holds of Hunsden's intentions. Perhaps the method is inherently flawed, for a distorted mind, one would expect, would also be a distorting mirror. There is another way to achieve the requisite duel presentation in autobiographical fiction - one used in <u>Jane Eyre</u> and <u>Villette</u>, and, it is here in <u>The Professor</u> too, although in a rudimentary way.

Feeling a need to bring Hunsden's supposed disdain out into the open, to force the testing of his marital choice, Crimsworth takes Hunsden to meet Frances Henri. Hunsden engages her in spirited but innocuous conversation, clearly trying to draw her out. He plays devil's advocate, or rather Utilitarian's advocate, recalling, by the way, Dickens in the mood of <u>Hard Times</u>: " 'Mademoiselle, what is an association? I never saw one, What is its length, breadth, weight, value - ay <u>value</u> - What price will it bring in the market?' " (XXIV, 250). Frances retorts bravely, winning the admiration of all, although Crimsworth is sure that Hunsden's banter is maliciously intended. Hunsden takes his leave of Frances: "Hunsden rose. 'Good bye,' said he to Frances, 'I shall be off for this glorious England to-morrow, and it may be twelve months or more before I come to Brussels again; whenever I do come I'll seek you out, and you shall see if I don't find means to make you fiercer than a dragon - you've done pretty well this evening but next interview you shall challenge me outright. Meantime you're doomed to become Mrs. William Crimsworth, I suppose; poor young lady! but you have a spark of spirit; cherish it, and give the Professor the full benefit thereof' " (XXIV, 255-256). He bows to her, which to Crimsworth recalls Sir Charles Grandison with Harriet Byron.

The tensions that Crimsworth has been keeping under control through all this burst forth as soon as he and Hunsden are alone. Marrying Frances represents his bid for dignity and independence. He projects his own doubts and fears of its validity onto Hunsden. Even his prejudiced report tells enough of the truth: "No sooner had we got into the street than Hunsden collared me. 'And that is your lace-mender?' said he, 'and you reckon you have done a fine, magnanimous thing in offering to marry her? You a scion of Seacombe, have proved your disdain of social distinctions by taking up with an ouvrière! (12) And I pitied the fellow thinking his feelings had misled him and that he had hurt himself by contracting a low match!' " (XXIV, 256-257).

To this high compliment to Frances and himself, this reply: " 'Just let go my collar, Hunsden.' On the contrary he swayed me to and fro; so I grappled him round the waist; it was dark; the street lonely and lampless. We had then a tug for it, and after we had both rolled on the pavement and with difficulty picked ourselves up, we agreed to walk on more soberly. 'Yes, that's my lace-mender,' said I; 'and she is to be mine for life - God willing' " (XXIV, 256-257). Hunsden picks this up, saying that Frances Henri is too good for him although not good enough for Hunsden himself, who has very special requirements. All of this is lost on Crimsworth - both Hunsden's ironic flattery and his intimation of his own romantic attachments. Later, in Daisy Lane, Hunsden will continue to treat William as an equal by telling him more of his intimate history, but Crimsworth is not yet self-assured enough to understand anything except in so far as it effects his own ego. The men part without salutation.

We learn of their future rapport years later in Daisy Lane, but during the intervening years Crimsworth's increasing maturity is signalled by his acceptance of Hunsden's help in securing pupils for the Crimsworths' school, and by his soliciting, one supposes, and acceptance of Hunsden's skilled and successful guidance of his investments (XXIV, 264, 271).

Guided by the tripartite design of The Professor to investigate the Hunsden-Crimsworth relationship, we have seen something of the method and meaning of the novel, although both are obscured by inadequate execution. But onto this skeleton frame Miss Brontë has overlaid another pattern, one on which we have barely touched, and which indeed makes up the bulk of the book.

3

Again the simple structural design of The Professor furnishes a clue. The opening chapter, titled "Introductory", and the only chapter in the novel to bear a title, is further set apart from the tripartite structure of the novel by both form and content. Some time after settling in Daisy Lane, Crimsworth wrote to an old friend, known only here and only as "Charles". His letter related the first part of the story of his life. Charles never answered the letter, and now, finding a copy of it in his desk, Crimsworth decides to present it, and the succeeding chapters, to "the public at large".

The letter tells of his history up to his move to X---- to join his brother's staff. His manner is calm, intelligent, mature - very much the happy man of Daisy Lane, far from the travails of Brussels. Thus the novel is framed between two narratives which cover the beginning and the end of the story, or the "before" and "after", and both these presented by a reliable William Crimsworth. Miss Brontë, rather preciously it must be said, links beginning and end by having Crimsworth switch to present tense in the closing pages. He tells us that he is now at his desk writing this very novel. Hunsden enters, orders Crimsworth to lay down his pen, and the novel ends.

But in between these sections, the Crimsworth who continues to write his memoirs in Daisy Lane makes hardly a mention of that fact, and rarely brings his mature judgment to bear in evaluating the narrative as it flows from him. The central section is almost exclusively a recreation of the past, as he understood it then, not a mature commentary on it. The letter points up the dual vision in use in the framing sections. In both the first and penultimate paragraphs of the letter, Crimsworth carefully contrasts his feelings "then" and "now". He italicizes the words in both cases there, and again in the central section of the novel. This dual point of view occurs only sporadically between the first and last chapters. Comparison with the techniques of Jane Eyre and Villette shows quite different methods in this important regard. In the later novels the narrator is continually shifting between the points of view of "then" and "now".

As the last chapter provides a key to his relationship with Hunsden, chapter one provides the necessary background for comprehension of Crimsworth's inner turmoil. His letter begins by sketching his early relationship to Charles:

> I think when you and I were at Eton together, we were neither of us what could be called - popular characters - ; you were a sarcastic, observant, shrewd, cold-blooded creature; my own portrait I will not attempt to draw - but I cannot recollect that it was a strikingly attractive one - can you? What animal magnetism drew thee and me together - I know not; certainly I never experienced anything of the Pylades and Orestes sentiment for you, and I have reason to believe that you, on your part, were equally free from all romantic regard to me. Still, out of school-hours, we walked and talked continually together; when the theme of conversation was our companions or our masters, we understood each other, and when I recurred to some sentiment of affection, some vague love of an excellent or beautiful object, whether in animate or inanimate nature - your sardonic coldness did not move me - I felt myself superior to that check <u>then</u> as I do <u>now</u>.

This relationship is curiously similar to that between Crimsworth and Hunsden, except that in the earlier case the pair understood each other and tolerated the discomforting quirks of the other party. It is hard to say that this parallel relationship is designed to signal the nature of the more complex Hunsden-Crimsworth relationship, and harder still to write it off as a bit of Angrian history that Miss Brontë uses, in effect, as space filler. Whatever its genesis may be, the little vignette which parallels the more important relationship, like the patterning of imagery often noted in <u>Jane Eyre</u>, functions as a small part of the artistic whole. The author's concentration on themes and ideas becomes displayed in variations on the central motif which appear as internal patterns in the component parts. But that this can be abstracted out by criticism, and displayed schematically, does not mean that the parts were put together according to such a schematic plan.

After Eton, Crimsworth had offers from his uncles to join the church, accept a comfortable "living", and agree to a marriage to a cousin that would suit the family's convenience. His refusal provoked "mutual disgust", and he turned to his older brother Edward, now owner of the business that had been their father's before his failure and death. Their mother had lived on for six months, in destitution, unaided by her husband's "aristocratical brothers", whom she had mortally offended by her union with Crimsworth" (I, 3). Crimsworth sums up his feelings on this subject in these stirring words: "As I grew up, and heard by degrees of the persevering hostility, the hatred till death evinced by them against my father - of the sufferings of my mother, of all the wrongs, in short, of our house - then did I conceive shame of the dependence in which I lived and form a resolution no more to take bread from hands, which had refused to minister to the necessities of my dying mother" (I, 4).

There is a tragic grandeur in that, achieved in part by the rhythm of the prose, the retarding effect of the periodic syntax, the simplicity of diction, the inversions in word order in the central phrases where the thought turns from past woes to future purpose, and the archaic "conceived shame of ". "Of our house", recalls English translations of Greek tragedy, and elicits a deeper nuance from the earlier reference to the proverbial friendship of Pylades and Orestes.

If the content of the speech did not itself require our close attention, Crimsworth's lyric eloquence, unparalleled in this novel, surely points to a theme of major importance to him and to the novel. We have seen how the portrait of Crimsworth's mother appears and reappears, generally in connection with Yorke Hunsden. The letter to Charles itself closes with this reference to the portrait: "The face, I remembered, had pleased me as a boy, but <u>then</u> I did not understand it; <u>now</u> I knew how rare that class of face is in the world, and I appreciated keenly its thoughtful yet gentle expression. The serious grey eye possessed for me a strong charm, as did certain lines in the features indicative of most true and tender feeling. I was sorry it was only a picture" (I, 10). If that last sentence achieves not the tragic but the "childish-pathetic", or worse, it nevertheless conveys strong emotion, emotion that during the course of the novel cannot and does not cease to exist, but hides behind what Crimsworth calls "a buckler of impenetrable indifference". (13)

The mixed metaphor is both psychological and heroic, for Crimsworth is a very modern knight, his quest psychological health. His sense of personal shame for his mother's unrevenged degradation is the nearest we come to the root of his discomfort. That such a cause should have results discernible in terms of sexual maladjustment should surprise no modern psychologists, nor should it cause consternation within The Brontë Society - Freud did not invent nor discover overt patterns of behavior that had no existence before his day, and any accurate portrayal of personality will not be at odds with psycho-sexual analysis. Crimsworth's abhorrence of the idea of financial dependence on his relatives, which he generalizes to the point of despising the idea of owing gratitude to Yorke Hunsden, is not the stuff of trauma, although it may easily stand for, or be a manifestation of, more deeply-seated emotional distress. Perhaps the unhappy history of his family's rise and fall is itself only Crimsworth's rationalization of earlier, pre-intellectual, unhappiness. The internal mechanics of Crimsworth's psyche we may well leave to an adventurous psychiatrist. But the symptoms that result, as they show themselves in the novel, it is our business to track.

William Crimsworth, settled in as second clerk in his brother's establishment, is invited to Crimsworth Hall, to take part in "a large party given in honour of the Master's birthday" (III, 19). He had previously met the lady of the house and had found her lacking. The best he can say of her is an amusing damnation by faint praise: "It was now further obvious to me that she had a good complexion, and features sufficiently marked but agreeable; her hair was red - quite red" (I, 8). William "watched (her) in vain for a glimpse of soul". No other views of Mrs. Crimsworth are given against which to weigh William's, but there is a hint of sexual jealousy, projected onto brother Edward, in this of William: "Having perused the fair page of Mrs. Crimsworth's face - a deep, involuntary sigh announced my disappointment - she took it as a homage to her beauty - and Edward, who was evidently proud of his rich and handsome young wife, threw on me a glance - half-ridicule, half-ire" (I, 9). With this William turns from the pair and walks over to the portraits of his parents, where he peruses the face of his mother with more satisfying results. If a post-Freudian novelist had done this he would risk the accusation of being unduly obvious.

At Crimsworth Hall the local belles are assembled, and William responds similarly:

> Dancing began - I should have liked well enough to be introduced to some pleasing and intelligent girl and to have freedom and opportunity to show that I could both feel and communicate the pleasure of social intercourse - that I was not in short, a block, or a piece of furniture but an acting, thinking, sentient man. Many smiling faces and graceful figures glided past me - but the smiles were lavished on other eyes - the figures sustained by other hands than mine - I turned away tantalised, left the dancers, and wandered into the oak-panelled dining-room (where the portraits, to which he turns, are hung.) (III, 20)

It is at this point that Hunsden makes his entrance. Later on these two discuss William's behavior at the party, and while William denies having had any interest in the girls, Hunsden's recollection of his behavior is the one we are bound to believe: " 'You had and have no pleasant address; there is nothing in you to induce a woman to be affable. I have remarked you sitting near the door in a room full of company, bent on hearing, not on speaking; on observing not on entertaining; looking frigidly shy at the commencement of a party; confusingly vigilant about the middle and insultingly weary towards the end' " (XXII, 215).

While in Brussels William is notable for holding very different views on his own attractiveness to the opposite sex, and, although his behavior is often "frigid", shyness is not its best description. This man, of whom we can safely say that his reactions to women are unusually sensitive and ambivalent, is soon to find himself surrounded by women and bombarded with thoughts of love. These feelings he expresses in terms of abstract dichotomies, "Reason" versus "Passion", "Slave" versus "Master", "Spiritual" versus exterior charms, dependence versus independence, "Love" versus sensuality, etc. As William comes to terms with his ambivalence, he also finds satisfactory intellectual middle grounds for these dichotomies, so that the progress of his thought and feelings, when analyzed, will yield a number of parallel lines.

His use of the word, "sensualist", for instance, clearly indicates the movement. At one point Frances Henri is "for a sensualist charmless", while later Crimsworth's feelings for her convince him that: "I too was a sensualist" (XIX, 177; XXIII, 240). Such progress in self-knowledge does not come easy. The realization itself is immediately followed by an epic, nine-day siege of "hypochondria". It is entirely accurate from a psychological point of view that Crimsworth himself cannot understand why the malady struck at just this time. That he wants very much to understand this is clinically unusual, but very helpful for the novelist. He credits his earlier attacks to the cheerless loneliness of his youth: "No wonder her spells <u>then</u> had power; but <u>now</u> when my course was widening, my prospect brightening; when my affections had found a rest; when my desires, folding wings, weary with long flight, had just alighted on the very lap of Fruition, had nestled there warm, content, under the caress of a soft hand - why did Hypochondria accost me now?" (XXIII, 241-242). Modern critics of <u>The Professor</u>, one after the other, ask the same question, and conclude that there was indeed no good reason for the attack, other than Miss Brontë's interest in the malady generally. (14) Is not his unconscious feeling of guilt clear? Crimsworth must pay the price for the emotions of aggression and lust which have surged through him. Of course he wonders why the attack should hit him just as he admits to himself feelings of sexual attraction for the heretofore pure and sexually neuter Frances Henri. Of course he cannot fathom it: the unconscious is precisely that - unconscious.

Lucy Snowe's attack of hypochondria, in <u>Villette</u>, similar in its symptoms to Crimsworth's, can be related to her feelings about Dr. John but this is obscured by the plot, and by various other explanations Lucy herself provides. While Crimsworth's story, like Lucy Snowe's, can be told in the abstract and intellectual terms which the protagonist chooses to employ, the result is an oversimplification and a tediously wordy one. Let us rather follow Crimsworth to Brussels and see what evidence passes intact through his rationalizing filter.

Crimsworth accepts Pelet's terms and finds himself happily teaching English to French and Flemish schoolboys. The bedroom to which he is assigned however, contains a window, boarded up, which faces the garden of the adjacent "Pensionnat de demoiselles". Once alone in his room: "The first thing I did was to scrutinise closely the nailed boards, hoping to find some chink or crevice which I might enlarge and so get a peep at the consecrated ground; my researches were vain for the boards were well joined and strongly nailed; it is astonishing how disappointed I felt" (VII, 64).

M. Pelet, Crimsworth soon reports, "had all a Frenchman's, all a Parisian's notions about matrimony and women" (VIII, 69). Pelet's mother, "ugly, as only continental old women can be", generally keeps to herself, but one afternoon she sends a servant up to invite Crimsworth to join her in the dining room for tea. Other than his own preoccupations, there is nothing to prompt his response: "Just as I laid my hand on the handle of the dining-room door a queer idea glanced across my mind. 'Surely she's not going to make love to me' said I, 'I've heard of old Frenchwomen doing odd things in that line - and the goûter? They generally begin such affairs with eating and drinking, I believe' "(VIII, 71). He enters the room: "Already the cold sweat started on my brow." Madame Pelet has other ideas and other company. Madame Reuter, whose daughter runs the neighboring girls' school is there with news for Crimsworth: he is to be offered a part-time position there.

With Pelet's approval, Crimsworth meets with Mademoiselle Zoraïde Reuter, at her school, to discuss such an arrangement. Her entrance makes him start "involuntarily" for he had been peering into the heretofore forbidden garden, but they cordially come to terms and Crimsworth leaves feeling that "Brussels seemed a very pleasant place" (IX, 80). For Crimsworth the courtesy and interest Zoraïde shows him makes her "charming" in his eyes. Quite soon he is impatient to see her again, and misunderstanding her egregiously. He thinks not only that he is falling in love with her but that she would favor his suit. After his fashion, he woos her in the garden, obscurely indicating his feelings by asking her to pluck a flower for him. It is painful to hear him credit her lack of comprehension of this private system of courtship to her naïveté (XIII, 109). Zoraïde Reuter is and has been secretly engaged to Pelet, but Crimsworth does not suspect this at all, in fact he has lately confided his interest in her to Pelet himself. Crimsworth's imagination leads him so far astray that one night he opens the windows of his room - including the boarded one he had convinced Madame Pelet was an unnecessary precaution in the room of the girls' teacher - and muses on Zoraïde Reuter's wifely possibilities. Deficiencies she has, but these are understandable if not all correctable, and easily outweighed by her merits. Crimsworth continues "in voiceless soliloquy":

"I know she is not what the world calls pretty, no matter, there is harmony in her aspect and I like it. . . . Then I respect her talent; the idea of marrying a doll or a fool was always abhorrent to me; I know that a pretty doll, a fair fool might do well enough for the honey-moon - but when passion cooled, (15) how dreadful to find a lump of wax and wood laid in my bosom, a half idiot clasped in my arms, and to remember that (16) I had made of this my equal - nay, my idol, to know that I must pass the rest of my dreary life with a creature incapable of understanding what I said, of appreciating what I thought or of sympathising with what I felt!" (XII, 110-111).

Such thoughts are interrupted by the entrance of Pelet and Zoraïde under his window and the revelation that they are planning their own wedding. They talk of and laugh at Crimsworth's pretensions, which Zoraïde only learns now from Pelet. A sleepless night ensues for Crimsworth: "Something feverish and fiery had got into my veins" (XII, 114), but the next day, after a cold bath, Crimsworth believes himself to be a better man for the experience. He has not the slightest inkling that the treachery, the deception, was largely of his own making.

It is interesting to note that the ideals of wedded love which Crimsworth had so strenuously insisted on in considering Zoraïde's matrimonial qualifications are no different than those he endlessly spouts when discussing his engagement and marriage to Frances Henri. His ideals do not change; there is nothing in the novel to eliminate the suspicion that his love for Frances is largely a result of another this time unobstructed projection of his own imagination. While his marriage endures and is satisfactory as far as we know, Crimsworth does seem more to force Frances Henri to fit his ideal of marriage, seems less to see her objectively or to derive his ideal from his experience. The extraordinary sensitivity he exhibits during courtship and after Hunsden meets Frances may have a component of fear, fear that she will prove a "deceiver" as did Zoraïde. If, to some degree he realizes that both amours have similar roots in his own wishful imagination, his uncontrollable apprehension of another disaster is, psychologically, shrewd characterization. On the other hand, unsentimental realism would dictate that for a man as traumatized as William Crimsworth, a stable marriage, whatever its foundation, is as much as can reasonably be hoped. This line of thought is one of the factors which casts doubt on the love Lucy Snowe finds with Paul Emanuel. The question of whether suffering injures or strengthens its victim, is examined in <u>Shirley</u> and <u>Villette</u>. Crimsworth assumes the latter opinion, although the novel permits us to differ with him.

It is Crimsworth's high good fortune to have found a girl as attractive as Frances Henri who is also responsive to his strange wooing. The curt, cold, formality of his courtship may be explained as the result of his almost heroic self-control of his teeming emotions, but the pairing with Frances does not entirely convince and verges on the painfully unreadable. It is a triumph of characterization, though essentially a work of salvage, that Frances Henri is attractive and believable, and yet does not elicit the reader's pity for her marriage with William.

Crimsworth's discovery and courtship of Frances makes up the bulk of the central section of the novel, and while there may be some interest in secondary characters and in the turns of the plot, his actions and his portrayal of them throw a veil of tedium over all. He is not entirely ignorant of contradictory impulses in his psyche and this results in long dialogues within himself, couched in the worst of eighteenth-century prose, and so laced with capitalized abstractions that the original typesetters silently reduced scores of them to lower case. His overt dialogue is equally stiff and tiresome. He is forever congratulating himself for insights and actions that are merely stupid, and the reader's exasperation soon turns to boredom. No man would wish his adventures longer.

We need not delay ourselves with instances of this. Everyone who knows <u>The Professor</u> knows them. It is in order however to note that Crimsworth's moralizing, on marriage, love, independence, "Reason", etc., is for the most part merely restatement of Calvinist commonplaces. Crimsworth is no revolutionary, but he finds some excuse for his declamation of <u>sententia</u> in the Roman Catholic culture - he assumes it to be morally degraded - which surrounds him and opposes his views. Frances Henri, of course, is a Protestant. Moreover his moral statements are to some degree self-defensive rationalizations, and given in an often "purple" rhetoric that is as unattractive to us as our own day's dialogues between id, ego, and superego, will doubtless be to readers a century hence.

Zoraïde Reuter and Frances Henri are not the only women who excite Crimsworth's sexuality, but these are the two who would make tolerably respectable brides. Sexual desire with respect to them can be freely expressed in terms of marriage. The discussions of marriage, love, and allied topics, masks the sexual attraction and repulsion which motivates the intellectual debate but which itself cannot be either admitted in "respectable" society or acknowledged by Crimsworth's distressed psyche.

More than once Crimsworth tells us the dire consequences of "sensual indulgence". It leads to "the acrid bitterness of hopeless anguish" (XIX, 166). He makes a point of telling us, even in the least suspicious of circumstances, that he is deliberately reining in his sexual drives. Both Zoraïde Reuter, before his suit's ignominious end, and Frances Henri, have a lack of physical beauty that is a positive merit in Crimsworth's system of ideal love, and both are also distinctly preferred for their capability of mind. In contrast to these is the "pretty doll", the "fair fool", whose physical charms, "might do well enough for the honey-moon", but are her only charms. There is no indication that Crimsworth has personal experience of the merits and demerits of such brainless beauty, but he puts forth his opinions on this with fervor. While he makes no direct connection between them and his two potential wives, Crimsworth is in fact surrounded during his courtships by many young women, his pupils.

With some exceptions, he despises them. They are lazy, slovenly, uncouth, and irresponsible. They are slow to learn, and fast to connive, back-bite, cheat, and deceive. What is also clear, although Crimsworth does not say so, is that while many of them are of marriageable age, they come from respectable families for whom Crimsworth's economic status would bar him from the role of suitor. Frances Henri is penniless and without family. Miss Brontë's Preface to The Professor tells us that she wanted a hero whose life would be like those of "real living men" for whom riches only replaced rags through their own efforts - no wealthy wives for them. Sudden change of fortune and fate was part of Miss Brontë's world, and obviously part of her other novels. The choice of Crimsworth for the hero of this one is what forces it to be realistic, or antiromantic. No amount of good luck or fate can essentially change Crimsworth, nor does he react significantly to coincidences that fall to his lot. The later novels move away progressively from this, and examine fate, instead of trying to avoid it.

Crimsworth's sexual feelings toward the pupils cannot be expressed in terms of marital love, and so cannot be expressed at all. His aggressive scorn of the girls points to his shame of his inferior, dependent status, and to related psychosexual roots; for his disdain is too strong to be covered by the stated basis for it: low morals, low habits, degraded national character, and these all related to the bad influence of the Roman Church.

It is as illustrations of these evils that Crimsworth describes his pupils for us. His first thoughts on such girls, before he had known his pupils, was that they were "a kind of half-angels", good and pure. "Good features, ruddy blooming complexions, large and brilliant eyes, forms full even to solidity seemed to abound. I did not bear the first view like a stoic, I was dazzled, my eyes fell" (X, 84). But his first closer look, at the trio nearest his desk, gives this: "Eulalie was tall and very finely shaped, she was fair and her features were those of a Low Country Madonna; . . . there were no angles in her shape or in her face, all was curve and roundness - neither thought, sentiment nor passion disturbed by line or flush the equality of her pale, clear skin; her noble bust heaved with her regular breathing, her eyes moved a little - by these evidences of life alone, could I have distinguished her from some large handsome figure, (17) moulded in wax" (X, 84-85). This last figure of wax is used again in Crimsworth's soliloquy on Zoraïde: a woman without mental or spiritual qualities, he says there, would become "a lump of wax and wood" soon after the honeymoon (XII, 110-111).

Then there is Caroline: "Caroline was little, though evidently full grown; raven-black hair, very dark eyes, absolutely-regular features, with a colourless olive complexion, clear as to the face and sallow about the neck, formed in her that assemblage of points whose union many persons regard as the perfection of beauty. How, with the tintless pallor of her skin and the classic straightness of her lineaments, she managed to look sensual - I don't know - I think her lips and eyes contrived the affair between them and the result left no uncertainty on the beholder's mind" (X, 85).

This first survey of his charges, and I could quote more of the same, has taken Crimsworth but five minutes, and in even less time than that, he tells us, he "had buckled on a breast-plate of steely indifference and let down a visor of impassible austerity" (X, 86). This is an expansion of the metaphor of chivalric combat Crimsworth had previously used to indicate his response to his brother's malice. The connection between the two virulent relationships is thus made through metaphor, perhaps the only way possible short of clinical analysis. After teaching his girls a while, Crimsworth is ready to give us his generalizations on them: "They were each and all supposed to have been reared in utter unconsciousness of vice. The precautions used to keep them ignorant, if not innocent, were innumerable. How was it then, that scarcely one of those girls having attained the age of fourteen could look a man in the face with modesty and propriety?" We are asked to ponder the portraits Crimsworth supplies of "selected specimens":

Aurelia Koslow . . . is of middle size, stiffly made, body long, legs short, bust much developed but not compactly moulded, waist disproportionately compressed by an inhumanly braced corset, dress carefully arranged, large feet tortured into small bottines, head small, hair smoothed, braided, oiled and gummed to perfection, very low forehead, very diminutive and vindictive grey eyes, somewhat Tartar features, rather flat nose, rather high cheek-bones, yet the ensemble not positively ugly. . . . I should say she is slovenly and even dirty; her outward dress, as I have said, is well attended to, but in passing behind her bench, I have remarked that her neck is grey for want of washing, and her hair, so glossy with gum and grease, is not such as one feels tempted to pass the hand over, much less to run the fingers through. . . . She seems resolved to attract, and, if possible, monopolise my notice; to this end, she launches at me all sorts of looks, languishing, provoking, leering, laughing; As I am found quite proof against this sort of artillery - for we scorn what, unasked, is lavishly offered - she has recourse to the expedient of making noises; sometimes she sighs, sometimes groans, sometimes utters inarticulate sounds for which language has no name; if, in walking up the schoolroom, I pass near her, she puts out her foot that it may touch mine, if I do not happen to observe the manoeuvre and my boot comes in contact with her brodequin, she affects to fall into convulsions of suppressed laughter; if I notice the snare and avoid it, she expresses her mortification in sullen muttering. (XII, 99-101)

I believe this passage tells us more about William Crimsworth than Miss Koslow. And here is Adèle Dronsart: "This is a Belgian, rather low of stature, in form heavy, with broad waist, short neck and limbs, good red and white complexion, features well chiselled and regular, well-cut eyes of a clear brown colour, light brown hair, good teeth, age not much above fifteen, but as full-grown as a stout young Englishwoman of twenty. . . . She was an unnatural-looking being, so young, fresh, blooming, yet so Gorgon-like. Suspicion, sullen ill-temper were on her forehead, vicious propensities in her eye, envy and panther-like deceit about her mouth" (XII, 101). This feline image links with Crimsworth's later metaphor for the power of uncontrollable sexual impulse, "a tiger-leap", which he uses when he begins to admit that "such impulses are seldom altogether bad", and to allow that he too has such drives (XXIII, 234).

I should draw attention here to another striking metaphor. We find Crimsworth debating with himself the great question of Good and Evil: "Rough and steep was the path indicated by divine Suggestion; mossy and declining the green way along which Temptation strewed flowers; but whereas, methought, the Deity of love, the Friend of all that exists would smile well-pleased were I to gird up my loins and address myself to the rude ascent, so on the other hand, each inclination to the velvet declivity seemed to kindle a gleam of triumph on the brow of the man-hating, god-defying demon" (XX, 198). The thought is abstract, the imagery heavily sexual. And so it is with Crimsworth's portrayal of his students - the stated purpose is moral evaluation, but the focus is very much on the physical, and the judgment is not sober but passionate, even aggressive. One can say much the same of <u>The Professor</u>; it tests, on an intellectual plane, the relationship between Sense and Reason, while its materials are emotional and sexual, and while its most effective insights are psychological. Similarly, <u>Jane Eyre</u> tests a moral imperative, <u>Shirley</u> a social question, and <u>Villette</u> a theological one, and these novels, and their heroes, can fruitfully be analyzed in psycho-sexual terms. The psychological approach encompasses most of <u>The Professor</u>, while it merely illuminates dark corners of the later novels which have much more insistent intellectual and philosophical contents than does <u>The Professor</u>.

In her attempt to write an "anti-romance", a truthful story of a plain and sober hero, Miss Brontë largely failed to do much else. Crimsworth, and later Frances Henri, are not only English Protestants in Catholic Europe, but realistic characters in the world of the lascivious French novels. <u>The Professor</u> is at odds too with the "Silver-Fork" school, for whom aristocratic French women are paragons of beauty and virtue. Crimsworth's pupils at the Pensionnat aggressively refute this. Crimsworth conquers by adherence to precepts that recall Isaac Watts: he works assiduously, and he curbs his passions. The moral of the novel is no more complex than that, but there is some doubt if Charlotte Brontë was entirely satisfied with this moral. She succeeds in eschewing romantic sensationalism - although Edward Crimsworth is a stock villain of melodrama. And she succeeds, against heavy odds, in making Frances Henri a credible figure. But the intellectual thrust of the novel goes no further than its opposition to "romance", and its simplified Calvinism. What makes Crimsworth come to life, both as a character and as a person, are his amorous fascinations. Zoraïde Reuter, and minor characters among the female pupils, are the most vivid people in the novel. Crimsworth "exists" for the reader primarily as he reacts to them. When he thinks, he is a fool; when he feels, he is at least a man.

That this should be so can be referred, not to Miss Brontë's naïveté, but to a certain subversive distrust she feels of Crimsworth's attitudes. Those spirited Frenchwomen, and the budding tempters in the classroom, have all the book's vitality. The portrayal of Frances Henri is devoid of sexual content. It is Crimsworth who is the "lump of wax". The pat ending of the novel does not redeem our sense of his odd insufficiency. He is an exhibit of how dull and foolish a life of sexual denial can be. Whether because of early psychological trauma, or because of economic and social deprivation - the novel allows both readings - Crimsworth is less then a whole man, immeasurably less than an attractive one. His victory, and The Professor's overt moral, is in serious conflict with the tacit moral the book exhibits. Miss Brontë denies the doctrinaire radicalism of George Sand, and the assured conservatism of Walter Scott, but she is also attracted toward both these poles. If this conflict is a cause of The Professor's failure, it is a conflict that occurs in Miss Brontë's other books, and there, it is a source of their success.

NOTES:

(1) The Athenaeum, XXX (June, 1857), 755.
(2) Kathleen Tillotson, Novels of the Eighteen-Forties (London, 1961), 282-283. Very much the same thing is said more bluntly by Melvin R. Watson, "Form and Substance in the Brontë Novels", in: From Jane Austen to Joseph Conrad, ed. Rathburn and Steinmann(Minneapolis, 1958), 106-117. Fannie Elizabeth Ratchford, The Brontës' Web of Childhood (New York, 1941), 200, does not enlarge upon the unusual finding that The Professor is "better constructed than any of her later books", although otherwise Miss Ratchford's comments are unexceptional: "delicate and firm in drawing; virtuous in its extreme sobriety, but pulseless, a cold, colorless, lifeless exercise."
(3) See for example, Margaret Lane, Introduction to the Everyman ed. (New York, 1965), ix.
(4) Earl Allen Knies, "The Art of Charlotte Brontë", unpub. doctoral diss., U. of Illinois, 1964, p. 92.
(5) May Sinclair, The Three Brontës (Boston and New York, 1912), 114.
(6) Robert Martin, Charlotte Brontë's Novels, The Accents of Persuasion (New York, 1966), 34, notes the "unusually frank" depiction of sexual drives in the novel, and Robert B. Heilman's "Charlotte Brontë's 'New' Gothic", in: From Jane Austen to Joseph Conrad, 118-132, points to instances of strongly sexual descriptions and confrontations in all the novels. Neither of these critiques however take their insights into structural analysis or reach unconventional interpretations of The Professor.
(7) W.A. Craik, The Brontë Novels (London, 1968), 48-69, 56-57, 62, 60.
(8) Martin, 39.
(9) Letters, III, 206-207.
(10) This is a point not made in M.M. Brammer's study of a microfilm copy of "The Manuscript of The Professor", RES, XI (1960), 157-170.
(11) Quotations are identified in the text by chapter and page nos. of the Shakespeare Head Brontë. Where the ms differs from the printed text, as it

does in my quotations only in punctuation and capitalization, I prefer the ms reading. Miss Brontë's punctuation is idiosyncratic, and occasionally seems careless, but the printed text's regularization is less than systematic, and the ms often indicates different pace and emphasis.
(12) The ms, p. 306, shows two short words vigorously canceled, and an untouched exclamation point here. "God damn!" would fit the space and be consistent with other deletions by Nicholls.
(13) III, 19. The paragraph continues the metaphor of chivalric battle, referring to "ammunition", "shafts", and a "quiver".
(14) Martin, 40; Craik, 52-53; Knies, 97.
(15) At this point in the ms, p. 129, 3 lines have been energetically deleted. Evidently Rev. Nicholls found something more offensively explicit here then in the surrounding matter. Whether he kept the lines from the world, or only from the typesetters, cannot be known.
(16) Here three words have been deleted. See previous note.
(17) "Handsome figure" had been "fine shape" before revision, probably by Miss Brontë.

V

Jane Eyre

1

"Currer Bell has given us one work, at least, which will endure with the prose literature of our language. That work is <u>Jane Eyre</u>." (1) So did Sydney Dobell, the poet of <u>The Roman</u> (1850) and of <u>Balder</u> (1853), assure the readers of <u>The Palladium</u> in 1850. Dobell's prophetic powers are often less impressive - in the same article he said that Thackeray had yet to write anything that would outlive his age, and despite Currer Bell's public denial, he insisted that <u>Wuthering Heights</u> and <u>The Tenant of Wildfell Hall</u> were both and in that order products of her immature genius.

But if Dobell's insight into the future is uneven, his view of his own age differs little from a common modern interpretation of the Victorian situation: this "generation, which having thrown to the winds the folly and the wisdom of its fathers, is in the awful predicament of learning all things anew", (2) The contemporary "will to believe", the result of the undermining of traditional beliefs, he then relates to the special value of <u>Jane Eyre</u> for its day: "There is no other book in modern prose which it is so absolutely impossible to disbelieve." Dobell has in mind both the vividness with which the story and characters strike the reader, and the moral and spiritual truths the book inculcates. Surely Currer Bell's "faculty of imposing belief" would not have the "power for good" he speaks of, if the only belief imposed was in the facts of the story.

Dobell is not alone in seeing Miss Brontë's moral contribution. Here is Charles Kingsley on Mrs. Gaskell's <u>Life of Charlotte Brontë</u>, and perhaps with <u>Jane Eyre</u> in mind too: "(It) will do good. It will shame literary people into some stronger belief that a simple virtuous practical home life is consistent with high imaginative genius; and it will shame, too, the prudery of a not overly cleanly, though carefully whitewashed age, into believing that purity is now (as in all ages till now) quite compatible with the knowledge of evil." (3)

If <u>Jane Eyre</u> has borne a moral message to its readers, the message has been one of revolution. The novel is an exhibit in the history of feminism, for Jane's plight points up the narrow scope, in employment and education, that was woman's fate in early Victorian England. And Jane insists too on a relationship with the male that, if not of equality, is a long way from simple submission. Jane is also in full revolt against the rigorous Protestantism of Brocklehurst and St. John Rivers.

The novel's feminism, as has often been pointed out, (4) reflects contemporary agitation for reform of the "governess question," and for wider educational opportunities for women. The criticism of hypocritical and extreme forms of Evangelical Christianity is also part of the increased attention novelists were paying to religious matters, and of the increased attention clergymen and enthusiastic believers were paying to the possibilities of prose fiction. Evangelical tracts had long existed in a form known as "the tale" - indeed the Rev. Patrick Brontë had published one - and, prompted in large measure by the Oxford Movement, and by the causes that made that possible, the quantity and quality of religious novels was enjoying a boom. In the 1840's, as opposed to later decades in which the problem of doubt occupied the center of this stage, sectarian argumentation was predominant. (5) Currer Bell's attack on Brocklehurst's "religion" has this relationship to its time, as well as one to the attack on hypocrisy and cruelty that is one of the preoccupations of the English novel. Dickens would not have handled Brocklehurst just as Miss Brontë did, but the man and his works would have appealed to Dickens as a most suitable target. Similarly, the virulent attacks on the Catholic church, by Crimsworth and by Lucy Snowe, are clearly part of the counterattack against the "Papal Aggression". (6) One can go a bit further and relate <u>Jane Eyre</u> to Disraeli's <u>Tancred</u>, also published in 1847. In this novel religious doubt and the perplexing sectarian wars are encountered by a highly idiosyncratic form of direct revelation. (7) The intervention of Providence in the world of <u>Jane Eyre</u> is another sort of direct revelation of Divine purpose. <u>Jane Eyre</u> is then a novel of reform and religious import in an age of such novels. But <u>Jane Eyre</u> has survived as its contemporaries have not, and not because of its feminism or its demonstration of Divine justice.

   The vividness of the story of Jane Eyre is attested by the continued popularity of the novel with the common reader and by the pronouncements of scores of professional readers. That the novel has, or even had, a coherent spiritual message has not been the focus of later Brontë studies however, although in recent years it has been announced that, far from being a novel of protest or rebellion as its surface meaning suggests, <u>Jane Eyre</u> is in fact conservative if not reactionary: "<u>Jane Eyre</u> and <u>Wuthering Heights</u> represent the ostensible triumph of the secular, moderate liberal, sentimental point of view over the mythical, tragic point of view." The marriage of Rochester and Jane is not a victory of Christian ethics, nor a consummation of love grounded in mutual affection and respect. It is a "domestication" of a passion that represents a threat to established values and structures of society: "Rochester's injuries are, I should think a symbolic castration." (8) The novel then, does carry a "message", though hardly the one Miss Brontë intended nor the one apparent to some early readers.

   <u>Jane Eyre</u>'s ending, the maiming of Rochester, the death of Bertha Mason and the marriage this makes possible, do not go down well with modern readers, common and professional. Not only does the fire at Thornfield, despite the novel's preparations for it, seem too pat a solution to the plot's intricacies, but Rochester's punishment seems unnecessarily severe to the liberal conscience. Jane's anguished decision to flee Rochester and her dazed wanderings in search of food and shelter seem to many sufficient homage to the moral imperative. The extenuating circumstances in her case need not require more punishment than this, and those who believe this often suspect that Charlotte Brontë believed it too. Jane's love of Rochester is indeed presented with a vividness that convinces us not only of its depth and ardor, but of its primacy over moral considerations. Jane should have stayed with Rochester - <u>Amor vincit omnia</u>. And does not Jane herself return to Rochester before she knows of Bertha Mason's death? <u>Jane Eyre</u> is no moral "Tale", but, like some of George Sand's novels, a daringly explicit portrayal and defense of passion. Its ending is merely, in this view, a half-hearted sop to prudish respectability.

   The "hysterically moralistic tone" of much criticism of Miss Brontë, Wayne Burns tells us, indicates that these critics "fully understand or sense the veiled sexuality in the novel". (9) He insists that Jane's response to Rochester's telepathic call is described in terms of sexual orgasm. Joseph Prescott points to Charlotte Brontë's deliberate use of obscene double-entendre. (10) Burns again, and Martin Day, relate their similar and remarkable findings to the novel's ending, both seeking to discover and defend its structural integrity. (11)

   Sydney Dobell was quite typical of his day in finding the book of highest excellence despite blunders of "construction" and verisimilitude. (12) If this was a paradox to him, it did not disturb his peace, but that a work of art should be successful and at the same time deficient in unity, structure, and technique, violates modern critical dogma and impels reëxamination and a search for heretofore unnoticed and unsought evidences of artistic competence. One suspects as well that the combination of high aesthetic value and at least a superficially "Victorian" moral outlook is another distasteful matter. How can a book satisfy moderns for whom its nominal moral stance is repugnant?

Many attempts to relate the undeniable power of Jane Eyre to modern theories of aesthetic unity and structure have been less ambitious and controversial, and highly rewarding. It has been often shown, for instance, that Rochester and St. John Rivers represent a balance of temptations to Jane, the one overly swayed by passion, the other overly repressive of passion. And Rivers' coldness repeatedly figured in terms of ice and marble, is linked to Brocklehurst through the metaphor, applied to both, of a "column". There are three families in the novel, the Brocklehursts, Ingrams, and Rivers, which consist of two daughters and one son, each family figuring with increasing prominence in each of the three main sections of the book. A network of cross references, many of them made directly by the narrator, exists between these and other parallel patterns. Hence various parts of the novel are pulled together toward unity.

Similarly, a network of verbal echoes seems to exist in the book. A casual remark by Rochester early in the Thornfield section: "I have all my limbs and all my features like any other man" (XIV; I, 168), is an ironic preparation for his catastrophe. Jane's curt, "No, sir" to Rochester's "do you think me handsome?" echoes her answer to Brocklehurst's earlier catechism. Parallel references to Jane's possible future in hell, by Brocklehurst and by Rivers, (13) further link the first and third sections of the novel and reinforce the felt continuity of Jane's character over the span of years. Many more instances of this sort have been noted, leading commentators to see the book as "a novel built on recurrences", (14) organized like "dramatic poetry" (15) or a "symphonic" (16) structure.

Another way in which unity is achieved, and the novel's power explained, is through prophetic dreams, omens, and symbols. The charades played at Thornfield for instance, shadow forth a possible future for the chief players and for the observing governess; the riven tree, still joined at its roots, is a complex but clear symbol of the lovers' fate, and even the pictures Rochester selects from Jane's portfolio have been said to be "prophetic visions". (17)

From such examination of the text emerges not only a wanted explanation of the novel's coherence, but also a strong indication that its composition was not impromptu, but carefully, even meticulously planned. Mrs. Tillotson in fact, taking into consideration these factors and the ways in which exposition is slowly and dramatically revealed, tells us that Jane Eyre, like Wuthering Heights, "must have been planned backwards". (18)

But another category of pattern, that of imagery, is to some critics evidence of an unconscious, perhaps fortuitous richness: that of the "mythic, natural, and unconscious strength of an earlier literature". (19) The moon as a symbol, albeit one with shifting, ambivalent, or ambiguous connotations, has received a good deal of this attention. (20) So have trees, and nature imagery generally, (21) and much has been said about patterns of meaning arising from patterns of metaphors of fire and ice. (22)

Despite these investigations of the aesthetic coherence of Jane Eyre the several investigators are often at odds with each other and are far from demonstrating either that such coherence is an important source of the novel's power, or from agreeing about its real moral attitude. An interesting attempt at consolidation of modern findings concludes by stating that "this nature imagery, along with its intense amatory elements, as it parallels the main events of the story of Jane Eyre clearly serves as the main source of the novel's power". (23) I doubt that many are convinced of this. And demonstrations of unity tend to overlook aspects of Jane Eyre,that are excrescent whatever sort of unity is being postulated.

Rochester's administration of a mysterious potion to the wounded Mason, a drug procured "at Rome, of an Italian charlatan" (XX; I, 277), is a cliché functioning at a low level of artistic integrity. Repeated reference to Bertha Mason as "the foul German spectre – the Vampyre", is a touch of low-level terror with but tenuous links to dominant patterns of imagery and thought. Jane learns Rochester's fate in the fire at Thornfield through an interview with the landlord of the local inn. "I was the late Mr. Rochester's butler", he tells her, and so provides a specious plot thrill as Jane thinks for a moment that her Rochester is the "late" one (XXXVI; II, 248). The butler's unthinking insistence on retailing his own rambling history instead of the information Jane is panting to learn - a standard Gothic device, used to more defensible effect in Otranto and Udolpho - produces suspense, but at some sacrifice in the reader's respect for the author. And there are other exhibits from the book that militate against attempts to see Jane Eyre as a well-made aesthetic object. To shrink from such flaws, while stretching to demonstrate coherence wherever possible, is to avoid the inescapable if unpleasing truth that a novel can succeed brilliantly and yet be riddled with naïve techniques and hackneyed attempts at meretricious effects.

It is surely a flaw for Charlotte Brontë's voice to intrude and break the continuity of the story. (24) Jane's isolated reference to her wish to earn her living by setting up a school of her own (XIX; I, 256), is a similar fault, and would be even if we did not know the other novels or the biography. Is it not a needless, non-functional coincidence that Miss Temple is acquainted with Mr. Lloyd, the apothecary of Gateshead? Mrs. Harden, the housekeeper at Lowood, "a woman after Mr. Brocklehurst's own heart, made up of equal parts of whale bone and iron" (XIII; I, 88), bears a name that is either unnecessarily coincidental, or else an unfunctional expression of Miss Brontë's private ire. The name of Lady Ingram's Irish friend, "Mrs. Dionysius O'Gall of Bitternut Lodge" (XXIII; II, 15), is a misplaced attempt at conventional humor which obscures the meaning of an important scene. Rochester had seriously considered sending Jane to Ireland - the comic address is not his joke but Miss Brontë's. Time and again the elevated rhetoric produces discordant and disturbing patches of purple. Rochester's speech, often very stiff, can intermittently adopt the tones of the Jacobean stage: "My seared vision! My crippled strength!" (XXXVII; II, 273), or be inadvertently comic: " 'Her very fingers!' he cried; 'her small slight fingers! If so, there must be more of her' " (XXXVII, 259). The reader who remains undismayed or confused by this last gaucherie will surely have his own example to offer.

Unlike the purple patches and striking shifts in rhetoric in say Joyce's Portrait of the Artist, Miss Brontë's lapses are often just that, not functional pointers to meaning. In fact, Joyce's autobiographical novel is in many ways a sophistication of techniques which exist in a crude form in Jane Eyre. His patterns of imagery, character names, literary echoes, and plot balances, possess a coherence much beyond Miss Brontë. Despite this, the meaning of his novel, specifically the location of its central irony, is a matter of much dispute. Analysis of Miss Brontë's meaning through the same critical methods of textual analysis which is enlightening but inconclusive for Joyce, faces considerable problems when Miss Brontë's crudities are not glossed over. The traces in Jane Eyre of obsessive motifs carried over from the Angrian tales, (25) can not be treated in the same way as Joyce's motif of flight, for example, in the Portrait. Nor is one always happy to agree to demonstrations of highly complex patterning of moon and nature images. How much of this is simply part of the tradition of Romantic and Pre-Romantic poetry, here used as conventional space-filler between dramatic episodes? How much of the echoing of imagery and dialogue is simply inadvertent repetition, a failure of invention?

The questions insistently remain with us. Why does Jane Eyre succeed as it does? What is its moral attitude?

2

Jane Eyre postulates a comprehensive if highly idiosyncratic relationship between man and Deity. It embodies a faith in a just although sometimes incomprehensible God, and a Puritan belief in the inexorable consequences of sin. The characters affirm or deny these principles, and, through the agency of the plot, reap reward or punishment accordingly. Jane and Rochester move from imperfect adherence to the novel's theology, through suffering, to enlightenment. Along the way a variety of alternate moral and theological positions are confronted and examined.

Jane Eyre is full of supernaturalism, much of it of the folklore variety. Jane, for instance, has a momentary fear that sounds of Rochester's approach are in fact signs of a "Gytrash", "a North-of-England spirit" who figured in "certain of Bessie's tales". The event soon dissipates her qualms, but the mature author of these memoirs takes the opportunity to explain: "In those days I was young, and all sorts of fancies bright and dark tenanted my mind: the memories of nursery stories were there amongst other rubbish; and when they recurred, maturing youth added to them a vigour and vividness beyond what childhood could give" (XII; I, 142).

This is but one of the novel's many statements of disbelief in the unearthly, and the same end is served by the deliberate deflation of the potentially mysterious: "Sometimes I saw her (Grace Poole): she would come out of her room with a basin, or a plate, or a tray in her hand, go down to the kitchen and shortly return, generally (oh, romantic reader, forgive me for telling the plain truth!) bearing a pot of porter" (XII; I, 139).

Such debunking of conventional superstition resembles Scott's practice. Natural explanations for strange events are delayed until after the storyteller has reaped their benefit. Other events remain unexplained. The author, who elsewhere lets the reader into his confidence about such matters, admits that even his sophisticated intelligence is baffled. His known cynicism, and his habit of familiar frankness with the reader, makes the residual supernaturalism highly effective.

Jane peers into Moor House and sees the Rivers girls for the first time: "I had nowhere seen such faces as theirs: and yet, as I gazed on them, I seemed intimate with every lineament" (XXVIII; II, 123). Young Jane ponders the sense of familiarity with these "strangers", as elsewhere she meditates on the possibility that Bessie's tales of wonder have some truth in them. The mature Jane enters the story at almost its exact center to give us her feelings on this point:

Presentiments are strange things! and so are sympathies; and so are signs: and the three combined make one mystery to which humanity has not yet found the key. I never laughed at presentiments in my life; because I have had strange ones of my own. Sympathies, I believe, exist: (for instance, between far-distant, long-absent, wholly estranged relatives; asserting, notwithstanding their alienation, the unity of the source to which each traces his origin) whose workings baffle mortal comprehension. And signs, for aught we know, may be but the sympathies of Nature with man. (XXI; I, 285)

The mature Jane has come to believe what she once only suspected. The "strange" "presentiments" to which she refers include the telepathic communication with Rochester and presumably the recognition of her cousins at Moor House. Both omens proved true.

That the telepathy occurred is irrefutable. Natural explanation is inconceivable. Significantly, on receipt of Rochester's mysterious summons, Jane's belief in its reality is coupled with a careful discrimination between it and other mysterious perceptions: " 'Where are you?' I exclaimed. The hills beyond Marsh-Glen sent the answer faintly back - 'Where are you?' I listened. The wind sighed low in the firs: all was moorland loneliness and midnight hush. 'Down superstition!' I commented, as that spectre rose up black by the black yew at the gate. 'This is not thy deception, nor thy witchcraft.' " The telepathy itself is of a different order of phenomena: " 'It is the work of nature. She was roused, and did - no miracle - but her best' " (XXXV; II, 240). Here Jane knows for sure what she had suspected earlier: the "sympathies of Nature with man" may show themselves in "signs". The prophetic and well-timed splitting of the great tree is additional evidence, as are other forms of accurate omens. Jane can not doubt the dream in which Nature herself appears personified as "Mother" and directly advises her to "flee temptation" (XXVII; II, 105).

For the context of thought in which what would usually be called miraculous is "no miracle", we may turn to the "Natural Supernaturalism" of Sartor Resartus. A real miracle, Carlyle held there, would be a violation of the Laws of Nature. But since these Laws are beyond even the most enthusiastic scientist's grasp, it is better to call all things miracles than to credit Deity whenever our own ignorance becomes most apparent. "Miracle? What is a miracle? Can there be a thing more miraculous than any other thing?" (26)

That Jane should describe the telepathic sensation in terms susceptible of a sexual reading in no way detracts from the religious orientation that the novel makes abundantly clear. As many poets have known, the sexual can figure the religious ecstasy - and no wonder: the varieties of ecstatic experience are few. Jane's discrimination of superstition from the work of Nature insists on the spirituality of Rochester's call. She denied that the sound of a voice outside of her mind, or the sight before her eyes, were suggestions of Nature. There is no confusion in her creed between the Sacred and the sensible.

If all things are "no miracles", we must so consider the fire at Thornton, the death of Bertha Mason, and the maiming of Rochester. All are to be presumed workings of Divine Law. As we cannot know this Law, we cannot know for sure why the events occurred, and Jane does not attempt to formulate reasons for them. "Some say it was a just judgment on him for keeping his first marriage secret, and wanting to take another wife while he had one living" (XXXVI; II, 252), but Jane makes no response to this report of local gossip. All she wants to know from the loquacious landlord of The Rochester Arms is if her master lives.

There is a passage in the novel in which Jane's views bear directly on the meaning of the catastrophe. Having fled from Thornfield, she finds herself "alone" and "absolutely destitute". After a meal of bilberries she retires to rest in the heath. Her "sad heart" will not let her sleep: "It trembled for Mr. Rochester and his doom: it bemoaned him with bitter pity; it demanded him with ceaseless longing." At this point Jane reënacts the spiritual crisis depicted in Lamartine's "L'infini dans les cieux". It is paraphrase bordering on translation:

> Worn out with this torture of thought, I rose to my knees. Night was come, and her planets were risen: a safe, still night; too serene for the companionship of fear. We know that God is everywhere; but certainly we feel His presence most when His works are on the grandest scale spread before us: and it is in the unclouded night-sky, where His worlds wheel their silent course, that we read clearest His infinitude, His omnipotence, His omnipresence. I had risen to my knees to pray for Mr. Rochester. Looking up, I, with tear-dimmed eyes, saw the mighty milky-way. Remembering what it was - what countless systems there swept space like a soft trace of light - I felt the might and strength of God. Sure was I of His efficiency to save what He had made: convinced I grew that neither earth should perish, nor one of the souls it treasured. I turned my prayer to thanksgiving: the Source of Life was also the Saviour of spirits. Mr. Rochester was safe: he was God's and by God would he be guarded. I again nestled to the breast of the hill; and ere long, in sleep, forgot sorrow. (XXVIII; II, 112-113)

"Rochester was safe . . . and would be guarded." Subsequent events do nothing to temper this simple faith.

As far as Rochester is concerned, God's hand has become equally apparent and trustworthy. The telepathic cry, he later tells Jane, was preceded by an acknowledgment of sin and a surrender of self to God. It was in many ways a typical Evangelical conversion, but rather more convincing than such reports generally are. Neither suicidal despair nor Rochester's desire for Jane is obliterated by his humiliation. That he should call Jane "the alpha and omega" of his "heart's wishes" at this moment of evidently successful communication with Deity is a blasphemy that Jane herself dare not repeat.

Her own comment on the relative priorities of human and Divine love is given in this judgment on her past errors: "My future husband was becoming to me my whole world; and more than the world: almost my hope of heaven. He stood between me and every thought of religion, as an eclipse intervenes between man and the broad sun. I could not, in those days, see God for his creature: of whom I had made an idol" (XXIV; II, 45). There is a Biblical echo in this, (27) as well as an echo of Rochester's reference, earlier in this chapter, to "The World Well Lost", the subtitle of Dryden's All for Love. (28)

Rochester too, after the catastrophe and after Jane's return, clearly states his agreement and confirms his new faith:

> "Jane! you think me, I daresay, an irreligious dog: but my heart swells with gratitude to the beneficent God of this earth just now. He sees not as man sees, but far clearer: I would have sullied my innocent flower - breathed guilt on its purity: the Omnipotent snatched it from me. I, in my stiff-necked rebellion, almost cursed the dispensation: instead of bending to the decree, I defied it. Divine justice pursued its course; disasters came thick on me: I was forced to pass through the valley of the shadow of death. His chastisements are mighty; and one smote me which has humbled me for ever. You know I was proud of my strength: but what is it now, when I must give it over to foreign guidance, as a child does it(s) weakness? Of late, Jane - only - only of late - I began to see and acknowledge the hand of God in my doom. I began to experience remorse, repentance; the wish for reconcilement to my Maker. I began sometimes to pray: very brief prayers they were, but very sincere. (XXXVII; II, 275-276).

The passage is rich with Biblical allusions and with echoes of earlier phrases in the novel. Rochester quotes from the Psalms, (29) a portion of the Bible that young Jane had told Brocklehurst was "not interesting" (IV; I, 37). Jane and Rochester are both wiser now.

What we have been examining here are two stories of faith, the progress of two Pilgrims. The precipitating event in the lives of each is the crossing of the other's path. This is the coincidence, the "miracle", that determines the form of the novel and which provides the crucial trials for each protagonist. Neither Jane nor Rochester think that they have been the victims of a capricious fate or a malicious deity, but neither do they make explicit their discovery that a stern but benevolent God has been shaping their ends. Nor does the author of the book draw the moral that heavenly intervention is the framework of the novel. Jane Eyre, the heroine of the book, and Currer Bell, the surrogate for its author, come together here. They share the same secret, the same conclusions about the world. What the characters say, and what the author "says" by the act of writing the novel are identical. Jane Eyre would defend her view of life in the same way as the author would defend the improbabilities of her novel's plot. The form and content of the book are indistinguishable.

Jane's story can be seen as the progressively wiser discrimination between superstition and revelation, and between perfect and imperfect creeds. Helen Burns, early in the novel, presents a faith which provides a corrective both to Brocklehurst's severity and to young Jane's Old Testament belief in an ethic of retribution: " 'I must dislike those who, whatever I do to please them, persist in disliking me; I must resist those who punish me injustly.' " The mature Jane would not disagree with Helen's dim view of this: " 'Heathens and savage tribes hold that doctrine; but Christians and civilized nations disown it' " (VI; I, 69-70). But Helen's stoicism and her idea of universal salvation are extremes that Jane skirts without abating her affection for Helen or her respect for her belief. Helen's early death seems to confirm Jane's belief that such saintliness is a special faith for special persons.

The suggestion that Rome is the proper haven for Eliza Reed's particular brand of asceticism is clear too. And Jane's last thoughts on Mrs. Reed are also within the Protestant framework. A sinner's deathbed is the scene of monumental interest and importance for the religious, particularly for the Calvinist. Mrs. Reed's turning away from the offered reconciliation with Jane, and her probable refusal, or inability, to take her last opportunity to turn in repentance to God, inspires in Jane pity and dread, "a grating anguish for her woes - not my loss - and a sombre tearless dismay at the fearfulness of death in such a form" (XXI; I, 312). The possibility of an eternity of hellfire was probably suggested to many early readers of this scene, although Jane does not elucidate the grounds of her "dismay".

Jane's reactions to proposals from Rochester and Rivers are often seen in terms of a clear-cut dichotomy: Rochester lets love of man rule him too much, Rivers too little. Jane's own characterization of the two relationships is more complex and brings into focus their ethical and religious implications: "I was almost as hard beset by him (Rivers) now as I had been once before, in a different way, by another. I was a fool both times. To have yielded then would have been an error of principle; to have yielded now would have been an error of judgment" (XXXV; II, 238).

Yielding to Rochester's proposal that she become his mistress would have run counter to her moral principles. Even if there had been no Bertha Mason, Rochester had been a reprobate and a moral anarchist: "I know my Maker sanctions what I do", he had said about his intended bigamy, and presumably he said the same about his European adventures. Rochester's attitude here, and some other of his attributes, are, as has often been stated and overstated, Byronic. His travel in Europe, seeking the love that eluded him with his mad wife, is a clear analogue to Byron's heartsick heroes.

If yielding to Rochester would have been an error of principle, St. John River's proposal only threatened to involve Jane in an "error of judgment". His morality is not in question any more than was Helen Burn's and indeed both earn Jane's respectful and heart-felt eulogies. Rivers presented another permissible variant of religious thought, one that again did not quite suit Jane. The portrayal of his doctrines, if it does not contain references to Carlyle directly, is certainly related to the body of thought of which he is a prime spokesman. (30) Rivers' choice of Biblical texts includes his namesake St. John's exhortation to work before "the night cometh, when no man can work", the same text which, slightly altered, ends Carlyle's chapter on "The Everlasting Yea". Further evidence of Rivers' commitment to the Gospel of Work occurs at every turn. The work must be, for one who has the capabilities, above mere domestic chores: " 'Don't cling so tenaciously to ties of the flesh; save your constancy and ardour for an adequate cause; forbear to waste them on trite and transient objects. Do you hear, Jane?' " Jane hears, but this is not her way: " 'Yes; just as if you were speaking Greek' " (XXXIV; II, 202).

As Rivers increases his insistent pressure on Jane, she repeatedly describes him as "earnest". The word itself appears five times in little more than a page (XXXV; II, 237-238). It seemed to Jane that, "He was of the material from which nature hews her heroes - Christian and Pagan - her lawgivers, her statesmen, her conquerors: a steadfast bulwark for great interests to rest upon" (XXXIV; II, 204). Jane understands the nature and importance of the "Hero", and is not immune to "Hero-Worship", but she chooses not to surrender herself to either.

Rivers is a good deal more than a simple portrait of Victorian "earnestness" in its Evangelical guise, nor is Jane's response to him one of simple defiance. It is clear to the reader, as it is clear to Jane and to Rivers himself, that his call has a good admixture of personal motivation. His reactions to Rosamond Oliver's physical presence, and to the idea of marrying her, have emotional and psychological components that would surely be of great interest to the psychoanalyst. The obsessive nature of his aspirations, the insistent egoism, seen in the way he repeatedly turns his conversations with Jane toward his problems, beg for consideration as signs of emotional distress.

In a psychological analysis of the novel, Rivers might be Jane Eyre's version of William Crimsworth. But the moral and intellectual framework of Jane Eyre is so much fuller and more insistent than that of The Professor that this framework is that to which criticism owes its first and primary attention. And unlike The Professor, Jane Eyre's coincidence-ridden plot makes a moral point and directs us to a moral rather than a psychological analysis. Jane Eyre's language is heavily Biblical, and its catastrophe seems to have been based on a Biblical text: "And if thy right eye offend thee, pluck it out, and cast it from thee: for it is profitable for thee that one of thy members should perish, and not that thy whole body should be cast into hell. And if thy right hand offend thee, cut it off, and cast it from thee: for it is profitable for thee that one of thy members should perish, and not that thy whole body should be cast into hell."

Miss Brontë and many of her readers were aware of the context in which these verses appear. It makes clear the centrality of the passage to the crime and punishment of the novel: "Ye have heard it was said by them of old time, Thou shalt not commit adultery: But I say unto you, That who soever looketh on a woman to lust after her hath committed adultery with her already in his heart. . . . It hath been said, Whosoever shall put away his wife, let him give her a writing of divorcement: But I say unto you, That whosoever shall put away his wife, saving for the cause of fornication, causeth her to commit adultery: and whosoever shall marry her that is divorced committeth adultery." (31) The Bible does not blink the power of sexual desire, even in woman, but the novel chooses not to relate Jane to this. It is the moral and religious import of human passion and sexuality that is examined in Jane Eyre, and we forget this at the risk of misreading.

Presumably near death, Jane stumbles onto the threshold of the Rivers. It has been an utterly random flight from Thornfield. It ends at the one threshold, out of all possible thresholds, that the plot and the heroine require. During the journey Jane is preoccupied with the dangerous results her departure may have on Rochester: "I had injured - wounded - left my master. I was hateful in my own eyes. Still I could not turn, nor retrace one step. God must have led me on. As to my own will or conscience, impassioned grief had trampled one and stifled the other" (XXVII; II, 108). There, writ small, is the story of Jane Eyre. It is a religious "tale", a spiritual autobiography. Its moral base is orthodox, its feminism and its treatment of sectarian differences are contemporary issues, not purely personal trail-blazing.

3

But for many, Charlotte Brontë, if not "the greatest writer of passion in the English language", (32) is at least the writer of a novel that "will long be remembered . . . among the most vivid masterpieces in the rare order of literary 'confessions' ". (33) Critics and readers, late and soon, speak of the intensity, the vividness, the passionate force of the novel's heroine, not of the book's moral lesson.

While one might question the statement that Jane Eyre was "a new kind of fictional treatment", bringing a new frankness and a new concentration on the personal as against the social aspects of life, a new functional use of the first person, (34) Miss Brontë's priority in these matters is of less moment than the fact that she did indeed excel in and through these particulars. Trollope, considering the tragic elements of both Jane Eyre and The Bride of Lammermoor, has this to say:

> But these stories charm us not simply because they are tragic, but because we feel that men and women with flesh and blood, creatures with whom we can sympathise, are struggling amidst their woes. It all lies in that. (35)

And what of the novel's moral content? It has been regularly ignored, disdained, and even interpreted, formally and tacitly, as a vindication of love's power and priority. Jane Eyre is the girl who loved Rochester, despite his history, despite his attempt to deceive her and his offer of concubinage, despite, at last, the cruel fate that maimed him. That other Jane Eyre, who recounts the story of her youthful error, suffering, and reconciliation in a stronger faith, does not interest us. And Charlotte Brontë's remarks on the reception of Jane Eyre suggest that it is not only the morally emancipated of our own day who admire the novel for the "wrong" reason: "As to the character of 'Lucy Snowe' my intention from the first was that she should not occupy the pedestal to which 'Jane Eyre' was raised by some injudicious admirers." (36)

In the last analysis we must refer the unintended apotheosis of Jane Eyre to the same subversive sympathy for sexual vitality that we glimpsed in The Professor. For it is the youthful and passionate Jane, not her moralizing older self, who is most vivid to the reader. The means by which this comes about are neither rhetorical nor ideological, but as I shall attempt to show, technical.

It has been repeatedly shown and acknowledged, it is axiomatic, that when a fictional character is presented from the "inside", and through dialogue which reveals his state of mind, that character engages the reader's interest and sympathy. He may be, in fact and by the author's design, an evil man, as evil as Ferdinand Count Fathom, as evil as Milton's Satan himself, but so presented, the reader is impelled if not to affection, at least to a judgment so generous that the author's intentions are foiled. Thackeray's Barry Lyndon is an example of the attempt to swim upstream against this axiom of fiction. Jane Austen, for Emma, took "a heroine whom no one but myself will much like", and produced one who, as W.D. Howells said, "takes the fancy". Just how Miss Austen managed this has been extensively shown, (37) but much of the credit must go to her harnessing of the power of our axiom: we like what we believe to be human, and in fiction to be human is to think.

The use of the first-person, autobiographic mode provides the opportunity to give a theoretically continuous interior view of the narrator-cum-hero, but the converse of our axiom is soon discovered: a character who praises himself is not liked. All her protestation of humility does not succeed in making us like Esther Summerson in Dickens's Bleak House. She is very good indeed, but we will not tolerate her telling us so, even if that is not the purpose of her revelations.

One way to avoid these pitfalls, and the one taken by Jane Eyre, is to combine the autobiographic with the objective mode in such a way that the axiom serves rather than hinders the aims of the novelist. This is done by splitting the heroine, not merely into the young Jane who acts and the mature Jane who reports, but into a continuum of Jane Eyres. At various stages of the story, young Jane acts and also comments and reports on her earlier actions and thoughts, and all of this is presented in turn by the mature Jane who is herself in a continuous state of action and change. For the mature Jane, in the process of reporting her story, reads herself back into it, forgets her present state, and relives her past, in ever-varying degrees. But she also judges her past, at times severely. Thus she creates in herself a continuum of attitudes, shifting between the poles of sympathetic identification with her young self and objective judgment of her past errors.

A great deal of criticism of Jane Eyre is effectively oblivious to this discrimination. "It is through Jane's consciousness that we see the other characters", (38) a critic writes, but the value of this insight is severely limited by the failure to attend to the temporal complexity of that consciousness. (39)

To oversimplify by extracting just two Janes, the young heroine and the mature narrator, permits us to indicate the novel's relationship to our axiom of the novel. The narrator never praises herself or the heroine. She censures, explains, excuses, and justifies the heroine's actions. The more the narrator's presence is felt, even when it is not actually censorious, the less we know young Jane, and the less uncritically do we view her. On the other hand, Jane the heroine, her mind, is also made present to us, and the more its presence is felt, the more sympathetically we take her. The plan of the novel requires that we eventually admire the composite Jane. We do so, even though all we know of her has come from her own mouth. She is not an entirely likable character, as she herself shows and tells us, but we have known her too well and too long for us to withhold sympathy.

It is also essential to the novel's purpose that we understand that we have here a story of the development of a "correct" moral and religious stance, and consequently a growth from a heroine defective in these regards. Our sympathy for the various Janes that appear in the course of this development is to be tempered by our understanding that Jane is imperfectly developed until she merges with the perfect Jane who is the narrator. The requisite control of the reader's response, the guidance of our sympathy and of our moral sense, is attempted by the manipulation of what we are calling for convenience, the narrative point of view of the two Janes.

This procedure, as Miss Brontë employs it in Jane Eyre, commits her to the avoidance of direct statement or evaluation by Currer Bell, the editor of Jane's memoirs, nor are we guided in any direct ways by Charlotte Brontë herself. The plan, by its self-contained subjectivity, runs the risk of ambiguity. Which Jane are we to believe when there is disagreement between them? In what way are we to evaluate the composite Jane? The terms of the world of the novel itself, its structure and its plot, are our only clues, and if for any reason we do not read this right, there is no other help.

There are, we shall say, two Jane Eyres, the young one who acts and who is often in error, and the mature one who reports and often points out this error. For the novel to succeed as planned, we must hear the voice of young Jane enough so that our sympathy is engaged in her behalf. Conversely, we must be conscious enough of the voice of the mature Jane so that an objective evaluation of young Jane is possible. A delicate balance is required, and it is evident from the generality of criticism of the novel that, if such a balanced view had been felt by some readers of the previous century, it has largely been lost for subsequent readers. We like Jane Eyre more than we should. The mature Jane is insufficiently known and characterized; she intrudes her voice and her consciousness too faintly for us to know her, like her, and believe her when she criticizes young Jane. The novel's plot and its message are not supported by the emotional reactions the book produces on the reader. Its intended unity is askew.

Among the ways young Jane's voice becomes present to us, direct dialogue is the most important and effective. It is the mode least affected by the fact that, from the viewpoint of the mature Jane, the dialogue is past rather than present. (The pun on "present" is useful here.) Each time we read a "she said", our sense of presentness is somewhat diminished, but even this reminder can be and is dispensed with often. As we read a page of dialogue in which Jane speaks or even listens, our sense of her presentness is very great. We enter and share the "time zone", as it were, in which she lives. She is as present to us, not as life itself, but as a character in a play or television play that we both watch and follow along with, word by word, in our copy of the script. Except that on the one hand we hear the dialogue delivered by another's voice, and in reading we hear it in our mind's ear as we read it ourselves, both experiences are psychologically very similar - the vivid impression of real life and presentness we experience in the theater is not much more vivid than the impression certain parts of certain novels can produce. In some circumstances, the novel's ability to present interior views and to manipulate time, may even tip this comparison in its favor.

Jane Eyre not only abounds in direct dialogue, it generally relies on this mode at crucial moments of the action. Supplementing direct dialogue is the high frequency of Jane's silent dialogue or soliloquy. This is presented within quotation marks although it is not in fact spoken. Such dialogue makes possible interior views of Jane that direct dialogue can only hint at, but generally at a lower level of presentness. We read silent soliloquy "silently", as it were, and it is less present also in that its content deals less with the present instant than with contemplation of the past or future.

In between direct dialogue and soliloquy, in terms of presentness, is indirect dialogue, the report of her mental processes that, while not in young Jane's voice, is so intimately portrayed that its voice, the voice of the mature Jane, is lost. A very great deal of what we know of Jane Eyre comes to us through these three modes. To categorize and compute the relative use of them and so to compare Jane Eyre with other novels would probably prove this statement, but the procedure is not one to be trusted. The degree of presentness produced is a more complex matter than my simplified categories imply. One page of dialogue in Jane Eyre may make Jane more present to us than a chapter of soliloquy by some other character. And one authorial intrusion at a crucial moment may distance us from Jane's present, and temper our sympathy for her for many pages of dialogue to follow.

Some sections of the narrative can only be categorized arbitrarily:

I had at heart a strange and anxious thought. Something had happened which I could not comprehend; no one knew of or had seen the event but myself: it had taken place the preceding night. Mr. Rochester that night was absent from home; nor was he yet returned: business had called him to a small estate of two or three farms he possessed thirty miles off - business it was requisite he should settle in person, previously to his meditated departure from England. I waited now his return; eager to disburthen my mind, and to seek of him the solution of the enigma that perplexed me. Stay till he comes, reader; and, when I disclose my secret to him, you shall share the confidence. (XXV; II, 47)

This begins as direct exposition by the mature Jane but its point of view becomes ambiguous as she enters into and identifies with young Jane. The past tense in the center of the paragraph is equally appropriate from either temporal point of view. The last sentence is inextricably ambiguous. It is an apostrophe to the reader, but by which Jane and from what time zone? The effect produced by such a passage has little to do with the appearance of quotation marks.

Another way in which young Jane's present is brought vividly to our consciousness is through the omission of significant and expected commentary. Jane makes no comment at all on discovering that the stranger she aided on the road is in fact the newly arrived master of Thornfield. At crucial moments in her relationship with him and with Rivers, a new bit of vital information comes to her, but she makes no comment on it at that time. The reader is led by such omissions to make the comment for himself, to figure out what young Jane must be thinking now. He is lured into her presence and into her time zone. A simple instance of this occurs on the night of the first party at Thornfield. Jane and Adèle are listening to its sounds from the top of the stairs: "The clock struck eleven. I looked at Adèle whose head leant against my soulder; her eyes were waxing heavy, so I took her up in my arms and carried her off to bed. It was near one before the gentlemen and ladies sought their chambers. The next day was as fine as its predecessor" (XVII; I, 216). Between the two last sentences, the reader may deduce that Jane stayed up until the party was over. More complex omissions of commentary at more crucial moments provide more intense cooperation, more forceful occasions for the reader to live the life of Jane's mind with her, to exclude the sense of Jane's pastness, to exclude the presentness of the mature Jane.

Young Jane is made present to us by direct physical description of her self and her surroundings. The description of the cold of the Lowood winters, and the sensations of exhaustion felt on the flight from Thornfield, are special cases of this. Although they are clearly in the mature Jane's voice, they are too personal, too intimate, to have the effect of authorial comment. Similar to this in effect are the detailed notations, nominally by the mature Jane, of young Jane's fine sense perceptions: "When I turned from it (the vista from the leads of Thornfield) and repassed the trap-door, I could scarcely see my way down the ladder; the attic seemed black as a vault compared with the arch of blue air to which I had been looking up" (XI; I, 135). Young Jane's acute perception is given us to share as she peers into the house at Marsh End: "This scene was as silent as if all the figures had been shadows, and the fire-lit apartment a picture; so hushed was it, I could hear the cinders fall from the grate, the clock tick in its obscure corner; and I even fancied I could distinguish the click-click of the woman's knitting-needles" (XXVIII; II, 123). It is a convention of fiction that the narrator has powers of knowledge and of memory that in other contexts would be incredible. Fiction depends upon our assent to this convention, but the feats here exhibited have a more important claim to legitimacy. Like the Proustian use of the memory of exquisite and delicate sensations, the mature Jane's memory serves to make young Jane present to the reader. Only she, we in fact believe, could report so intimately, and only when the sensation was fresh in her mind.

This technique is used by Charlotte Brontë in conjunction with another method of recapturing and recreating the past, namely the shift from past to present tense. Such a shift need not intensify the sense of the presentness of past events. It can be a means of drawing attention to the detached author's role as a deliberate arranger of an aesthetically pleasing panorama of a scene that is not only past, but fictional. (40) The present tense is used this way in <u>Jane Eyre</u> (XI; I, 117), but more often its function is quite different. Chapter twenty-three begins with an extensive use of present tense as Jane, on Midsummer Eve, walks in the garden prior to Rochester's entry and the interview during which the lovers will become affianced. The absence of quotation marks around the following does not keep the location of the narrative voice from being ambiguous: "Sweet-briar and southernwood, jasmine, pink, and rose have long been yielding their evening sacrifice of incense: this new scent is neither of shrub nor flower; it is - I know it well - it is Mr. Rochester's cigar. . . . I hear a nightingale warbling in a wood half a mile off; no moving form is visible, no coming step audible; but that perfume increases. . . . A great moth goes humming by me; it alights on a plant at Mr. Rochester's foot: he sees it, and bends to examine it" (II, 11).

And here is another variant on this technique. The voice is clearly the mature Jane's, but as she relives the past, the reader does too: "What charade Colonel Dent and his party played, what word they chose, how they acquitted themselves, I no longer remember; but I still see the consultation which followed each scene: I see Rochester turn to Miss Ingram, and Miss Ingram to him; I see her incline her head towards him, till the jetty curls almost touch his shoulder and wave against his cheek; I hear their mutual whisperings; I recall their interchanged glances; and something even of the feeling roused by the spectacle returns in memory at this moment" (XVIII; I, 238). It remains for the reader to name the "feeling roused". The passage has an internal dramatic plot of its own, as the mature Jane moves from objective reporting to identification with her past and then slides back to the state with which she began.

It has often been noted that a good deal of the complicated exposition of <u>Jane Eyre</u> is presented gradually and as part of a scene which serves other functions as well. This dramatic presentation of exposition gets high marks for the skill by which Miss Brontë satisfies the notions of such critics as Henry James and Percy Lubbock. From our present standpoint, the technique clearly serves the desired function of increasing our sense of young Jane's presentness. It avoids the intrusion of the mature Jane's voice that conventional exposition would require. Even if young Jane herself voiced exposition in large blocks, it would shift our interest from the particular moment in which she is to the time zones she is recalling.

The avoidance of large blocks of exposition is most common in early portions of the book, and it serves the purpose of immediately engaging our affections for its heroine. But it is also in the early chapters that Jane's behavior is most obviously subject to critical evaluation by the mature Jane. We are constantly being reminded of the child's shortcomings, for they are in embryo the same failings that will continue to appear in her conduct. This is most often done briefly and gingerly. The mature Jane's corrections take the form of justifications and explanations, and provide verbalizations of emotions young Jane could not then have expressed: "What a consternation of soul was mine that dreary afternoon! How all my brain was in tumult, and all my heart in insurrection! Yet in what darkness, what dense ignorance, was the mental battle fought! I could not answer the ceaseless inward question - why I thus suffered; now, at the distance of - I will not say how many years, I see it clearly" (II; I, 12-13). The repeated comment on the special ways children think and feel serves to introduce us to the child's mind, but they do not excuse the child's moral failings. The explanation does not obscure the sin: "I reflected. Poverty looks grim to grown people; still more so to children: they have not much idea of industrious, working, respectable poverty. . . . poverty for me was synonymous with degradation. . . . I could not see how poor people had the means of being kind. . . . I was not heroic enough to purchase liberty at the price of caste" (III; I, 24-25). During the flight from Thornfield over ten years later, Jane struggles against this same pride. Only starvation is enough to force her into the salutary humiliation of begging.

An area of thought that has shifted dramatically since 1847 is the attitude toward the moral responsibilities of children. The early chapters of Jane Eyre are full of intrusions like those quoted, which, however gently expressed, portray a culpably deficient moral being. Jane's youth, the need to keep her an object of the reader's affection, plus the natural sympathy of the mature Jane for the young, clothe the moralist's hand in velvet, but censure is indeed clearly intended. Brocklehurst, Mrs. Reed, and other characters judge Jane harshly, but that they are overly severe does not mean that Jane is perfect or that more respect is not due them than she offers. We are constantly being reminded of Jane's faults, and so prepared for their more drastic consequences that threaten her later.

But we are not in fact prepared. We are not convinced that, however hard pressed, Jane's early rebellion was not only sin, but a sign of true spiritual calamity to come. Brocklehurst's religion, his practices notwithstanding, was not more severe than that followed in many an English household, (41) and even in its milder form, the child who was less than respectful to authority, or who was habitually gloomy or scornful, was held to be sinful. (42) It is Charlotte Brontë's purpose to depict young Jane as kindly as possible, but she also wants us to see the early flaws of character. Many of these were too obvious to elicit comment from the mature Jane, but explicit comment is not lacking. The modern reader especially tends to overlook this and the evidence of young Jane's defects. Even the casual reader will remember John Reed's throwing a book at Jane, but how many realize that the next blow was struck by Jane, and in a frenzy of rage: "I received him in frantic sort. I don't very well know what I did with my hands, but he called me 'Rat! rat!' and bellowed out aloud" (I; I, 6). Jane is indeed then, as later, what the Reed servants call her: " a picture of passion". Her loss of control and consciousness is a most serious sign to those concerned with their election to Calvin's heaven.

Not only in the early chapters of the book, and not only by direct comment by the mature Jane does Charlotte Brontë try to lead us toward a critical as well as an affectionate evaluation of Jane. Especially at the beginning and end of the novel, moral judgments are common and explicit. Complementing the effect this has of distancing us emotionally from young Jane, are the continued intrusions by the mature Jane. Even when such intrusion is not for a moral comment, its effect is to draw us from young Jane's time zone toward that of the mature Jane. The more our attention is led to the mature Jane, and to the "correct" moral stance that she has achieved, the more we tend to judge young Jane. The balance between sympathy and judgment is not achieved - affection strongly predominates in the reader's mind. Yet a battery of interesting techniques has been enlisted in aid of such distancing, and it remains to survey them.

Comment and explanation that is unambiguously by the mature Jane, whatever the content, distances us from young Jane. Sententious commentary, often without much connection with the narrative at hand functions in the same way. Psychological analysis of young Jane leads us from affection toward a clinical objectivity (IV; I, 43). Summary and block exposition, even if given by young Jane, reduces the intensity with which we empathize with the child. The phrase, "in those days", and variants of it, echo like a chorus throughout the novel, drawing us toward the broader and wiser viewpoint of the mature Jane. So do the brief jumps ahead in time, which break the generally chronological narrative as only the mature Jane can do. Digressive commentary, often disruptive in tone, serves similar purposes, as do explicit references to the writing of this "novel" or "autobiography" (both words are used to describe it). Comparison of Jane's story with other stories, and the use of literary and Biblical allusions remind us that Jane's case is not unique, and force us to consider the larger issues her story raises.

Quite often the mature Jane's authorial intrusions are strategically placed at and before climactic points of the action. Rivers asks to speak to Jane privately. She knows that some revelation of his attitude to her is about to be given. But first we have this: "I know no medium: I never in my life have known any medium in my dealings with positive, hard characters, antagonistic to my own, between absolute submission and determined revolt" (XXXIV; II, 214). This has no other real function but to lead the reader's judgment of the relationship which is just beginning to come to light.

On the eve of Jane's wedding day, she sleeps with Adèle. In the morning, "I remember Adèle clung to me as I left her" (XXV; II, 61). The first two words of this sentence are not gratuitous. Among their tonal effects is that of distancing. Similar distancing, reduction of the reader's involvement in Jane's plight, immediately follows: "I suppose" Rochester was impatient, "the church, as the reader knows" was nearby, "I wondered what other bridegroom ever looked as (Rochester) did", "I know not whether the day was fair or foul", "and now I can recall", "I remember", "I have not forgotten" (XXVI; II, 62-63). Some of this serves to indicate that the emotions of that morning were so intense that the mature Jane still recalls it vividly, but more important is the function of these intrusions in decreasing our sense of young Jane's presentness, in decreasing our uncritical affection for her as her time of trial approaches. It is essential, if the novel's moral purpose be effective, that our sympathy for young Jane does not obscure our moral considerations. We must be wrenched from her time zone into a point of view where objectivity is possible.

The most obvious, and to many readers the most disconcerting authorial intrusions, are the frequent apostrophes to the reader. As we have seen, some of these intensify rather than diminish the drama before us, but most are of the latter type, Such intrusions are common in Fielding and Thackeray, to name the greatest, as well as in Miss Brontë. On many grounds critics have rebuked the practice, but it is more than coincidence that the writers named have something else in common: they are all dedicated moralists. Vividness of presentation is only one of their aims.

So we may turn to almost all the crucial points in Jane Eyre and expect to find intrusions by the mature Jane there, and these often in the form of a comment to the "reader". They function as if they said: Reader, you are reading a book now, and Jane Eyre's crisis is long passed. Your sympathy is admirable but it comes too late. Read what follows to see what it all meant, for its lesson.

There is, we may conclude, a tension in the novel, in the reader, and evidently in the author too, a tension between contrary pulls toward the two Janes. Young

Jane proves the more attractive to modern readers, but the opposing pull does not cease to exert its force. The tension itself is an important source of the novel's power, both as it involves the reader activity in the design of the book's force field, and as the mature Jane's voice acts, in fact if not in intention, to set young Jane's voice off in high relief. To the wholly sympathetic reader of young Jane's story, the mature Jane provides an "interference" that can be resisted only by increased involvement in the younger's fate, by increased empathy with her.

Jane Eyre is Charlotte Brontë's most popular novel, and despite the special interest that attaches to Villette, probably her best. It is a novel that expresses an unquestioning faith in Divine justice and in orthodox morality. Yet its heroine is an exemplar of "passion". Jane Eyre does not subdue this conflict in its author's psyche but embodies it. To a significant degree, the passionate heroine is made possible, one suspects, because of the insistent and overt moral framework which controls, if it does not in the end contain her. This conflict between what is "right" and what is vital and attractive, "passionate" if you will, is part of Shirley and Villette too, but in these books the perfect faith in Divine justice is gone. The conventional framework of the moral "tale" is no longer possible, and Miss Brontë is faced with the dilemma of constructing a novel upon new principles. Her disdain of contemporary fiction had led her in Jane Eyre to the older form of the moral exemplum, to the fiction in her Aunt's "mad Methodist Magazines full of miracles and apparitions, and preternatural warnings, ominous dreams, and frenzied fanaticism". (43) Here was a simple narrative tradition, far from the fashionable fiction she would not imitate, and yet one which sanctioned the use of what we are used to call "Gothic" terror and melodrama. For reasons too complex to describe with assurance, after Jane Eyre, that form and the faith behind it were no longer available. Charlotte Brontë's sympathy with the passionate life is increasingly admitted into her consciousness, and continues to undermine what orthodox faith and comfort she can summon.

NOTES:

(1) Sydney Dobell, "Currer Bell", The Palladium (Sept. 1850), in Life and Letters of Sydney Dobell, ed. "E.J.", 2 vols. (London, 1878), I, 164.
(2) Dobell, I. 165. This view is almost a commonplace of intellectuals as early as the 1830's, and intellectuals of the present would generally agree with it. See Walter E. Houghton, The Victorian Frame of Mind, 1830-1870 (New Haven, 1957), esp. 93-109.
(3) Letter to Mrs. Gaskell, in E. M. Delafield (pseud.), ed., The Brontës, Their Lives Recorded by Their Contemporaries (London, 1935), 259.
(4) Kathleen Tillotson, Novels of the Eighteen-Forties (London, 1961), 258 ff.
(5) Margaret M. Maison, The Victorian Vision, Studies in The Religious Novel (New York, 1961), 3, 89.
(6) Robert A. Colby, Fiction with a Purpose (Bloomington and London, 1967).
(7) Maison, 324-325.
(8) Richard Chase, "The Brontës, or Myth Domesticated", in: Forms of Modern Fiction, ed. William V. O'Connor (Minneapolis, 1948), 118,108.
(9) Wayne Burns, "Critical Relevance of Freudianism", Western Review, XX (1956), 310.
(10) Joseph Prescott, "Jane Eyre, A Romantic Exemplum with a Difference", in: Twelve Original Essays on Great English Novels, ed. Charles Shapiro (Detroit, 1960), 87-102.
(11) Martin S. Day, "Central Concepts of Jane Eyre", Personalist, XLI (1960), 503; Burns, 313-314.
(12) Dobell, 165-167.
(13) Tillotson, 302-303.
(14) Arnold Shapiro, "A Study in the Development of Art and Ideas in Charlotte

Brontë's Fiction", unpub. doctoral diss., Indiana U., 1965, p. 158.
(15) Mark Schorer, Introduction to Jane Eyre, Riverside ed. (Cambridge, Mass., 1949), xvii.
(16) Earl Allen Knies, "The Art of Charlotte Brontë", unpub. doctoral diss., U. of Illinois, 1964, p. 136. Summaries of this approach as well as additions to its findings are given by Robert B. Martin, Charlotte Brontë's Novels (New York, 1966), and by W.A. Craik, The Brontë Novels (London, 1968).
(17) Thomas Langford, "The Three Pictures in Jane Eyre", VN, # 31 (Spring, 1967), 47-48.
(18) Tillotson, 289.
(19) Charles Burkhart, "Another Key Word for Jane Eyre", NCF, XVI (1961), 177-179.
(20) Robert B. Heilman, "Charlotte Brontë, Reason, and the Moon", NCF, XIV (1960), 283-302, and Charles Burkhart, "Brontë's Villette", Explicator, XXI (1962), item 8.
(21) Schorer; Donald H. Ericksen, "Imagery as Structure in Jane Eyre", VN, # 30 (Fall, 1966).
(22) David Lodge, "Fire and Eyre: Charlotte Brontë's War of Earthly Elements", in Language of Fiction (New York, 1966), 114-143, and Eric Solomon, "Jane Eyre: Fire and Water", CE, XXV (1963), 215-217.
(23) Ericksen, 18.
(24) Craik, 83-84, quotes the two most obvious instances of this.
(25) Fannie E. Ratchford, The Brontës' Web of Childhood (New York, 1941), 200-214.
(26) Carlyle's Journal, in: Froude, Thomas Carlyle, A History of the First Forty Years of his Life, 1795-1835, 2 vols. (London, 1882), II, 81.
(27) Rom. I.25, "Who changed the truth of God into a lie, and worshipped and served the creature more than the Creator."
(28) II, 31. "Did she (Mrs. Fairfax) think, Janet, you had given the world for love, and considered it well lost?" This has biblical echoes too: "For what shall it profit a man, if he shall gain the whole world, and lose his own soul?" (Mark VIII.36).
(29) "Yea, though I walk through the valley of the shadow of death, I will fear no evil."
(30) Houghton, esp. chs. X and XII, provides full documentation of the contemporary matrix of "Earnestness" and "Hero-Worship". Tillotson, 309, sees Carlyle's influence in Jane's remark to Rochester: "We are born to strive and to endure."
(31) Matt. V.27-32. Curiously Rochester loses his left arm, and the use of an unspecified eye. One suspects that the vagaries of Charlotte's punctuation and capitalization owe something to Bible study.
(32) Henry H. Bonnell, Charlotte Brontë, George Eliot, Jane Austen (London, 1902), 52.
(33) F. Harrison, Studies in Early Victorian Literature (London, 1906), 162.
(34) Bruce McCullough, "The Subjective Novel: Jane Eyre", Representative English Novelists (New York and London, 1946), 170.
(35) Anthony Trollope, An Autobiography, The Oxford Trollope (London, 1950), 228.
(36) Letters, IV, 52.
(37) See Andrew H. Wright, Jane Austen's Novels, A Study in Structure (London, 1953), esp. 137-161. The preceding quotations in my text are from p. 137. See also Wayne Booth on Emma in The Rhetoric of Fiction (Chicago, 1961), 243-266.
(38) Ericksen, 18.
(39) Discrimination between Jane the actor and Jane the narrator has been often made as a passing comment. Craik, 73-75, deals carefully with the subject and has both suggested and confirmed my own investigations of it. J. Hillis Miller's "Time and Intersubjectivity", in his The Form of Victorian Fiction (Notre Dame and London, 1968), while it does not deal with the Brontës, has been richly

suggestive for such formulations as, "A novel is a structure of interpenetrating minds" (p. 2).
(40) This occurs in Vanity Fair, in Adam Bede (chs. XII, XVI, and elsewhere), in set pieces in Dickens, and is common in other Victorian fiction.
(41) Winifred Gérin, Charlotte Brontë (London, 1967), 12-14.
(42) The Improvement of the Mind; With a Discourse on the Education of Children and Youth (London: Scott and Webster, 1751), 320-321, 33.
(43) Mrs. Gaskell, Life of Charlotte Brontë, Everyman ed. (London, 1960), ch. VII, 80.

VI

Shirley

1

"One of the great achievements - perhaps the greatest- in the art of the novelist is unity." (1) This rather un-Romantic principle is not uncommon among early Victorian critics, (2) and George Henry Lewes, who more usually sought "truth" of content rather than excellence of form, (3) found it the key to the failure of Charlotte Brontë's Shirley: "In Shirley all unity, in consequence of defective art, is wanting. There is no passionate link; nor is there any artistic fusion, or intergrowth, by which one part evolves itself from another. . . . Shirley cannot be received as a work of art. It is not a picture; but a portfolio of random sketches for one or more pictures. The authoress never seems distinctly to have made up her mind as to what she was to do." (4)

This finding could serve as a summary of modern opinion on the novel, (5) and it points as well to the further direction modern investigations often take. Branwell, Emily, and Anne Brontë died before Shirley was completed. This alone would account for the novel's wavering direction and purpose, even if it were not clear to many commentators that, as Mrs. Gaskell reported, Shirley Keeldar was a portrait of "what Emily Brontë would have been, had she been placed in health and prosperity". (6) This identification has since become the subject of dispute. E.A. Baker, arguing from the evidence of Emily's writings, says that Shirley is not Emily even if Charlotte intended such portraiture. (7) Ivy Holgate argues that Shirley's failure stems from the attempt to portray both Emily Brontë and Mary Taylor in the character of Shirley Keeldar. (8) Mrs. Gaskell also suggested the identification of Caroline Helstone with Ellen Nussey, and there is some controversy here as well. J.M.S. Tompkins makes a tightly argued case for Anne Brontë as the model, (9) and evidence of self-portraiture would not be far to seek.

One theory, which like the others starts with the radical imperfection of the novel's structure, is so ingenious that it serves not only as explanation of the novel's lack of unity, but almost as a proof of it. (10) The original plan, we are asked to consider, was for Caroline Helstone, that is Anne Brontë, to die of a broken heart. When the real Anne died, it would have been intolerable for her sister to portray Caroline's death for inevitably she would be using the experience of recently witnessed decline and death for the purposes of her fiction. In addition, there was the chance that Anne's memory would be tarnished by the implication that she had died of unrequited love. (11) The text of Shirley does not require these interpretations, but it does not deny them either, and such theorizing has provided the most convincing explanation of Shirley's peculiar deficiencies.

Another popular way of accounting for the felt deficiencies of Shirley is also biographical, but of a more literary cast. G.H. Lewes is for some the villain of the piece. (12) Inconsistent as are his critical formulations, unsatisfactory by his own canons as is his own novel of 1848, (13) Shirley can be seen as a reaction to his strictures on the sins against realism perpetrated in Jane Eyre. Miss Brontë's letters to Lewes generally defend her practice and resist the homage to Jane Austen that Lewes strongly recommends, but the second paragraph of Shirley can be read as acquiescence: "If you think, from this prelude, that anything like a romance is preparing for you, reader, you never were more mistaken. Do you anticipate sentiment, and poetry, and reverie? Do you expect passion, and stimulus, and melodrama? Calm your expectations; reduce them to a lowly standard. Something real, cool, and solid lies before you; something unromantic as Monday morning, when all who have work wake with the consciousness that they must rise and betake themselves thereto." The "sentiment" and "poetry" of life, Miss Brontë's touchstones of value in her consideration of Scott, Jane Austen, and George Sand, (14) seem to be repudiated here, but the novel itself does not follow these severe precepts, and we recall that long before Miss Brontë had heard of Lewes she had made similar pronouncements in The Professor. (15)

Miss Brontë's enthusiastic regard for Thackeray, made public in the Preface to Jane Eyre's second edition, together with some formal and tonal similarities between Shirley and Vanity Fair, point toward influence from that quarter too. But by moving from personal to public themes, from autobiography to panorama, from romance to realism, Charlotte Brontë was putting her worst foot forward. As Earl Knies sums up this position, "she was not really a novelist in the Victorian tradition, and Lewes and Thackeray were not satisfactory models". (16)

Whatever the degree of intended imitation, Shirley was, in form and content, a very modern novel in 1849. Charlotte Brontë would not write a "fashionable" novel, but, as Asa Briggs deftly puts it, "society novels were giving way to novels about society", (17) and Shirley is most readily classified in this latter category. Like Mary Barton, it surrounds its core of social concern with melodrama and romantic courtship. But Shirley is also a historical novel which, in the manner of Scott, Thackeray, and the Dickens of Barnaby Rudge, selects the time of its action both for its inherent interest and for its relationship to contemporary preoccupations.

The criticism of clerical practices is carried over from Jane Eyre, but it is here subsumed under the larger head of social criticism. The broader moral aims of Shirley are reflected in its wider canvas. The third-person mode is that prescribed by such aims and the one regularly used in related works by Miss Brontë's contemporaries. The revolutionary example of Vanity Fair provided a model for the criticism of life and for the criticism of contemporary fashionable fiction, and Miss Brontë attacked her new project with an élan that matches her early enthusiasm for Thackeray. She did the necessary historical research in newspaper files, and as historian has received high marks. (18) From the beginning she saw the need for organizing her material into a coherent whole. Her defense of the opening portrait of the curates is not only that it is amusing and true - "photographed from the life" (19) - but "neither is that opening scene irrelevant to the rest of the book - there are other touches in store which will harmonize with it". (20)

Miss Brontë had insisted to Ellen Nussey that her characters were not to be identified with real models: "You must be satisfied if that young person (i.e. Caroline Helstone) has furnished your mind with a pleasant idea; she is a native of Dreamland, and as such can have neither voice nor presence except for the fancy, neither being nor dwelling except in thought." (21) The matter, particularly with regard to Shirley Keeldar, is far more complex than that, and there can be no doubt that Jessie Yorke exists in the novel solely as a portrait of and tribute to Miss Brontë's friend Martha Taylor. But the use of real-life models need not have resulted in artistic failure for Charlotte Brontë when it did not detract from the success of her contemporaries who did as much.

Looking back on Shirley, its author acknowledged failures of execution. Her male heroes "probably" lacked "distinctness" and "impressiveness", she says. (22) Shirley's "nervousness" about the bite of a supposedly mad dog is defended for its psychological soundness, but the telling of it is "badly managed". (23) Miss Brontë's last known words on the novel are these: "I took great pains with 'Shirley'. I did not hurry; I tried to do my best, and my own impression was that it was not inferior to the former work; indeed I had bestowed on it more time, thought, and anxiety: but (a) great part of it was written under the shadow of impending calamity, and the last volume I cannot deny was composed in the eager, restless endeavour to combat mental sufferings that were scarcely tolerable." (24) The fruits of Miss Brontë's "time, thought, and anxiety", and the consequences, to the novel, of "impending calamity" will repay examination.

2

The text of Shirley abundantly exhibits the results of the taking of "great pains". Its first chapter is a marvel of dramatic exposition. The religious establishments of the community, and their relationship to each other, are given in broad outline and colorful detail. Civil, social, and economic problems are all presented. The connection between the religious and the economic disputes is made clear by the report of Mike Hartley's drunken tirades. Hartley is not only an "Antinomian weaver", but also "a violent Jacobin and leveller". He is "not unacquainted with history", and he is "hankering" to add Robert Moore to the list of murdered "tyrants" and "crowned heads". It is not until the last chapter of the novel that we learn that Hartley, here again described as "a frantic Antinomian in religion, and a mad leveller in politics", had been Moore's assailant. Helstone's report of Hartley's "vision" is a clear if apocalyptic foreshadowing of the political climax of the book. It is a vision, said Hartley, of "bloodshed and civil conflict" to come, and the curates are not inclined to deny the possibility.

The behavior of the curates, as presented and as reported, is ironically commented on by references to the more successful religious opposition. Supplehough and Barraclough bellow like possessed bulls and beat their tubs to an increasingly larger audience, and what we know of the curates, even by the end of the first chapter, furnishes a reason for this popularity.

The plot and characters sketched in the first chapter are rapidly filled in by what follows. The Caroline Helstone-Robert Moore relationship is all before us by the end of chapter six. Well before then we have heard, at least twice, of the absentee landlord of Fieldhead, and we know that Robert Moore has a brother Lewis, now a tutor in a private family. The first of a long series of hints about Caroline's mother has been dropped. A similar attempt to hint about the future events of the novel without eliminating suspence or surprise has been noted with regard to the Shirley-Lewis Moore romance. Seemingly idle comments about Shirley's inclinations are verbally echoed later in descriptions of Lewis, (25) and the reader is prepared for the unexpected.

As we read further, Miss Brontë's care for organization of her materials remains evident. She gives us a good number of secondary characters whose lives and comments relate to the preoccupations of the leading figures. Love and marriage, social justice and injustice, selfishness and dedication, ambition and resignation, are continually being examined and exemplified. Reactions to thwarted or disappointing love surround the story of Caroline and Shirley like so many lessons and warnings. There is an implicit parallel between clergyman, industrialist, and aristocrat, for each has responsibilities to his "flock". The proposition that "Misery generates hate", is applied to the reactions of distressed labor, but it has a bearing too on other instances of misery and frustration. None of this patterning of themes and incidents is done schematically, although the dramatis personae is carefully and often numerically balanced. There are three imperfect curates, two solitary spinsters, two unwed sisters living with their brothers. There are two Helstone brothers and two Moore brothers. Both heroines are fatherless, have unaffectionate uncles, and both attract young admirers who are involved with the progress of their love affairs.

The care with which Shirley was written is evident in such smaller matters as the titling of chapters, a new departure of Miss Brontë. By and large these titles provide an organizational principle for the chapter. "Two Lives" makes explicit an intended comparison, much in the manner of Middlemarch. Other titles are ironic, clearly in the tradition of Tom Jones and Vanity Fair. The chapters themselves often exhibit their own neat structure. One may deal with a single plot thread of the multiple plot, others focus on a single family or a single class. A dramatic opening, a movement to exposition and analysis, and a modulation to a peaceful close as a day ends, or a character exits, is a pattern superimposed on many chapters of dramatic action. Some chapters end on an ominous or suspenseful note, but rarely is the pause between chapters without significant function.

Stylistically Shirley is a veritable storehouse of detachable exhibits. There is a variety and flexibility in the narrator's tone, style, and attitude that, while far from as successful as that of Vanity Fair, is at times of the same kind. Shirley's omniscient and detached narrator gives Miss Brontë opportunities that the form of The Professor and Jane Eyre denied her. Narrators in those novels were also characters, and what they could say was limited by the parts they had to play. The narrator of Shirley is avowedly a professional writer, and has the freedom indeed the responsibility to her contemporary readers, to exhibit a professional's virtuosity.

Miss Brontë responds eagerly to this new opportunity. Shirley's very first page gives us the ironic title "Levitical", the "abundant shower of curates", the metaphor of the book's parts as courses of a meal, and the placing of the story in its historical and literary contexts, and there are dozens of pages in Shirley with as much interest, variety, humor, charm, and close observation of detail.

Particularly in the first half of the book, there are notable attempts at verbal wit and local irony. Moore's new industrial equipment is described as "his grim, metal darlings" (XXII; II, 74). Servants hurry in to give their grotesquely exaggerated account of the battle of the mill: "Both women rushed into the parlour to announce these terrible facts to the ladies, terminating their clear and accurate narrative by the assertion that they were sure" of the immensity of the catastrophe (XX; II, 39). Caroline Helstone rather romantically laments her lost youth: " 'But when we are young,' added the girl of eighteen, 'our minds are careless and our lives easy' " (XXI; II, 62-63).

Only a detached narrator can permit himself such luxuries, not to mention those like the following which have no relationship at all to the themes of the novel: "Certainly Miss Mann had a formidable eye for one of the softer sex: it was prominent, and showed a great deal of the white, and looked as steadily, as unwinkingly, at you as if it were a steel ball soldered in her head" (X; I, 198). "Dora being the one whom he secretly hoped one day to call Mrs. David Sweeting, with whom he dreamt of taking stately walks, leading her like an empress through the village of Nunnely: and an empress she would have been, if size could make an empress" (VII;I, 129).

This sort of comedy is not attempted simply through metaphoric wit, but employs careful control of prose cadence, syntax, and sound. Here is a striking example of what Miss Brontë can do with style alone: "The rectors passed to the full front - the parish clerks fell to the extreme rear; Helstone lifted his shovel-hat; in an instant out clashed the eight bells in the tower, loud swelled the sounding bands, flute spoke and clarion answered, deep rolled the drums, and away they marched" (XVI; I, 331-332). Another example, somewhat reminiscent of the famous report of George Osborne's death which ends the ninth number and the thirty-second chapter of Vanity Fair, ends the thirtieth chapter of Shirley: "A fierce flash and sharp crack violated the calm of night. Yorke, ere he turned, knew the four convicts of Birmingham were avenged" (II, 246). The important "avenged" is delayed until the sentence ends, but "violated" has prepared us for it. The alliteration of "fierce flash" is apt; "calm" provides an opposition to "crack" in both sound and meaning. The delay produced by "ere he turned" is a masterful and necessary touch.

Another new opportunity that Shirley's nominally detached narrator provides,

and which Thackeray's example warranted, was authorial comment for wisdom
and direction. Here is Miss Brontë's version of the moral guidance that Victorian readers were used to hearing:

> It is happy that ("the true poet") can have his own bliss, his own society with
> his great friend and goddess, Nature, quite independent of those who find
> little pleasure in him, and in whom he finds no pleasure at all. It is just, that
> while the world and circumstances often turn a dark, cold side to him - and
> properly, too, because he first turns a dark, cold, careless side to them -
> he should be able to maintain a festal brightness and cherishing glow in his
> bosom, which makes all bright and genial for him; while strangers, perhaps,
> deem his existence a Polar winter never gladdened by a sun. (IV; I, 50)

More commonplace wisdom, excellently expressed, was an order of the day,
and Miss Brontë, at her best, is as good at it as any: "For however old, plain,
humble, desolate, afflicted we may be, so long as our hearts preserve the
feeblest spark of life, they preserve also, shivering near that pale ember, a
starved, ghostly longing for appreciation and affection" (X; I, 200).

3

The examples I have been quoting as illustrations of Charlotte Brontë's successful handling of the new possibilities the form of Shirley allowed her, have been
most mercifully selected, for this new freedom was also the occasion for egregious failure. As Currer Bell, the celebrated author of Jane Eyre, Miss Brontë
now had a platform from which to air her grievances and to speak her piece on
a number of personal and contemporary issues. Shirley is full of authorial comments that bear the marks of beliefs passionately held and impatiently annunciated. Too often the tone is that of anger. Miss Brontë's targets include a wide
range of human, social, and institutional failings, and adverse criticism of
Jane Eyre often seems to be the motive behind the aggressiveness: " 'Obtrusiveness is a crime; forwardness is a crime; and both disgust: but love! - no
purest angel need blush to love! And when I see or hear either man or woman
couple shame with love, I know their minds are coarse, their associations debased. Many who think themselves refined ladies and gentlemen, and on whose
lips the word "vulgarity" is for ever hovering, cannot mention "love" without
betraying their own innate and imbecile degradation: it is a low feeling in their
estimation, connected only with low ideas for them' " (XVII; I, 351).

This is but one of a number of remarks that relate more to contemporary fiction and criticism than to the story of the novel, and like many such diatribes,
it appears as a speech of one of the book's characters. It is Caroline Helstone
who steps out of character to make the oration quoted above. The question of
"coarseness" and "vulgarity" has but tenuous links with the story, but this does
not prevent Shirley from taking up with enthusiasm what is in fact Charlotte
Brontë's crusade: " 'You describe three-fourths of the world, Caroline.' 'They
are cold - they are cowardly - they are stupid on the subject, Shirley! They
never loved - they never were loved!' 'Thou are right, Lina! And in their dense
ignorance they blaspheme living fire, seraph-brought from a divine altar.' 'They
confound it with sparks mounting from Tophet!' " Shirley's inclination to debate
Caroline here cannot withstand Miss Brontë's desire to agree with her.

Interchanges like this, and such outbursts are often equally uncharacteristic
of their spokesmen, make for glaring improbability and a severe loss of verisimilitude. A very long silent soliloquy of Caroline Helstone culminates in this:
" 'King of Israel! your model of a woman is a worthy model! But are we, in
these days, brought up to be like her? Men of Yorkshire! do your daughters
reach this royal standard? Can you give them a field in which their faculties
may be exercised and grow? Men of England! look at your poor girls' ", and

so on to the end of the page (XXII; II, 84). Caroline Helstone would never speak so, and it is a disappointment to know that Miss Brontë was capable of it.

There is a good deal of authorial comment that is more pertinent to what we know of Charlotte Brontë's private life than to the story before us, and many cases in which explanatory comment on an action seems, in tone and comment, far in excess of what the action requires. This is a form of sentimentality, an indulgence which is most clearly seen in the narrator's pausing, as she does twice, to tell us of the future death of Jessie Yorke:

Mr. Yorke, if a magic mirror were now held before you, and if therein were shown you your two daughters as they will be in twenty years from this night, what would they think? The magic mirror is here: you shall learn their destinies - and first that of your little life, Jessy.

Do you know this place? No, you never saw it; but you recognize the nature of these trees, this foliage, - the cypress, the willow, the yew. Stone crosses like these are not unfamiliar to you, nor are these dim garlands of everlasting flowers. Here is the place. (IX; I, 164-165)

And on then slowly to the discovering of Jessie's grave.

All this is strikingly similar to the scenes and the rhetoric of Dickens' Christmas Carol. Scrooge, we recall, is transported to scenes highly charged with emotion and asked if a particular "place" is familiar to him. The culminating scene is the disclosure of Scrooge's own grave. The scene in Shirley is not unlike that look ahead to the grave of Helen Burns in Jane Eyre, but in the mouth of our omniscient narrator it is not self-characterization but an assault on the reader's emotions. It is in the worst tradition of grave-side maudlin, without the justification that Dickens' context may be said to give him.

The form of Shirley allows, even encourages, authorial digression, and the narrator accepts this freedom without qualm. Digressions are sometimes acknowledged as such: "But what has been said in the last page or two is not germane to Caroline Helstone's feelings, or to the state of things between her and Robert Moore" (VII; I, 116). We read on for the expected justification of the digression. There is none. A good deal of the important published prose of the period, that of the reviews and articles in the great periodicals, operates as if digression were a prime requisite. The nominal issue, usually a book under review, is no more than a springboard from which the writer takes off in whatever direction strikes his fancy. The author of Shirley and many of its characters operate on similar lines. Unfortunately what Miss Brontë has to say, and the way she chooses to say it, lack the poise, stability, and calm good sense of a Macaulay, nor is her exuberant use of exclamation points as effective as Carlyle's. Her style is often highly idiosyncratic, despite the obvious debts to other writers. There are passages of supercharged rhetoric, and some, particularly those on Milton's Eve, and much of Louis Moore's journal, that can be characterized as cosmic bombast. Its source, if there was one in particular, has not survived among standard authors.

Even the care for style and wit which we have sampled at its best, often misfires. Miss Brontë is unable to wring any charm from the commonplace smirking reference to affairs of love and biology as "interesting" incidents. Her care for the sound of her prose is oddly misguided with regard to the uses of alliteration. Time and again we come across disconcerting excess: "On the silvery space slept two sable shadows" (XIII; I, 255). What makes all these matters worse is the evident enthusiasm, at times even passion, with which the disconcerting and the unreadable are perpetrated. Miss Brontë's debut as an avowedly professional author is a virtuoso performance, but an immature and erratic one.

The more complex tasks of exposition and characterization the panoramic form required are often handled with high skill. But the freedom to choose one's own limits involves a temptation too. There is nothing to authorize the space given, for example, to the portrayal of the personality of Mr. Yorke. The fact that lengthy passages of block exposition are required for this signals his lack of functional connection with the rest of the novel. It may be that a larger part in the climax of the book had been at one time intended for Yorke. We may suspect this because of the inordinate space given to him early in the novel, and because of a curious and otherwise wholly perplexing fact that we learn at the novel's close. We have long known that Yorke and Helstone had both courted a Mary Cave. Helstone won her, evidently ignored and mistreated her, and she did not survive the marriage by many years. In the formal announcement of the double marriage which ends the novel, we learn that Shirley is the daughter of the late Charles Cave Keeldar. Is this a remnant of a connection between Shirley and Caroline that existed in an earlier and incompletely expunged version of the story? (26) Miss Brontë admitted that once her work was completed, it was "next to impossible (for her) to alter or amend (it)". (27) But neither were the first chapters of Pickwick or Waverley thoroughly revised.

The reader of Victorian novels can, or should, excuse any amount of inadvertence, any evidence of over-hasty composition and less than thorough revision, as long as other qualities are provided. Among the chief compensations of the typical expansive novel of the eighteenth and nineteenth centuries, is the felt presence of the narrator. As much recent criticism has been pleased to point out - to counter charges of undramatic authorial intrusion - the narrator of a Tom Jones or a Vanity Fair is himself a chief character in the book. The same is partly true of Shirley, with the crucial difference that this narrator is all too often without the charm and personal attractiveness of Fielding or Thackeray. Both these narrators achieved a rapport with their readers, as did Dickens in his own way, that is not achieved in Shirley. Thackeray's mature serenity and ironic urbanity give way in Shirley to ill-tempered and violent harangue. Thackeray, Fielding, and Dickens have the good sense to leave metaphysics to the philosophers and to successfully disguise their personal animosities and emotions. Their judgments are unexceptional, though far from commonplace in expression. Miss Brontë's ambitions are unwisely far less limited, and for such reasons she makes a much less agreeable companion.

As has recently been pointed out in the case of Fielding, (28) his narrator invites the reader to join with him in his satiric attacks on his characters and on the human foibles they represent. Any reader however can become an "inside" reader, escaping the moral criticism that is directed not only at society in the novel and by analogy at society in general, but also at a particular class of readers, the "outside" readers. To comprehend the author's irony is to escape it, and those who escape become collaborators and friends of the author. This is also true of Vanity Fair, although Thackeray's narrator specifically makes himself - and his coterie of "inside" readers - examples of moral imperfection. But his chief self-accusation is of sin no more alarming than a comfortable and complacent laziness, failings that good friends would tolerate and many readers envy.

Except when the narrator of Shirley succeeds in recapturing the ironic tones of Fielding or Thackeray, and so reaps their sort of reward, she has only "outside" readers. Miss Brontë is not angry at the whole world of course, although we have seen her damn three-fourths of it, but her vituperation is hurled widely, and most often without the irony that lets the reader escape it. Not only does she make no exception for those readers who are ready to penetrate her irony and join forces with her, but her tone is so militant that, far from being the reader's friend, she is a clear and present danger to his peace. It is this, I submit, rather than Shirley's lack of unity, that makes the novel unpopular and unsuccessful. Could a book be less unified than Pickwick or Waverley? If we love our omniscient narrators they can do no wrong. If they are disagreeable, they can do no right.

Shirley differs from the panoramic novels of Dickens, and from _Vanity Fair_, in that its emphasis is soon concentrated on the courtship adventures of its central figures. Miss Brontë had recently read her first novel by her great predecessor in this speciality, Jane Austen. (29) Although in her letters to Lewes Miss Brontë's response to Jane Austen's work is never more than mixed, _Shirley_'s description of Yorke as "proud and prejudiced" (XXI; II, 58) may be something of an acknowledgment of influence, and there are some similarities in technique that suggest that Miss Brontë may have learned something from her new acquaintance.

Shirley's technical methods are in a number of instances comparable to those more successfully used by Jane Austen. We have a nominally uncommitted and omniscient author whose report is nonetheless highly selective. It is necessary in _Shirley_ that the release of suspense be carefully controlled. We must not know what lies behind Mrs. Pryor's slightly strange solicitude for Caroline Helstone, so our omniscient narrator avoids giving us an interior view of Mrs. Pryor. The trick is to draw no attention to such omissions. In _Pride and Prejudice_, and even more so in _Emma_, Jane Austen does this with an art Miss Brontë does not approach. Shirley Keeldar's feelings, especially those toward Robert Moore, and the reasons for her decline and preparation for death, are central mysteries of the plot, but the reader is increasingly conscious, and resentful, of the narrative strategy that makes this suspense possible.

A narrator's "suggestive reticence", (30) which lets us know a character well without suspecting his crucial secret, is a dangerous technique. The sign of its use is the discovery, on rereading, of retrospective irony. There is much of this in _Jane Eyre_, and in the Mrs. Pryor thread of _Shirley_, but especially with regard to Shirley herself, clues are either too unobtrusive to count or too revealing to maintain the reader's unsuspecting ignorance. It may occur to the reader - but it very likely will not occur to him - that the reason Shirley does not tell Caroline that Louis Moore is the tutor in the Sympson family is that she cherishes some feelings for Lewis that make her overly careful about referring to him. Robert Moore notices that the sound of this name makes Shirley blush. He mentioned this to her, and "Not for _your_ sake!" is her enigmatic response (XXX; II, 238). This seems to be a veiled hint that it is the name Moore, that Robert shares with his brother Lewis, that brings the blush, but this is at once too clear and too ambiguous a hint. If we read it as a clue it is so clearly an avowal of Shirley's interest in that quarter that we will suspect such a reading is wrong. It is equally possible, in retrospect, to say that Shirley blushes on behalf of Caroline whose love of Robert is so strong that it sensitizes Shirley to the sound of his name. The mystery remains unsolved at the end of the novel, at which time we can call it a confusion.

Shirley's reticence on the subject is so perplexing to Caroline that she asks about it directly. The answer she receives is unconvincing: " 'I never made it a secret: I had no reason for so doing. If you had asked me who Henry's tutor was, I would have told you: besides, I thought you knew' " (XXVI; II, 150). Shirley's reasons for keeping Mrs. Pryor's identity a secret are almost as suspicious, as is her assertion that she had sensed that Mrs. Pryor was Caroline's mother. Charlotte Brontë's defence of all this could be no better than an admission that her plot needed some mystery.

Miss Brontë's manipulation of selective omniscience is not only crude and unsuccessful, but she seems to have felt that she had hinted not too subtly but too broadly. Especially in the last third of the novel there is an obvious and distressing attempt to blow sand in the reader's eyes. Here is Miss Brontë trying to obscure an issue that is already sufficiently obscure:

> Flattered and fawned upon as Shirley was just now, it appeared she was not absolutely spoiled - that her better nature did not quite leave her. Universal

report had indeed ceased to couple her name with that of Moore, and this silence seemed sanctioned by her own apparent oblivion of the absentee; but that she had not quite forgotten him - that she still regarded him, if not with love yet with interest - seemed proved by the increased attention which at this juncture of affairs a sudden attack induced her to show that tutor-brother of Robert's, to whom she habitually bore herself with strange alternations of cool reserve and docile respect: now sweeping past him in all the dignity of the monied heiress and prospective Lady Nunnely, and anon accosting him as abashed school-girls are wont to accost their stern professors. (XXVII; II, 183-184)

Any progress the diligent reader has made by this time in deciphering the tangled relationships of the characters is thwarted by this endlessly ambiguous passage. On rereading, one feels that it is Charlotte Brontë's deliberate obfuscation of matters that Shirley's deviousness had left far from clear.

The mystery of Shirley's supposed hydrophobia, like these other mysteries, requires one thing from the narrator and that is silence. Instead Miss Brontë feels impelled to comment: "Certainly, (Shirley) was not a little changed from what she had been two hours before. This change, accounted for only by those three words ("a little sick"), explained no otherwise; this change - whencesoever springing, effected in a brief ten minutes - passed like no light summer cloud" (XXVIII; II, 195). Miss Brontë heightens suspense, but also brings the narrator's profession of ignorance out into the open. The prose approaches incoherence, and the repeated use of litotes is unfortunate. It hints at comic irony when neither comedy nor irony is present.

Repeated confessions of authorial ignorance, often with a casual "for some reason", make it too obvious to the reader that he is being manipulated, if not cheated. And the entrance of a maid, "bustling in with the tea things", just as some crucial revelation is to be made, is an even cruder and less acceptable narrative procedure (XVI; I, 321). What is needed is a better sense, on the author's part, of what the reader has been able to discover of the novel's secrets. And more care is necessary to keep the machinery that makes suspense possible out of view.

Jane Austen merges her narrator's point of view with that of one of her characters. When some information is to be withheld, the narrator is not there at all. She has disappeared and left the telling to a character who obviously could not unravel the mystery. The third-person mode slides successfully and unperceived into first person. While there is some use of this technique in Shirley, and much variation on it in Jane Eyre, Miss Brontë's characterization of her narrator is very uneven. Often she is simply omniscient and detached; often she adopts the point of view of Caroline Helstone, particularly with regard to Mrs. Pryor. At times Shirley's narrator is explicitly an author writing an historical novel. Then again she is a most interested and sympathetic onlooker to events in which she had some personal but unspecified part. Lewis Moore begins to write in his diary: "Come near, by all means, reader: do not be shy: stoop over his shoulder fearlessly, and read as he scribbles" (XXIX; II, 221). The authorial "I" makes sporadic appearances throughout the novel, but nowhere near consistently enough to affect a feeling of familiarity with him.

There are numerous confessions of authorial ignorance - some justify important omissions of information, many seem gratuitous, the borrowing of a mannerism. In fact Miss Brontë often seems to be doing no more than that. The tone of voice of her narrator recalls contemporary essayists, and Austen, Thackeray, Scott, Dickens, and Fielding, but all this with no coherent plan. Surprisingly, for such an experienced writer, Miss Brontë seems to have little intuitive grasp of the fact that an omniscient narrator can be, and must be, coherently characterized, if characterized at all. This question solved itself in the Angrian narratives. There, the narrator is a character in the story itself or is at least known to the reader from other tales in the cycle. In The Professor and Jane Eyre, the form made characterization of the narrator a prime business of the novel. The seemingly simple narrative form of Shirley required either a great deal of intuitive tact or a conscious consideration of problems that in 1849 had not become a matter of critical attention.

Miss Brontë came to Shirley with neither of these advantages, nor with any inkling that such was needed. But she was less innocent when the novel was completed. The simple technical problems intruded themselves into plain sight. A scene designed to accomplish one purpose threatened to unravel a mystery that had been carefully planted and concealed. Obfuscation seemed imperative. Other narrative stances were tried, but there was no acceptable way to hide the required narrative maneuvers. There was no narrative personality for Charlotte Brontë to hide behind - and novel readers are like Keats in objecting to literature which "has a palpable design upon us". Obfuscation and significant omission are neither good nor bad when a character uses them. When it is done by someone who we have no reason to believe is anyone but Currer Bell, it is intolerable. A novelist is like a magician in this respect: nothing can help him if his unacknowledged mechanical aids show.

The obfuscations and the borrowing of authorial tones which Miss Brontë resorts to in the last volume of Shirley are necessary - at least she thought so - to the simple working-out of her plot. It was no better than first-aid for a patient in need of radical surgery. We recall her admission that the affair of Shirley's mad dog was "badly managed". But for her next novel, even if it was a retreat into the safer ground of fictional autobiography, the lesson of Shirley's debacle would be of value.

5

Failures of technique, style, and characterization, and an inconsistent and often overly aggressive narrative voice go a long way toward explaining why Shirley is no competitor to Vanity Fair. Yet there is an intensity in Shirley that relates it to Miss Brontë's other works, and the emergence of a moral ambiguity for which Shirley's chosen form is not only inadequate but restrictive. The suspicion of a conflict within the author that attaches to the endings of The Professor and Jane Eyre is confirmed by the confusions and contradictions that run throughout Shirley, and it is to this conflict that the failures of tone and execution may be, in the last analysis, referred.

If Caroline Helstone and other characters are made the speaking puppets of Charlotte Brontë's didacticism, the fault lies not in the irrelevance of the content of such speeches as we have noted, but in the irrelevance of the intensity of emotion exhibited in them. Neither the question of the social place of women, nor the question of the relationship between capital and labor, is digressive, for both are pointedly related to each other and are subsumed under the novel's larger theme. "Selfishness" (31) is a good description of this theme, for it indicates that the common ground for the novel's social themes is the idea of personal morality. And "selfishness" also represents Charlotte Brontë's generally negative moral evaluation of the species.

Robert Moore is the epitome of economic selfishness, but merely the most prominent of many characters similarly infected. Martin Yorke's strange adolescent infatuation with Caroline Helstone is not unrelated to the theme of selfishness in love, and his father's love of Mary Cave, as well as Helstone's marriage, are further variations on this theme.

Marriage motivated by economic ambition is at the heart of the relationship of Robert Moore and Shirley, and this is echoed, in the background, by Yorke, the curates, and Mr. Sympson. We hear of the management of the discontented laborers by organizers who have only their private advancement in mind, and of local magistrates who prefer security to social justice. We have fastidious curates for whom the rich man's table is not a temptation but a deliberated goal.

It is selfishness again which moves the leaders of the "ranter's" church: their liquor is more important to them than the saving of souls. Even Shirley's odd secretive behavior can be assimilated to the theme. She knows full well that Caroline loves Robert, yet she permits her to believe that Robert is destined for herself. Caroline suffers from the erroneous presumption of an intimacy between these two that Shirley does not dispel. It is her selfish pride which accounts for her insistence on her own perfect privacy, cost what it may to others. "All men, taken singly", Shirley's narrator tells us, "are more or less selfish; and taken in bodies they are intensely so" (X; I, 184). With some possible exceptions, "all the characters are linked by their relationship to the theme of selfishness". (32) I quote Dickens' biographer, writing on Martin Chuzzlewit, to point up the similarities between the two novels.

The similarity in plan is much greater than in execution. Pecksniff and Jonas Chuzzlewit are of a different order of meanness than are Robert Moore and the Rev. Helstone. Moore, in fact, is the novel's hero.

Comparison with Vanity Fair points up another curious aspect of Shirley. Thackeray's Dobbin merely rejects the world of sham and selfishness and goes his own way. Robert and Lewis Moore, both lovers of virtue in their own special ways, are outspoken in their defiance of the conventional ways of the world, yet Robert is a vindictive oppressor of labor and, under the pressure of financial crisis, makes a mercenary proposal of marriage. Louis Moore's disdain of wealth and social position threatens to become the dominant motive in his life. He is far from comforted by the knowledge of his own righteousness. Becky Sharp's childhood experiences, and her early life as a dependent are not without significance for her later life, but Caroline Helstone's experience, and its meaning in moral and pragmatic terms, are central and crucial to Shirley. To the panoramic view of society as the embodiment of a pervasive moral flaw, Charlotte Brontë has added a philosophic inquiry into the genesis of that flaw. In order to do this, she takes as her leading figures not the typical case nor the grotesquely concentrated example, but the recalcitrant particular which brings the general proposition under scrutiny.

Caroline Helstone is the central focus of Miss Brontë's investigation, and herself an ardent student of the subject. Around her Caroline sees the working out of the proposition that misery generates hate, that frustration induces bitterness and selfishness. Caroline sees in Miss Ainley's selflessness not virtue but "a terrible hollowness", and concludes that Miss Mann's long life of suffering has brought her no nearer to Christian resignation than "a certain lethargic state of tranquillity". Her habitual pleasure is malicious gossip (X; I, 194, 199). Frustration in love has had, she sees, much to do with the shaping of the personalities of her uncle, her mother, and Hiram Yorke, and the bitterness engendered in the economically downtrodden provides further collaborating testimony.

In the face of all this Caroline ponders with special care her own story. She counts herself the victim of her uncle's indifference, her mother's desertion, Robert Moore's unfair and uncommitted flirtation, and the social barriers that thwart her desire to find a meaningful role in the world. There is a special urgency in her self-evaluation because she is in love with Robert Moore and through most of the novel afraid that she will lose him. Have the deprivations in her life made her already undesirable to him? Will her meekness and sensitivity make the strong-willed and self-assertive mill-operator turn away? And what will this added blow make of her in the long years to come?

Unlike the other characters in Shirley, we are given an almost continuous interior view of Caroline. We hear the questions she raises for herself, and she is the recipient of the narrator's special attention. There is an alternate view of the effects of suffering and frustration that is applied to her situation:

Every joy that life gives must be earned ere it is secured; and how hardly earned, those only know who have wrestled for great prizes. The heart's blood must gem with red beads the brow of the combatant, before the wreath of victory rustles over it . . . .

In short, at eighteen, the school of Experience is to be entered, and her humbling, crushing, grinding, but yet purifying and invigorating lessons are yet to be learnt.

Alas, Experience! No other mentor has so wasted and frozen a face as yours: none wears a robe so black, none bears a rod so heavy, none with hand so inexorable draws the novice so sternly to his task, and forces him with authority so resistless to its acquirement. It is by your instructions alone that man or woman can find a safe track through life's wilds: without it, how they stumble, how they stray! On what forbidden grounds do they intrude, down what dread declivities are they hurled! (VII; I, 106-107)

Experience is then a chastening but necessary power: it teaches and it purifies. Another authorial comment suggests that suffering will provide strength, but of an aggressive and bitter sort:

For the whole remnant of your life, if you survive the test - some, it is said, die under it - you will be stronger, wiser, less sensitive. This you are not aware of, perhaps, at the time, and so cannot borrow courage of that hope. Nature, however, as has been intimated, is an excellent friend in such cases; sealing the lips, interdicting utterance, commanding a placid dissimulation: a dissimulation often wearing an easy and gay mien at first, settling down to sorrow and paleness in time, then passing away and leaving a convenient stoicism, not the less fortifying because it is half-bitter.

Half-bitter! Is that wrong? No - it should be bitter: bitterness is strength - it is a tonic. Sweet mild force following acute suffering, you find nowhere: to talk of it is delusion. There may be apathetic exhaustion after the rack; if energy remains, it will be rather a dangerous energy - deadly when confronted with injustice. (VII; I, 114-115)

Robert Moore, having survived his trials, has this more optimistic and pragmatic contribution to the debate: "I believe - I daily find it proved - that we can get nothing in this world worth keeping, not so much as a principle or a conviction, except out of purifying flame, or through strengthening peril" (XXX; II, 244). The immediate evil results of frustration are opposed by an eventual and greater good, but as Moore continues, and as the lives of others in the novel prove, only if the individual is strong: "If the soul has strength, it conquers and rules thereafter."

There is yet one more view to be considered, one which moves from the psychological level:

Most people have had a period or periods in their lives when they have felt thus forsaken; when, having long hoped against hope, and still seen the day of fruition deferred, their hearts have truly sickened within them. This is a terrible hour, but it is often that darkest point which precedes the rise of day; that turn of the year when the icy January wind carries over the waste at once the dirge of departing winter, and the prophecy of coming spring. The perishing birds, however, cannot thus understand the blast before which they shiver; and as little can the suffering soul recognize, in the climax of its affliction, the dawn of its deliverance. Yet, let whoever grieves still cling fast to love and faith in God: God will never deceive, never finally desert him; "Whom He loveth, He chasteneth." These words are true, and should not be forgotten. (XX; II, 36)

The narrator goes on to paraphrase the text which may be interpreted as saying that special suffering is a mark of special grace.

This has special relevance to Caroline Helstone who alone among the nominal Christians in the novel is specified as devout: "Caroline was a Christian; therefore in trouble she framed many a prayer after the Christian creed. . . . This world, however, we all know, is the scene of trial and probation; and, for any favourable result her petitions had yet wrought, it seemed that they were unheard and unaccepted. . . . At moments she was a Calvinist, and, sinking into the gulf of religious despair, she saw darkening over her the doom of reprobation" (XX; II, 36). With such a faith, suffering may be comprehended, and even if death proves the only deliverance, God's justice is sure. This is the problem Caroline Helstone and the novel itself set out to confront. Caroline Helstone's "earnest wish was to see things as they were, and not to be romantic" (X; I, 191). The fearless confrontation of things as they are, which brings to mind Arnold's secular version of the same honestness, (33) is at the heart of *Shirley*. Charlotte Brontë, like Caroline Helstone, "will determine to look on life steadily, as it is; to begin to learn its severe truths seriously, and to study its knotty problems closely, conscientiously" (VII; I, 116). What it is that Caroline Helstone sees is a loveless selfishness, cruelty, and unearned and unrewarded suffering. Her faith in justice is tried, and the culminating stroke, Robert Moore's apparent shift of affection from her to Shirley, proves nearly fatal. Caroline takes to her bed and it is made clear that only the discovery that Mrs. Pryor is her long-lost mother saves her.

This extraordinary coincidence elicits no significant comment from either Caroline or the narrator, nor do either persist much longer in considerations of the significance of her fate. This shift is matched by the novel's shift from the moral panorama to the love adventures of the four principals. Chapter twenty-five, in which, under her mother's care, Caroline recovers, is titled, "The West Wind Blows", evidently in allusion to the deliverance figured earlier as "the prophecy of spring" coming at the "darkest point" of "icy January". The chapter opens with authorial comment on Mrs. Pryor's earnest prayers for her daughter's survival. A vision of prayers unheeded, of signs of death on a patient's face, is invoked only to be abruptly dismissed - Caroline wakes refreshed and better. It is as if the questions of Divine justice and human suffering had been shifted from their wider applications onto the simple question of Caroline's survival. She lives and the subject is essentially closed.

As Caroline recuperates, Lewis Moore and Shirley Keeldar take the center of the stage, and we watch them make the difficult adjustments their love requires. It is some hundred pages before Caroline is in significant action again. She contrives with Martin Yorke to gain the forbidden entrance to Robert Moore's sickroom, and their engagement is soon upon us. Evidently her suffering has given her a new strength of purpose, but by now such considerations are beside the point. What began as a social and moral novel, and moved toward a philosophical novel, ends as romance.

As this end nears, Miss Brontë increases the tempo of her attacks on the conventions of romantic fiction in which she herself has become enmeshed. She scores some minor victories along the way. The curates continue to be painted "warts and all". As they come forward in the last chapter's "Winding-Up", the narrator insists on the fact that they do not get the punishment that simple novelistic convention would require: "Were I to give the catastrophe of your life and conversation (the narrator says to Peter Malone), the public would sweep off in shrieking hysterics, and there would be a wild cry for sal-volatile and burnt feathers. 'Impossible!' would be pronounced here: 'untrue!' would be responded there. 'Inartistic!' would be solemnly decided. Note well! Whenever you present the actual, simple truth, it is, somehow, always denounced as a lie" (XXXVII; II, 346). A romantic resolution of Malone's fate is avoided by an ironic trick, but this will not do for *Shirley*'s leading figures.

Shirley is a didactic, a moralistic novel, but one whose force is undercut by its concluding movement. By the end it is hopelessly ambiguous, or rather, the moral has simply disappeared: "The story is told. I think I now see the judicious reader putting on his spectacles to look for the moral. It would be an insult to his sagacity to offer directions. I only say, God speed him in the quest!" That final irony, with its smug self-congratulation, is neither earned nor convincing. It does not obscure the fact of the novel's failure of coherence. No doubt the author's "mental suffering" had much to do with the third volume of Shirley, but the realistic, third-person mode itself may have contributed to the failure to carry the moral stance through to the end. The "reality" Shirley discovers is too complex for panoramic treatment, and the faith toward which Caroline Helstone initially strives is not one readily enforceable in a realistic work. The mode will not tolerate unrealistic symbolic manifestations of Divine purpose or judgment. The attempted assassination of Robert Moore does not function as did Rochester's maiming, nor does the coincidental discovery of Caroline's mother carry implications akin to those involved when Jane Eyre arrives at the door of the Rivers.

Shirley is hardly the only novel that frustrated its author's intentions, and there was a most interesting example of this at hand. Miss Brontë had read G.H. Lewes' Rose, Blanche and Violet soon after it was published. (34) Here are the opening words of Lewes' Preface: "When a distinct Moral presides over the composition of a work of fiction, there is great danger of its so shaping the story to suit a purpose, that human nature is falsified by being coerced within sharply defined limits of some small dogma." Lewes saw this happening to the work under his pen, he goes on to say, and he changed his plan for the novel, abandoning his original purpose in mid-stream: "the Moral has been left to shift for itself."

Charlotte Brontë had been forced, for related reasons, to do the same, although it was no "small" dogma she had in mind. For Lewes, realism could not live with moral purpose, and, as he was not up to the invention of Naturalism, he wrote criticism and tutored George Eliot. Charlotte Brontë tried again and wrote Villette.

6

There is yet another factor at work in Shirley that militated against continuance of its moral focus. A subversive sympathy with characters who are strong, willful, and attractive, however morally deficient, is at work in Shirley as it is in Jane Eyre and The Professor. Before the novel opens, Caroline is attracted to Robert Moore, and nothing he does prevents that attraction from becoming passionate love. Neither Robert's thinking and unthinking cruelties, nor the surrounding examples of marital discord caused by just such a selfishness as he displays, affect Caroline's love. Her choice has nothing to do with moral evaluation. There are some gestures that suggest that Robert has come to a wiser appreciation of the rights and hardships of labor, and hence to a moral stance worthy of Caroline, but this does not substantially alter the impression he makes. He is a man defined by his strength of will. Morality is irrelevant to him. Shirley Keeldar adds to a similarly indomitable will, personal attractiveness and high social and economic position. Caroline is drawn to both these characters, and if there is any conversion in the novel, it is Caroline's dropping of her moral scruples and religious strivings, and her unquestioning acceptance of Robert and Shirley.

Both these characters are far from unselfish or blameless in their treatment of Caroline. But neither the narrator nor Caroline herself lets such considerations affect them. Their attractiveness preëmpts blame. And if Caroline can be said to reach a conclusion about the meaning of suffering, it is Robert Moore's thesis she embodies. Her own "strength" of "soul" she relies on to turn suffering to profit. It brings her neither faith nor despair, but a stronger and more agressive will.

The world of Shirley is in turmoil, and human selfishness is clearly the culprit. Caroline Helstone and Shirley's narrator preach submissive faith to the sufferers, and Christian charity to the oppressors, but the novel itself questions these prescriptions. Submission itself, we are shown, can be an act of selfishness, it does not enrich life. Charity, even the program Shirley undertakes to forestall antagonism toward Robert, is by no means the clearly wisest and eventually most "charitable" policy. The Christian posture which Shirley nominally supports, and of which Caroline is the focus, breaks down, as does Caroline herself. After her recovery, it is ignored. The question of Divine justice, the very basis of Faith, has been brought to the fore, and to some degree, repudiated. Personal grief, an unsuitable form, and the moral conflict in the author herself, have prevented Shirley from carrying its social and moral investigations through toward consideration of the problem of evil. The derision of conventional romantic fiction with which Miss Brontë ends Shirley is largely directed at herself. She will do better next time.

NOTES:

(1) "English Novels", Fraser's, XLIV (1851), 382.
(2) See the early chapters of Richard Stang, The Theory of the Novel in England, 1850-1870 (New York, 1959).
(3) Describing the special virtues of Jane Eyre and Mary Barton, Lewes displays the criteria that he most commonly uses, and that which he argues for in his correspondence with Miss Brontë. She and Mrs. Gaskell, he found, had "given imaginative expression to actual experience - they have not invented, but reproduced; they have preferred the truth, such as their own experience testified, to the vague, false, conventional notions current in circulating libraries" ("The Lady Novelists", Westminster Review, n.s., II (1852), 138).
(4) "Currer Bell's Shirley", Edinburgh Review, XCI (1850), 159. Miss Brontë was much put out by this review, primarily it would seem because of its lengthy discussions of the author's sex (Letters, III, 67-68, 93). She could not have been pleased either by Lewes' uninformed insistence that Shirley, unlike Jane Eyre, was based more on imagination than on the author's experience.
(5) Jacob Korg, "The Problem of Unity in Shirley", NCF, XII (1957), 125-136, posits some thematic unity in the novel, but he is far from demonstrating or even suggesting that the theme of "romantic egotism" appreciably unifies the book. His thesis forces him to find Shirley's dog Tartar, "the character who most perfectly embodies Charlotte Brontë's romanticism and who occupies the central point about which the three concentric rings of characters seem to be arranged" (130). Korg allows that this is an odd procedure.
(6) The Life of Charlotte Brontë, ch. XVIII, 277.
(7) History of the English Novel, XIII, 50.
(8) "The Structure of Shirley", BST, XIV (1962), 27-35.
(9) J.M.S. Tompkins, "Caroline Helstone's Eyes", BST, XIV (1961), 18-28. Lawrence and Elisabeth Hanson, The Four Brontës, 293, see Caroline as "a romanticized synthesis of Ellen Nussey and Anne".
(10) Janet Spens, "Charlotte Brontë", Essays and Studies by Members of the English Association, XIV (1929), 54-70.
(11) Tompkins refines this theory. She thinks Caroline was intended for a long but single life.
(12) The point is emphasized in Earl A. Knies, "The Art of Charlotte Brontë", and is important to Franklin Gary, "Charlotte Brontë and George Henry Lewes", PMLA, LI (1936), 518-542.
(13) Rose, Blanche and Violet, 3 vols. (London, 1848). The Berg Collection in the New York Public Labrary holds a copy with marginal notations by Thomas Carlyle. Lewes had presented it to Jane Carlyle. Overblown or insipid dialogue, and melodramatically romantic situations can be easily spotted for they drew

Carlyle's "hoohoo", "O dear!" and "how exceedingly natural". Nevertheless Carlyle worked his way to the last page of the third volume on which he wrote: "a book of some talent and much folly, je suis plus fou que toi!" (for reading it?).
(14) Letters, II, 179-180, 255; III, 172-173.
(15) Ch. XIX, 166.
(16) Knies, 167.
(17) "Private and Social Themes in Shirley", BST, XIII (1958), 206.
(18) Asa Briggs, 214.
(19) Letters, II, 313.
(20) Letters, II, 319.
(21) Letters, III, 68.
(22) Letters, II, 312.
(23) Letters, III, 17, 19-20.
(24) Letters, III, 154. Charlotte had earlier worried about the possible ill effects of the "long break" in the writing of Shirley (II, 313).
(25) W.A. Craik, The Brontë Novels (London, 1968), 153.
(26) The re-use of the name "Cave" may be merely inadvertent. The student of Jane Eyre will recall that there are two minor characters in that novel who for no apparent reason bear the name "Wood".
(27) Letters, III, 20.
(28) Arthur Sherbo, " 'Inside' and 'Outside' Readers in Fielding's Novels", a paper read at the convention of the Modern Language Association, New York City, 27 Dec., 1968.
(29) Letters, II, 179-180.
(30) Quoted by Andrew Wright, Jane Austen's Novels (London, 1961), 146, from Harold Child in CHEL, XII, 267.
(31) Arnold Shapiro, "A Study in the Development of Art and Ideas in Charlotte Brontë's Fiction", 189, uses the word in this context.
(32) Edgar Johnson, Charles Dickens, his Tragedy and Triumph, 2 vols. (New York, 1952), I, 469-470.
(33) See the first paragraph of "The Function of Criticism" (1865), "to see the object as in itself it really is".
(34) Letters, II, 200, 204-206.

VII

Villette

1

"The interest of the tale is metaphysical and subjective rather than external, and evinces a clear perception of the causes of mental suffering in a highly sensitive and conscientious mind." (1) "The novel begins out of the key in which it is composed." (2) Villette is "a book for which we can scarcely find measured language to express our admiration", (3) but: "the defect of plot is a want of continuity." (4) These contemporary responses to Villette point to the absence of critical consensus, and to a problem of literary theory, that remains with us to this day.

"Villette", says David Cecil, is Charlotte Brontë's "most consistently successful book . . . and it is nearly incoherent". (5) "To imply", says Melvin Watson, "that Villette is as important as Jane Eyre . . . leads toward, if it does not represent, a distortion of critical values." (6) Yet Robert Heilman makes Villette the prime example of Miss Brontë's "original, intense exploration of feeling that increases the range and depth of fiction", (7) and Robert Colby agrees to the historical significance of the novel: "It . . . opened up the subconscious to later novelists. Looking simultaneously backward and forward, Villette is at once an ancestral voice and a prophetic voice in the house of fiction, speaking of what was past and passing and to come." (8)

It was widely apparent to contemporary reviewers that Villette was deliberately, even aggressively, a response to, and a judgment on, the fiction for which the words "Circulating Library" provide both identification and damnation. (9) It denied the common reader's expectations, "with a mocking little short of sarcasm", (10) and modern research into the read and long unread sources of such expectations agrees whole-heartedly: Villette "recapitulates (the contemporary) reader's literary experience of the past half-century". (11) It is "most fruitfully approached as Charlotte Brontë's literary, not her literal, autobiography". (12)

The "contempt of conventions in all things, . . . even in the art of story-telling", (13) is immediately apparent in the character of Lucy Snowe and of that most unheroic hero, Paul Emanuel. The "story-telling" itself is less clearly successful. There is often an inconsequence to the events portrayed; characters appear and disappear without regard to the traditional differentiation between major and minor characters. (14) "Loose ends" abound. Some critics have suggested a most intriguing insight into the special values of Villette by calling it a "genuine autobiography", (15) that is, one which reproduces the inconsequence, perhaps even the incoherence, of life itself. On the other hand, the refusal, or failure, to follow the prime aesthetic principle that art is the ordering, not the reproduction, of disorder, can be taken as evidence of artless naïveté. The shifts of interest in Villette, as in Shirley, have been related to the author's change of plan or mood as composition progressed, (16) and the autobiographical parallels that exist in Villette as in all Miss Brontë's novels, suggest that personal motives rather than aesthetic ones lay behind the strange form of the plot.

The testing of a novel's coherence can look past its means to the results produced, and here Miss Brontë's success is validly open to question. Sensitive, careful, and sympathetic readers of the novel generally retreat from the larger problems it raises. There are, to be sure, other matters of interest. The handling of the supernatural, particularly the structural uses of the ghostly nun, (17) and of the moon, (18) have attracted recent critics. Villette's unusual place-names, (19) its geographic and personal "originals", (20) and its relationship to contemporary fiction and to public concerns, (21) have been carefully treated. The conflict between "Reason" and "Imagination" or "Passion", which looms larger and more explicitly in Villette than in the earlier works, is a popular focus, (22) although there is little agreement on the degree to which the conflict is resolved.

One of the few attempts to grapple with the aesthetic questions the novel raises was that of G.H. Lewes in 1853. Lewes begins his joint review of Villette and Mrs. Gaskell's Ruth by some earnest but inconclusive discussion of the question Villette prompted him to put to himself: "Should a work of Art have a moral?" He uses the ending of Paul et Virginie, a book pointedly alluded to in Villette, (23) as an example of a novel whose ending is inconsequential, for the death of Virginie does not mean, Lewes says, (24) that her love for Paul was wrong. "Art proves nothing" is Lewes' conclusion, which he hedges by insisting nevertheless that poetic justice should satisfy the reader's moral sense. (25) The ending of Villette involves a similar problem, one made no simpler by its famous "ambiguity", or by Miss Brontë's remarkable comments on it.

Charlotte Brontë was delighted to tease the ladies who asked for elucidation: "Since the little puzzle amuses the ladies, it would be a pity to spoil their sport by giving them the key." (26) But her irony in another treatment of the subject is less transparent:

> With regard to that momentous point M. Paul's fate, in case any one in future should request to be enlightened thereon, he may be told that it was designed that every reader should settle the catastrophe for himself, according to the quality of his disposition, the tender or remorseless impulse of his nature: Drowning and Matrimony are the fearful alternatives. The merciful . . . will of course choose the former and milder doom - drown him to put him out of pain. The cruel-hearted will, on the contrary, pitilessly impale him on the second horn of the dilemma, marrying him without ruth or compunction to that - person - that - that - individual - "Lucy Snowe." (27)

This surely may be put beside Miss Brontë's description of her "dread" of using even her pseudonym on Villette's title page as "the transcendentalisms of a retired wretch". (28) Her strange brand of irony attempts, unsuccessfully, to disguise and discredit intensely held and deeply personal feelings. Lucy Snowe can never be, even if her intimate relationship to Charlotte Brontë is ignored, so simply dismissed. None of Miss Brontë's expressions of dislike and disdain for her (29) require our acquiescence, and Villette itself will not permit it. (30)

However complex a judgment Lucy's story may require, there is room to doubt whether the narrator, or the author, confront the need for such judgment. Put another way, one questions whether or not the novel itself presents a coherent attitude to Lucy. Is her love for Paul a fulfillment or a delusion, a proof of her view of what love should be, or an acceptance of what love for such as she could be? The question immediately involves evaluation of the other major characters in the book, and eventually requires us to locate the irony, the degree of reliability of the narrator. If Lucy Snowe is not reliable, is Currer Bell? Is Charlotte Brontë? Is its moral the inconsequence of life, or is Villette an attempt to justify a point of view with which its author was not entirely in agreement? More specifically, if Lucy preferred Paul Emanuel to Dr. John Bretton, did Charlotte Brontë, consistently, in the book, either agree or disagree? The question that arises over the endings of The Professor and Jane Eyre, and that is brought forward in the first two volumes of Shirley, is again embedded in Villette.

Villette represents a return to the autobiographical mode of The Professor and Jane Eyre. From the former novel comes the setting in Brussels, from the latter the plain-looking and orphaned heroine. A most valuable letter from Charlotte Brontë to Ellen Nussey indicates that Villette was designed to produce a result which the method of Jane Eyre had failed to produce: "As to the character of 'Lucy Snowe' my intention from the first was that she should not occupy the pedestal to which 'Jane Eyre' was raised by some injudicious admirers. She is where I meant her to be, and where no charge of self-laudation can touch her." (31)

As I argued in my discussion of that novel, the mode of presentation of the young and the mature Jane Eyre is such that, despite the mature Jane's pointing of young Jane's failings, and despite the plot manipulations that support the mature Jane's viewpoint, it is young Jane who is most "present" to us, and who gains our sympathies. Villette employs a number of narrative techniques which effectively reduce the felt presence, and thereby the reader's admiration, of young Lucy.

Direct dialogue and silent soliloquy of young Lucy is much less frequent in Villette than was the corresponding case in Jane Eyre, and what direct presentation of young Lucy's psyche there is is typically of shorter duration and surrounded and interrupted by a variety of distancing devices. The use of the present tense is reduced, and where it does occur, it is the present of the mature Lucy more often than that of young Lucy. There are in fact only three extended instances of young Lucy's present tense. Two of these frame her drugged midnight wanderings in the park of Villette (XXXVIII; II, 256-259, II, 280-281), and the third introduces the rising storm at the novel's end. The effect of the tense of these passages is not to make Lucy vividly present to us so much as, in the former case to suggest the hallucinatory distortion of the scenes surrounded, and, in the later case, to suggest that Lucy's life has in some way stopped, become fixed, at that point in time in which she waited on the shore for Paul's return.

The most obvious narrative technique, in these regards, is the shift from first to third person. This is most striking when the mature Lucy refers to young Lucy, not as "I" but as "Miss Snowe" (XXIX; II, 112). But a more frequent version of this distancing of the mature Lucy from young Lucy, is the simple movement from the limited knowledge of the first person to the omniscience of the third. Parallel to this is the shift from what young Lucy knows to the wider vision possible to the mature Lucy.

Early in the book there are brief interior views of characters which are ambiguous as to point of view. We cannot tell if we are being given what the mature Lucy learned or what young Lucy is deducing. More extended presentation of information that young Lucy could not have known directly is quite common, and in the early chapters there are some attempts to justify such unexpected knowledge, attempts highly reminiscent of the Angrian narratives. Villette's narrator "caught a snatch" of a dialogue murmured across the room (XXX; I, 30, 21). The narrator describes the parting of a man she does not know and "his daughter, niece, or whatever she was". Two sentences later we are told that the man is in fact the father, and this sudden access of knowledge is explained in a lame parenthesis: "I afterwards knew that it was her father" (IV; I, 62). Again a parenthesis justifies a seeming slip when, newly arrived in Villette, Lucy forgets that she could not then understand French (VII; I, 79), and soon we are given a blanket justification of such gaucheries: "The sensible reader will not suppose that I gained all the knowledge here condensed for his benefit in one month, or in one half-year!" (VIII; I, 90).

Even this cannot justify the verbatim report of conversations at which Lucy was not present, or extended interior views which Lucy would never be in a position to learn, (32) but after the early chapters the narrator has stopped justifying her omniscience. We are given many blocks of exposition and lengthy analyses of character which are clearly based not only on what young Lucy knows at that point of the novel, but also on what the mature Lucy has learned in the years subsequent to those covered in the novel. Paul, Polly, and Dr. John, are repeatedly described and evaluated in a past tense that gives not one particular action but the summation of habitual actions. We learn not what they "did", but what they "used to do".

To a much larger extent than in Jane Eyre, crucial confrontations occur off-stage, or are reported in fragments of dialogue interspersed with summary statements. Remarking on this Craik notes: "It may be said that Charlotte Brontë is again showing truth to emotion and recollection, rather than to fact: it is much more natural for Lucy to forget the words used at the moments of greatest feeling, than for Jane Eyre to remember them." (33) The emphasis then is on the mind of the mature Lucy. But a good deal of the narrative is based on a different principle: "Reader, if in the course of this work, you find that my opinion of Dr. John undergoes modification, excuse the seeming inconsistency. I give the feeling as at the time I felt it; I describe the view of character as it appeared when discovered" (XVIII; I, 242). Miss Brontë felt her characterization of Dr. John was insufficient to justify his actions, (34) and the above description of method seems a rather feeble attempt to justify a failure of execution. The novel's method is inconsistent. Like the early justifications of authorial shifts into omniscience, such comments betray an uneasiness with a restricted point of view, and the rather cavalier asides to the reader do not excuse the practice nor disguise the uneasiness. This seeming struggle with simple problems of method is remarkably like the self-conscious amateurism of the Angrian tales.

The indecision over point of view is soon dismissed from the public arena, and inconsistencies and lapses are perpetrated without excuse. Generally it is the mature Lucy's voice and point of view which we are given, but with a reticence, a selective withholding of information which matches the state of young Lucy's knowledge. Suspense is maintained when wanted, but the reader justly feels put upon by the narrator's conveniently selective memory. Direct dialogue reproduces young Lucy's point of view, but unlike the practice in Jane Eyre, there is no ambiguity about the voice we are hearing. The mature Lucy does not identify with, or melt into, young Lucy. Apostrophes to the reader are clearly by the mature Lucy at the time of the writing of the novel. The mature Lucy does not censure young Lucy, but keeps her at a sufficient distance from herself, and from the reader, so that our regard for her is kept, for the most part critical. No one adores Lucy Snowe.

The distancing of the potential appeal of young Lucy is accomplished by content as well as by form. Lucy's aloofness, which is so noticeable in the chapters in Bretton, recalls the Angrian narrative's method of characterization of the narrator, and sets up here a major theme of the book. Lucy is not only "cool" and "cold", but unattractively so. Polly Home is a much more engaging child than young Lucy finds her: "I thought her a busy-body" (II; I, 14), and Polly's separation from her father is more pathetic than Lucy allows: "During an ensuing space of some-minutes, I perceived she endured agony. . . . I, Lucy Snowe, was calm" (III; I, 22).

The mature Lucy makes it clear that this disengagement from the emotional aspects of life is a matter of temperament: "These sudden, dangerous natures - sensitive as they are called - offer many a curious spectacle to those whom a cooler temperament has secured from participation in their angular vagaries" (II; I, 11). Even as a child, as far as we know a content and comfortable one, Lucy "liked peace so well, and sought stimulus so little, that when the latter came I almost felt it as a disturbance, and wished rather it had still held aloof" (I; I, 2).

Lucy watches a touching scene between Polly Home and her father: "Seeing that he continued to talk, apparently unconscious of her return, she took his hand, opened his unresisting fingers, insinuated into them the handkerchief, and closed them upon it one by one. He still seemed not to see or feel her; but by-and-by, he lifted her to his knee; she nestled against him, and though neither looked at or spoke to the other for an hour following, I suppose both were satisfied" (II; I, 13). Here we see that it is the mature Lucy too who disdains such simple emotional satisfactions.

Despite the mature Lucy's explanation to the contrary, there is some reason to suspect that the calm detachment from emotional involvement which both the mature Lucy and the Lucy of the Bretton chapters exhibit, and which young Lucy is forced to put aside in Villette, is in fact a mask, a deliberate repression of emotional needs, a refusal to expose tender and much wounded sensibilities. The extremity of the detachment is itself suspicious, and this reading is supported by a number of clear statements of Lucy's attitude: In the garden of the Pensionnat, Lucy recalls her youth in "Old England": "Oh, my childhood! I had feelings: passive as I lived, little as I spoke, cold as I looked, when I thought of past days, I could feel. About the present, it was better to be stoical; about the future - such a future as mine - to be dead. And in catalepsy and a dead trance, I studiously held the quick of my nature" (XII; I, 134). Speaking of her extraordinary visit to the Catholic confessional, Lucy reveals that restraint she imposed on herself: "the mere relief of communication in an ear which was human and sentient, yet consecrated - the mere pouring out of some portion of long accumulating, long pent-up pain into a vessel whence it could not be again diffused had done me good" (XV; I, 203-204).

As far as we know, young Lucy Snowe of the Bretton chapters had suffered no trauma, but was merely temperamently shy of emotional involvement. The role of temperament is stressed elsewhere as well. Lucy sees in the King of Labassecour a fellow "silent sufferer - a nervous melancholy man", a victim of hypochondria. The cause of this affliction Lucy knows well: "Some might say it was the foreign crown pressing the King's brows which bent them to that peculiar and painful fold; some might quote the effects of early bereavement. Something there might be of both these; but these as embittered by that darkest foe of humanity - constitutional melancholy" (XX; I, 269). Here temper and trauma are both indicted as contributing causes with temper the prime agent. More frequently however, trauma alone is given as the root of Lucy's anguish.

Miss Brontë defended the "external coldness" of her heroine this way: "You say that she may be thought morbid and weak, unless the history of her life be more fully given. I consider that she is both morbid and weak at times; her character sets up no pretensions to unmixed strength, and anybody living her life would necessarily become morbid. It was no impetus of healthy feeling which urged her to the confessional, for instance." (35) Miss Brontë avoids the question about filling in more of the details of Lucy's history, and continues to give both temper and trauma as the reasons for Lucy's morbidity.

Despite this, Lucy's trauma both during the eight years between the Bretton and Villette sections, and during the course of the novel, is so much more vividly present to us, and so much more vivid to Lucy herself as she laments her sorrows, that her temperament seems to be a reaction to the trauma, not the cause of her intense reaction to it. Lucy's temperament however accounts for her peculiar coldness in the Bretton chapters. If Lucy's sorrows are merely the result of her temper, all the operations of trauma and of fate about which she and the novel make so much, are in effect a false lead, merely the rationalizations of a disturbed personality who will not admit that she is the only offender against herself. (36) Some other support for this reading can be found in the novel, but far from enough for us to take it as the novel's real plot. Yet the suspicion that the novel is primarily Lucy's fantasy, the projections of a grotesquely sensitive temperament onto quite ordinary people and events, probably adds something to the peculiar intractability of the novel.

Putting this ambiguity aside, we come upon another. Lucy has lost her family, has no friends, and is disappointed in her love for Dr. John. The emphasis she herself gives to these various afflictions is inconsistent. It may be psychologically realistic that as she approaches the climax of her relationship with Dr. John she should be reminded of her lost loved ones, but our attempt to understand her is made extremely difficult. This ambiguity is seen in the various meanings the word "Imagination" has for Lucy. Often it means merely "hope", hope that Dr. John loves her. Often its referent is vague, but apparently some special kind of pleasurable day-dreaming. Yet we have been told quite definitely that "I, Lucy Snowe, plead guiltless of that curse, an overheated and discursive imagination" (II, I, 10).

The theme of loneliness goes a long way toward resolving these questions, for loneliness can be a common denominator for all Lucy's afflictions, and the force which drives her to the pleasures of imagination. This theme is reinforced by the fact that none of the major characters are part of an intact marital pair, but emphasis on this thematic unity undervalues Lucy's complexity. Her engagement to Paul provides the promise of companionship but it seems that more than simple loneliness lay behind her violently emotional response to Dr. John. Lucy settles for the hope of companionship, and then for the mere memory of it, as if the passionate nature she showed in her response to Dr. John had utterly disappeared or been transcended or repressed. Dr. John and Polly then come together, but strangely shorn of qualities that had earlier made them so attractive. The novel clearly celebrates the love Lucy finds with Paul, but also seems to operate by manipulations of other elements in the story, to question this proposition. And at last, if Lucy is meant to be the novel's heroine, why did Charlotte Brontë scorn her so?

There is a richness of complication below the surface of Villette which, one is tempted to say, is more like life than like a fiction. What young Lucy says and does, and what the mature Lucy says and does, are often each and mutually inconsistent. It is as if two different interpretations of Lucy were being simultaneously presented by two different authors, neither of whom were entirely convinced that their opponent was not closer to the truth. The techniques which emphasize the point of view of the mature Lucy do not entirely still the desperate voice that cried out for Dr. John.

3

The plot and structure of Villette do however provide the basis for an interpretation which covers the preponderance of the evidence. Lucy Snowe's story is predominantly that of a shrinking from life. The tragedies and disappointments that beset her however, force her from her chosen role as spectator into that of actor. Paul Emanuel's insistence that Lucy take a part in the school play is a paradigm of this movement.

Lucy is well aware of the pressure brought to bear upon her: "There remained no possibility of dependence on others; to myself alone could I look. I know not that I was of a self-reliant or active nature; but self-reliance and exertion were forced upon me by circumstances, as they are upon thousands" (IV; I, 40). (37) Lucy's disasters appear both literally and figuratively as storms. Her response is this: "the tempest took hold of me with tyranny: I was roughly roused and obliged to live" (XII; I, 134).

The death of Miss Marchmont thwarts the strategic withdrawal from life that Lucy had envisioned, and she draws a moral lesson from this which future events reinforce:

It seemed I must be stimulated into action. I must be goaded, driven, stung, forced to energy. My little morsel of human affection, which I prized as if it were a solid pearl, must melt in my fingers and slip thence like a dissolving hailstone. My small adopted duty must be snatched from my easily contented conscience. I had wanted to compromise with Fate: to escape occasional great agonies by submitting to a whole life of privation and small pains. Fate would not so be pacified; nor would Providence sanction this shrinking sloth and cowardly indolence. (IV; I, 43)

It is a moot question if this pattern is repeated or transcended by the end of the novel. That her proposed withdrawal of Miss Marchmont's companion was cowardly and slothful, Lucy is here ready to admit, but is her love of Paul Emanuel another instance of acceptance of "a too easy chair"? The torments to which Fate has lead her soon cause Lucy to lose sight of the value of Fate's intervention. She believes that she is one of those for whom Fate will deal harshly, and she is not usually proud or pleased to be among those so chosen.

For Polly Home, it is quite otherwise. Lucy assures her that she can trust "to Time and your kind Fate. I also have noticed the gentleness of her cares for you: doubt not she will benignantly order the circumstances and fitly appoint the hour" (XXXII; II, 159-160). Polly herself treats the problem of human justice, although in tones which betray the style and presence of the narrator:

"Life," she went on, "is said to be full of pain to some. I have read biographies where the wayfarer seemed to journey on from suffering to suffering; where Hope flew before him fast, never alighting so near, or lingering so long, as to give his hand a chance of one realizing grasp. I have read of those who sowed in tears, and whose harvest, so far from being reaped in joy, perished by untimely blight, or was borne off by sudden whirlwind; and, alas! some of these met the winter with empty garners, and died of utter want in the darkest and coldest of the year."

Lucy takes up the theme to this conclusion: " 'I think it is deemed good that you two should live in peace and be happy - not as angels, but as few are happy amongst mortals. Some lives <u>are</u> thus blessed: it is God's will: it is the attesting trace and lingering evidence of Eden' " (XXXII; II,158-160). "Human Justice" is also the topic selected for Lucy's impromptu theme, and her sketch is a vividly bitter image of human injustice:

"Human Justice" rushed before me in novel guise, a red, random beldame with arms akimbo. I saw her in her house, the den of confusion: servants called to her for orders or help which she did not give; beggars stood at her door waiting and starving unnoticed; a swarm of children, sick and quarrelsome, crawled round her feet and yelled in her ears appeals for notice, sympathy, cure, redress. She had a warm seat of her own by the fire, she had her own solace in a short black pipe, and a bottle of Mrs. Sweeny's soothing syrup; she smoked and she sipped and she enjoyed her paradise, and whenever a cry of the suffering souls about her pierced her ears too keenly - my jolly dame seized the poker or the hearth-brush: if the offender was weak, wronged, and sickly, she effectually settled him; if he was strong, lively, and violent, she only menaced, then plunged her hand in her deep pouch, and flung a liberal shower of sugar-plums. (XXXV; II, 193-194)

Lucy's bitterness here is in direct contradiction to her remarks to Polly. It can be accounted for by considering Lucy's emotional state and private purposes, as she makes these statements. The orthodox position is that alluded to in <u>Shirley</u>: "Whom the Lord loveth He chasteneth." And severe affliction has been traditionally taken as a good if not a necessary sign of Providential care. Lucy reverses the position, seeing the blessings Fate bestows on Polly and Dr. John as a sign, not of their insignificance, but of God's ability to create a Paradise on earth. This is a logical enough view, but Polly and Dr. John, in this part of the book, display exactly that kind of insipid insensitivity that one would expect to see related to their relative lack of trial by suffering.

Not only does Lucy forget that Fate had done well to rouse her to action, but she becomes convinced that her fate will be uniformly antagonistic. The word "Fate" appears at least nineteen times in <u>Villette</u>, most often in reference to Lucy, and with this burden: "that evening (during 'the long vacation'), more firmly than ever fastened into my soul the conviction that Fate was of stone, and Hope a false idol - blind, bloodless, and of granite core" (XV; I, 201). Fearful that Paul will leave her without a last farewell, Lucy has the "cruel conviction that fate and pursuing furies . . . would suffer me to see him no more" (XXXVIII; II, 254).

But in other moods, Lucy can ironically dismiss the entire concept of Fate: " 'It was not Madame Beck's fault,' said I; 'it is no living being's fault, and I won't hear any one blamed.' " But when Dr. John presses for an explanation - " 'Who is in the wrong then, Lucy?' " - Lucy hides, or forgets, her usual complaint against Fate: " 'Me - Dr. John - me; and a great abstraction on whose wide shoulders I like to lay the mountains of blame they were sculptured to bear: me and Fate' " (XVII; I, 233). Still elsewhere we are told that Lucy takes the orthodox comfort of the sorrowing: "How I used to pray to Heaven for consolation and support! With what dread force the conviction would grasp me that Fate was my permanent foe, never to be conciliated. I did not, in my heart arraign the mercy or justice of God for this; I concluded it to be part of his great plan that some must deeply suffer while they live, and I thrilled in the certainty that of this number, I was one" (XV; I, 198).

This is a summary statement by the mature Lucy and it seems demonstrably false. On the previous page is described Lucy's "sorrowful indifference to existence", a longing for death. But this is followed by an explanation to the "religious reader", acknowledging Lucy's heresy, but insisting that, in her position, anyone would have committed it. It is hard to avoid the suspicion that Charlotte Brontë is merely forestalling criticism by explaining away or denying Lucy's blasphemies.

Young Lucy herself makes no distinction between the "justice of God" and "Human Justice" and she most surely, and in her "heart" has arraigned its mercy. This is not an isolated conflict between what the book says and what the author of the book says, but it is the clearest instance of such conflicts. More often, as in the characterization of Polly and Dr. John, and in the case of the value of suffering, the opposing views are inextricably intermingled. Oppositions of this sort are not simply dialectical, but many-sided, and most positions have some supporting evidence in the text. The problem of interpretation becomes one of choosing the alternative reading best supported by the greatest amount of the evidence. The more coherent and simple our interpretations however, the more we run the risk of missing important elements in the book. In this sense, <u>Villette</u> can be said to be a poetic novel, one which <u>is</u>, but does not simply <u>mean</u>. In varying degrees the same can be said of Miss Brontë's other novels too.

Regardless of the mature Lucy's simplistic imputation of orthodoxy, young Lucy struggles to understand the cause, the value, the meaning, of her suffering. The experience itself affects her reasoning, and while she searches for understanding as the plot proceeds, the reader, standing outside that plot, watches her mind at work. The Fate that brought Jane Eyre to the threshold of the Rivers is even more actively at work in the world of <u>Villette</u>. Fate had deprived Lucy, but from the moment she leaves English soil, it works, in the guise of coincidence to repair that deprivation. On the <u>Vivid</u>, Lucy meets Ginevra Fanshawe, a cousin of Paulina Home and a link with Lucy's nearest living connection, her godmother Mrs. Bretton. The random flight from England takes Lucy to the new home of John Graham Bretton and it is Dr. John himself who is on hand to help her in the first moment in Villette. Coincidence brings Dr. John to the Pensionnat, and it is he who passes by as Lucy collapses in the street.

The climactic coincidence, the end of the chain of coincidences that bring Lucy to her reunion with the Brettons, is crucial to our understanding of Lucy's mind and to comprehension of <u>Villette</u>'s narrative technique. Brought unconscious to Dr. John's home at La Terrasse, Lucy wakes to a strange familiarity in "an unknown room in an unknown house". She knows the bric-à-brac intimately, and even sees her own old pencil-drawings. She makes the connection between these furnishings and those of her godmother's house at Bretton, but it all smacks too much of the unbridled imagination which created Bedreddin Hassan for Lucy to believe that she has been transported to England.

She sleeps, and wakes again to still more evidences that she is in the Bretton household, but it does not occur to Lucy, as it does to the reader, that the Bretton furnishings have been moved to Villette, Graham Bretton along with them. His portrait hangs on the wall and Lucy recognizes it. Mrs. Bretton enters and Lucy fears to trust her senses. She does not announce her identity to Mrs. Bretton, nor does she indicate that she has recognized her godmother. What is most remarkable about Lucy's reluctance to trust her reason - she fears all this may be a trick of her imagination - is that, unlike the reader, Lucy had long known that Dr. John was Graham Bretton: "I knew what manner of figure would enter, and for whose aspect to prepare my eyes. The discovery was not of today, its dawn had penetrated my perceptions long since." Lucy goes on to explain her keeping this knowledge to herself:

> To say anything on the subject, to hint at my discovery, had not suited my habits of thought, or assimilated with my system of feeling. On the contrary, I had preferred to keep the matter to myself. I liked entering his presence covered with a cloud he had not seen through, while he stood before me under a ray of special illumination, which shone all partial over his head, trembled about his feet, and cast light no farther.
>
> Well I knew that to him it could make little difference, were I to come forward and announce "This is Lucy Snowe!" So I kept back in my teacher's place; and as he never asked my name, so I never gave it. (XVI; I, 219)

We need not take this entirely at face value, any more than we take a very similar explanation by Shirley Keeldar. (38) Lucy has been unusually reluctant to admit to herself that Fate has led her back to the Brettons. She refuses to consider the possibility that her identity would be of the slightest interest to Dr. John. Her desire to avoid the risks of life have made her unable to allow herself to hope, even to see the true grounds for thanksgiving.

The handling of the narrative at this point has elicited a comment from E.M. Forster:

> As an example of mistaken triumph, I think of a slip - it is no more than a slip - which Charlotte Brontë makes in Villette. She allows Lucy Snowe to conceal from the reader her discovery that Dr. John is the same as her old playmate Graham. When it comes out, we do get a good plot thrill, but too much at the expense of Lucy's character. She has seemed, up to then, the spirit of integrity, and has, as it were, laid herself under a moral obligation to narrate all that she knows. That she stoops to suppress is a little distressing, though the incident is too trivial to do her any permanent harm. (39)

It is difficult to agree with Forster about this being a trivial "slip", for the narrator's withholding of information, and then her providing it out of chronological order at a dramatic moment, is a repeated method of this novel.

The growth of rapport and affection between Lucy and Paul is often told out of chronological order. We learn, long after Lucy learns it, that Paul had been surreptitiously putting books and pamphlets into Lucy's desk (XXIX; II, 116). Soon we learn that Paul's offerings included not only books but that traditional suitor's gift, "many a paper of chocolate comfits" (XXIX; II, 121). Earlier still Paul had presented Lucy with that other symbol of affection, "a little knot of white violets". Lucy "dried the violets, kept them and had them still", but she only lets the reader know this when she and Paul have been brought close together over the affair of the ghostly nun (XXXI; II, 145).

Our knowledge of Paul, as of Dr. John and Polly Home, often comes to us in summary statements of what Lucy has learned over a long period of time. That Paul liked to work in the garden and that a pet dog followed at his heels, are facets of his character that the reader learns long after Lucy did. It is a requirement of autobiographical fiction that the narrator withhold information from the reader. The narrator knows everything that the hero will ever know, but the form requires that he tell us what he knows in the same chronological order he himself learned it. In Villette the narrator often enters the story to sum up information that is both old and new to the reader, and young Lucy too gives voice, and therefore recognition, to both old and new information. The revelations about Paul Emanuel's interest in Lucy, and the attractive details about his character, are divulged to us neither when Lucy learns them nor merely at convenience or at random. We learn them at the time that Lucy's fears that Dr. John is destined not for herself but for Polly Home have become, to Lucy, increasingly well-founded. Before then, Paul, whatever his nature and his interest in her, was without significance to Lucy. Only as her hopes dim with regard to Dr. John, does Lucy permit herself to recognize signs of Paul's charms. (40) The narrative method is to tell us not what Lucy learns when she learns it, but what is important to her when it becomes important to her.

Lucy's failure to tell the reader, or Dr. John, that she had recognized him, can be interpreted as her failure to attach any significance to the recognition herself. Her withdrawal from life, her belief that Fate is her perpetual foe, make the recognition of no practical consequence. "To know" can be a complex matter, especially for one like Lucy who is vigilantly on guard against imagination and hope, those seducers to risk, those distorters of reason. Whether or not Lucy did in fact "know" long since that Dr. John was Graham Bretton is not a question that can be answered with a categorical yes.

We turn to the ending of Villette for whatever guidance it can provide as a check on our interpretation. As in the ending of Shirley, there is a refusal here to follow the conventional demonstration of poetic justice: "Madame Beck prospered all the days of her life; so did Père Silas; Madame Walravens fulfilled her ninetieth year before she died. Farewell." Nor does either poetic or human justice vindicate the deprivations of Paul and Lucy. That Lucy's sufferings have brought wisdom, or a resignation beyond regret or bitterness, is not unequivocally demonstrable. The denial of human and poetic justice, which the end of the novel makes finally manifest, would, through the strongest of "conventions", the belief in an ordered universe, imply the granting of Divine justice, but the text offers little support for that belief. Instead there is an "ambiguous" or open ending, but one which only the most blindly sentimental can take as Paul's safe return and a long and blissful life with Lucy. That the novel insists on denying mortal or poetic justice - and by the trap of "ambiguity" points the foolishness of those who believe in it - does not mean that Divine justice is also denied. But Villette, in the end, can bring only silence to its support.

Mrs. Gaskell reported a conversation with Charlotte Brontë in which she said that:

> Mr. Brontë was anxious that her new tale should end well, as he disliked novels which left a melancholy impression upon the mind; and he requested her to make her hero and heroine (like the heroes and heroines in fairy-tales) "marry and live happily ever after." But the idea of M. Paul Emanuel's death at sea was stamped on her imagination till it assumed the distinct force of reality; and she could no more alter her fictitious ending than if they had been facts which she was relating. All she could do in compliance with her father's wish was so to veil the fate in oracular words, as to leave it to the character and discernment of her readers to interpret her meaning. (41)

That the "ambiguity" of the ending was primarily a sop to her father's sensibilities, the text of the novel denies. There is a pattern in <u>Villette</u> that calls, not only for Paul's death, but for the "ambiguity" of its telling. Paul leaves Europe on a boat named the <u>Paul et Virginie</u>. The ending of that book has Paul on shore watching the ship carrying his beloved back to him. She does not survive the storm, and their intended marriage is not consummated. It is an explicit preparation for the ending of <u>Villette</u>.

The second page of the novel begins a series of preparations for Lucy's tragedy: "I believe (Mrs. Bretton) then plainly saw events coming, whose very shadow I scarce guessed." And this is followed by the figure of peace as calm water - "Time always flowed smoothly for me at my godmother's side; not with tumultuous swiftness, but blandly, like the gliding of a full river through a plain" - a figure which, with its converse, reverberates all through the novel and culminates on its last page.

Lucy's experience with Miss Marchmont provides a preparation for Lucy's future, for the love of Miss Marchmont's life also died prematurely and violently before her planned marriage. (42) On the eve of her own death, Miss Marchmont reveals to Lucy the story of her lost Frank. This narrative is juxtaposed with Lucy's premonition of impending doom, so that while the storm outside proves yet another true omen of death, this time Miss Marchmont's, it also becomes associated with Frank's death.

The most important foreshadowing of the end of the novel occurs in the period between the episodes in Bretton and Villette and appears in the beginning of the chapter on Miss Marchmont. During the intervening eight years, unspecified tragedy strikes Lucy. The feeling that the storm presages disaster, the storm imagery itself, and the ironic invitation to the reader to imagine that Lucy's peace went undisturbed, is a direct parallel to the disaster that strikes at the novel's close:

> On quitting Bretton, which I did a few weeks after Paulina's departure, . . . I betook myself home. . . . It will be conjectured that I was of course glad to return to the bosom of my kindred. Well; the amiable conjecture does no harm, and may therefore be safely left uncontradicted. Far from saying nay, indeed, I will permit the reader to picture me, for the next eight years, as a bark, slumbering through halcyon weather, in a harbour still as glass - the steersman stretched on the little deck, his face up to heaven, his eyes closed: buried, if you will, in a long prayer. . . .
>
> Picture me then idle, basking, plump, and happy, stretched on a cushioned deck, warmed with constant sunshine, rocked by breezes indolently soft. (IV; I, 39).

At the novel's end we are reminded of Lucy's experience that stormy weather warns of tragedy, and in a style again reminiscent of the nature studies of Bernardin de St. Pierre: "The skies hang full and dark - a rack sails from the west; the clouds cast themselves into strange forms - arches and broad radiations; there rise resplendent mornings - glorious, royal, purple as monarch in his state; the heavens are one flame; so wild are they, they rival battle at its thickest - so bloody, they shame Victory in her pride. I know some signs of the sky; I have noted them ever since childhood. God, watch that sail! Oh! guard it!" (XLII; II, 312).

We are told that this storm "achieved his perfect work", that "the Atlantic was strewn with wrecks". The ironic invitation to disbelief provides the final note: "Here pause: pause at once. There is enough said. Trouble no quiet, kind heart; leave sunny imaginations hope. Let it be theirs to conceive the delight of joy born again fresh out of great terror, the rapture of rescue from peril, the wondrous reprive from dread, the fruition of return. Let them picture union and a happy succeeding life." The conclusion of the passage from chapter four might well have been repeated at this point, so near is it in content and tone:

However, it cannot be concealed that, in that case, I must somehow have
fallen over-board, or that there must have been wreck at last. I too will remember a time - a long time, of cold, of danger, of contention. To this hour,
when I have the nightmare, it repeats the rush and saltiness of briny waves
in my throat, and their icy pressure on my lungs. I even know there was a
storm, and that not of one hour nor one day.

Here the narrator's use of her present tense links with the similar usage as the
last storm of the novel begins. In both cases, after tension and expectation are
raised by this revelation of the narrator's own excitement, her own presentness
in events of the past, the narrative reverts to past tense for the denouement:
"For many days and nights neither sun nor stars appeared; we cast with our own
hands the tackling out of the ship; a heavy tempest lay on us; all hope that we
should be saved was taken away. In fine, the ship was lost, the crew perished."
This is more explicit, but no more certain, than the dire results of Paul's bout
with the stormy sea. We are justified in reading the earlier passage as a gloss
on the later, not only for what happened but for the tone in which Lucy reacted
to it. And the echoes of Cowper's "Castaway" and of St. Pierre's tale enriches
and connects both scenes.

The placement of the first storm in the chapter about Miss Marchmont, the
association of storm and omen with her death, and the parallel between her fate
and Lucy's, all lead us to read with special interest Miss Marchmont's commentary on the significance of her life. Lucy has learned to discern and appreciate
Miss Marchmont's kindness and good sense despite her faults: "I found her a
furrowed, grey-haired woman, grave with solitude, stern with long affliction,
irritable also, and perhaps exacting. . . . A vein of reason ever ran through
her passion. . . . She gave me the originality of her character to study: the
steadiness of her virtues, I will add, the power of her passions, to admire, the
truth of her feelings to trust" (IV; I, 40-43).

All this leads us to see Miss Marchmont as a prefiguration of what Lucy Snowe
will become after Paul's death. She loves memory, and finds solace and "delight"
in reliving her days of bliss: "I renew the love of my life - its only love - almost
its only affection; for I am not a particularly good woman: I am not amiable. Yet
I have had my feelings, strong and concentrated. . . . This I can now see and
say - if few women have suffered as I did in his loss, few have enjoyed what I
did in his love. It was a far better kind of love than common" (IV; I, 45).

On the loss of Frank and on her life of loneliness and pain, Miss Marchmont
has much to say, but she even now doubts that all has been for the best:

"For what crime was I condemned, after twelve months of bliss, to undergo
thirty years of sorrow? I do not know," she continued, after a pause: "I cannot - cannot (43) see the reason; yet at this hour I can say with sincerity, what
I never tried to say before - Inscrutable God, Thy will be done! And at this
moment I can believe that death will restore me to Frank. I never believed
it till now. . . .

I doubt if I have made the best use of all my calamities. Soft, amiable natures
they would have refined to saintliness; of strong, evil spirits they would have
made demons; as for me, I have only been a woe-struck and selfish woman.
. . . . I still think of Frank more than of God; and unless it be counted that
in thus loving the creature so much, so long, and so exclusively, I have not
at least blasphemed the Creator, small is my chance of salvation" (IV; I,
45-47). (44)

That Lucy came to feel the way Miss Marchmont did, that these passages are
the "key" to Villette to which Miss Brontë referred, is much less convincing
when the novel is read than structural analysis suggests. The narrator of Villette
does, as we have seen, sometimes echo Miss Marchmont's sentiments, but not

often enough or with the conviction that would make them the clear moral of the tale, or the obvious final position of Lucy Snowe. The mature Lucy generally avoids discussion of ultimate things, and indeed, Miss Marchmont takes thirty years and the near approach of her own death to bow to the "Inscrutable God". Even then she has some doubts about her own fitness to receive His mercies.

The ending of <u>Villette</u> recalls the Marchmont chapter but not Miss Marchmont's commentary. In fact so little of her hard-won wisdom is present in Lucy's tone at the novel's end that even the structural importance of chapter four can be doubted. (45) If Lucy Snowe ever achieves Miss Marchmont's position, she keeps this to herself, and projects a bitter sadness more often than a peaceful resignation. The ambiguity of <u>Villette</u> does not reside in the events of its ending but in the moral evaluation of Lucy and her fate. The "overt" structure and meaning of the novel can be demonstrated, its coherence and meaning shown, but such analysis succeeds in this only by a selective use of the evidence. A good deal of the novel exists outside of its major pattern, and not only confuses but undercuts the overt moral. Miss Marchmont's final view of life is not the undisputed moral of <u>Villette</u>.

4

The conflict between what the novel says and what it does, between its structure and its effects, is paralleled in Miss Brontë's earlier novels. The conflict can be seen as one between orthodox Protestantism and Charlotte Brontë's unique version of Byronism, between Christian morality and romantic amorality. In the case of <u>The Professor</u>, Crimsworth is both a pilgrim on a progress to the earthly symbol for the Heavenly City, and an emotionally distressed man whose fulfillment can be interpreted in terms of sexual and psychosexual frustrations and release. I have chosen to take the latter alternative in the belief that this is the predominant meaning of the novel.

In <u>Jane Eyre</u> on the other hand, the moral meaning of the novel predominates. As I have tried to show, Rochester's progress is a religious conversion based on a Biblical text, and Jane's story is one of sin, sorrow, and redemption. Miss Brontë knew that she had largely failed to show young Jane's moral defects - " 'Jane Eyre,' was raised by some injudicious admirers" to a moral pedestal. The structure of the novel does indeed point to a moral interpretation, but one that is in conflict with part of its content. The author, or the narrator, reveals a sympathy with Jane that is at odds with the novel's overt plot and meaning. Not only has Jane, to her creator's chagrin, been uncritically adored, but modern critics have explored the novel's moral contradictions and explicated its high and heretofore unremarked component of sexuality. I have generally disagreed with the conclusions of these critics, in the conviction that they unwisely try to force the rest of the novel to conform to the sexual component, but they are responding to an amoral sexuality that is undoubtedly embedded in this very moral book.

<u>Shirley</u>, like <u>Jane Eyre</u>, has an explicit Christian meaning, again related to a Biblical text, but here the romantic component is so far increased that neither the moral nor the social aspects of the book can predominate. The extraordinary behavior of the principles, and of lesser characters like Martin Yorke and Lewis Moore, is most readily interpreted in terms of sexuality, but the moral theme of the novel provides its own significant thematic unity. The problem of unity in <u>Shirley</u> is not only one of an unsuccessful revolt from conventions of fiction, but of an abortive revolt from conventions of morality. The problem of a coherent moral interpretation of Robert Moore and Shirley Keeldar reflects Charlotte Brontë's honest but repressed understanding of the power of passion and physical attraction, a power felt regardless of moral considerations. <u>Shirley</u> expresses such passion with an accuracy that undermines the "correct" moral interpretation of the novel. (46)

Villette is an attempt to return to and improve upon the narrative methods of the novel which, despite its failure to be so received, was Charlotte Brontë's best attempt to write a religiously orthodox moral story. Villette is a very logical step for Miss Brontë, one which deals with the problem raised but not solved by Shirley, and which incorporates themes from The Professor and Jane Eyre. Despite the fact that much is new in Villette, it can be said to be an intensification of tensions that were in the earlier works, but less near the surface. In many instances, Villette is the best available gloss on the other novels.

Villette's relationship to the other novels, and to the personal and literary experience behind them, is in many ways obvious. Even more than in the earlier work, Biblical allusion and echoes abound. Indeed The Christian Remembrancer censured Currer Bell for the quantity of her "irreverent" quotations from Scripture. (47) Colby has indicated the relevance to Villette of Isaac Watts's Doctrine of the Passions Explained and Improved. (48) The word "reflet", which I suggested points a debt to Lamartine was introduced into English by Villette; the word "reflex" carries the meaning of the French original and appears here no less than seven times. The influence of Scott can be seen in the device of the ghostly nun, an undercutting of supernaturalism which yet provides Gothic terror and suspense. And there are important similarities between Lucy Snowe and Scott's Lucy Ashton. (49)

Like the other novels, Villette bears a certain if complex relationship to Charlotte Brontë's personal experience. "Originals" for persons and places have been often noted, and there are, to a greater degree even than in Shirley, references that seem to require biographical interpretation. We are told little about the disaster that struck Lucy Snowe during the eight years between the Bretton and Miss Marchmont episodes, but the many references to Lucy's "single-handed conflict with Life", imply her loss not only of friends, but of family. Lucy's most terrible attack of hypochondria includes a morbid dream: "Amidst the horrors of that dream I think the worst lay here. Methought the well-loved, who had loved me well in life, met me elsewhere, alienated" (XV; I, 201). We know nothing about the relationship with the well-loved dead that might explain such a dream, in fact this is their only "appearance" in the novel. We can guess that their number was three: "Three times in the course of my life, events had taught me that these strange accents in the storm - this restless, hopeless cry - denote a coming state of the atmosphere unpropitious to life" (IV; I, 43). It is difficult not to recall the trio of Branwell, Emily, and Anne. (50)

There is another class of allusion whose referent seems to be outside the novel: "I seemed to hold two lives - the life of thought, and that of reality; and provided the former was nourished with a sufficiency of the strange necromantic joys of fancy, the privileges of the latter might remain limited to daily bread, hourly work, and a roof of shelter" (VIII; I, 92-93). Lucy repeatedly describes herself as "thinking meantime my own thoughts, living my own life, in my own still, shadow-world" (XIII; I, 146), and of the "Imagination" that "holds my secret and sworn allegiance" (XXI; I, 290).

On the first of May in 1843, Charlotte Brontë wrote from Brussels to Branwell, concluding with one of the very rare overt references to their Angrian "web of childhood": "It is a curious metaphysical fact that always in the evening when I am in the great dormitory alone, having no other company than a number of beds with white curtains, I always recur as fanatically as ever to the old ideas, the old faces, and the old scenes of the world below." (51) Charlotte Brontë's famous "Farewell to Angria" is dated late 1839, (52) and there exist few strictly Angrian manuscripts after that date, and none covering the Brussels period (1842-43). (53) But the fact that the manuscript of some Angrian tales were found in Brussels and titled in French on their binding suggests that if actual composition was not going on in Brussels, at least that Miss Brontë had some of her work on hand there. (54)

Elucidation of the veiled references to Lucy's secret imaginative life is of more consequence than the autobiographical parallel it reveals, for Villette not only refers to Lucy's exercise of an Angrian imagination but itself illustrates the Angrian imagination in action. The peculiar relationship of the narrator and her material noted earlier is remarkably like that of the typical Angrian tale. Young Lucy is the same sort of oddly detached and mildly antagonistic observer of life in Bretton as are the old narrators of life in Verdopolis. This is very much less so in later chapters of Villette, and, together with the changes in the characterization of Dr. John and Polly Home, suggests the possibility that the first section was written long before the rest of the novel. Whatever the facts are about its composition, it can be said that Villette's movement is toward technical and emotional emancipation from Angria.

If Angrian style of narration declines after the early chapters, and if Miss Brontë succeeds in producing increasingly realistic effects and characters, there remains a continued fascination with some of the hallmarks of the Angrian world. I refer to the seemingly gratuitous malice, selfishness, and violence which is a staple of life in Angria. There is not only a world without God, but one without morality. (55) Its politics are based simply on power and intrigue, its leading figures are concerned only with attracting, conquering, and exercising dominion over territory and people. Love is a matter of sheer and often short-term physical desire. Liaisons are commonly adulterous. Zamorna pursues and deserts at will, and those deserted never think to invoke moral or traditional sanctions. All here understand that the world is simply a stage on which human will strives for fulfillment, and the prize goes to the strongest and to the most charismatic. Those with power, political or personal, exercise control, never compassion. Love is a matter of personal magnetism; it in no way insures kindness, but is more likely to result in mistreatment, the selfish taking of pleasure, and the ruthless disregard of those who have fallen victim to the hero's charms. Physical and verbal violence pervade the world of Angria.

Miss Brontë's fascination with her Angrian kingdom did not simply end with her last Angrian tales, but found continued expression in her novels. Overt acts of immorality could not continue to be tolerated now that these were public writings, but in less obvious forms, the grotesque cruelty of the Angrians as well as the categorical power of their personal attractiveness is discernible in the four novels. The narrator of Shirley, for example digresses needlessly to tell the story of the dog Tartar, and of his "torn and bleeding eye, just above and below which organ the vengeful fangs were inserted" (XX; II, 44). We wonder why we have been taken so far out of the story's way, and whether our shock has anything to do with the story. Shirley's self-cauterization of her wound, although it is said to have been based on an incident in Emily's life, indicates the underlying intensity of the emotional life that is rampant in Angria and below the surface in the post-Angrian work. Tartar's fate is a surfacing of the fascination with brutality.

In Villette we come across this kind of incident: "I knew that action would give a turn to his mood. (Paul) never liked to see me mend pens; my knife was always dull-edged - my hand, too, was unskillful; hacked and chipped. On this occasion I cut my own finger - half on purpose. I wanted to restore him to his natural state, to set him at his ease, to get him to chide" (XXXVI; II, 212). Lucy's motives here are similar to those of Yorke Hunsden in The Professor, of Jane Eyre teasing the maimed Rochester, of Robert Moore and Shirley Keeldar in their relationship with Caroline Helstone. Reasonable and even generous motives explain actions that in another context could be seen as signs of sadism. Lucy Snowe cuts her finger with a dull knife in order to take Paul's mind off his troubles. Lucy Snowe cuts her finger to demonstrate the strength of her will, to shock Paul, even, perhaps, in Angrian fashion, to taunt him with his meekness. Dozens of passages in Charlotte Brontë's novels will bear such dual interpretation, and this is truer still of Wuthering Heights.

One of the most remarkable scenes in Villette concerns Lucy's reactions to her first letter from Dr. John. She takes it up to the grenier where, alone and undisturbed, she can savor it to the full. The "nun" appears and Lucy runs for help, forgetting the letter. When she returns with Madame Beck, her mother and brother, and Dr. John, the letter is gone and Lucy cannot restrain herself: " 'My letter! my letter!' I panted and plained, almost beside myself. I groped on the floor, wringing my hands wildly. . . . 'Oh! they have taken my letter!' cried the grovelling, groping, monomaniac" (XXII; I, 311-312). The scorn which the narrator displays here is an Angrian disdain of the weak and unattractive.

Dr. John, who has seen Lucy frantic and in tears over her lost letter, and who is hiding that letter in his coat, is singularly untouched. Smiling, he asks her why the letter is so important, and he presses her till new tears come. At last he relents and returns the letter. But what is stupid if not cruel to us, is not so to Lucy: "Curious, characteristic manoeuvre! His quick eye had seen the letter on the floor where I sought it; his hand, as quick, had snatched it up. He had hidden it in his waistcoat pocket. If my trouble had wrought with a whit less stress and reality, I doubt whether he would ever have acknowledged or restored it. Tears of temperature one degree cooler than those I shed would only have amused Dr. John" (XXII; I, 313). Lucy understands Dr. John and admires his "quickness". He is her superior, by Angrian standards, for he regards her as Lucy regarded Polly Home at Bretton, and as Lucy regards her younger self. Dr. John's coolness is disdain of weakness, and so is Lucy's.

Another incident of gratuitous and really cruel "teasing" occurs when Mr. Home, who has already agreed to Polly's engagement to Dr. John, interviews that apprehensive suitor. The scene has its comic aspects, as absurdity and cruelty often have, and at its end the participants agree to Polly's wish that they shake hands: " 'Indeed, indeed, you are friends. Graham, stretch out your right hand. Papa, put out yours. Now, let them touch. Papa, don't be stiff; close your fingers; be pliant - there! But that is not a clasp - it is a grasp! Papa, you grasp like a vice. You crush Graham's hand to the bone; you hurt him!' He must have hurt him; for he wore a massive ring, set round with brilliants, of which the sharp facets cut into Graham's flesh and drew blood" (XXXVII; II, 236). This could have come directly from an Angrian tale. The conflict between the hero and his wife's father is a particularly virulent one in Angria. The wife and daughter relationship complicates the struggle of wills and produces Angria's greatest battles and holocausts. Here in <u>Villette</u> it is almost completely "naturalized", with its undue violence perhaps referred to the characteristic Yorkshire personality of its author.

Dr. John is well aware of the tender state of Lucy's "nerves". He has seen her in hysterics over his letter, and knows of her collapse outside the Catholic church. Yet from the night of the fire in the theater, and of his meeting with Polly Home, he utterly ignores Lucy - for three months! Lucy had been so moved by his earlier slight attentions that she could say: "A new creed became mine - a belief in happiness" (XXIII; II, 1). Seven weeks of neglect later, she is more convinced than ever that "these blanks were inevitable: the result of circumstances, the fiat of fate, a part of my life's lot, and - above all - a matter about whose origin no question must ever be asked, for whose painful sequence no murmur ever uttered. Of course I did not blame myself for suffering: I thank God I had a truer sense of justice than to fall into any imbecile extravagances of self-accusation; and as to blaming others for silence, in my reason I well knew them blameless, and in my heart acknowledged them so" (XXIV; II, 19-20).

It does not occur to Lucy that Dr. John should be blamed for his inattention, his cruel teasing, his unthinking and misleading kindness to her, his infatuation with the shallow Ginevra Fanshawe, his engagement to the rich Polly Home. None of these diminish his appeal, if anything they increase it. The "strange, sweet insanity" associated with that first letter more than balances his other acts. Lucy loves him. She "would not seriously infer blame. No; (Dr. John) might sadden and trouble me sometimes; but then mine was a soon-depressed, and easily-deranged temperament", and she tries "to keep down the unreasonable pain which

thrilled my heart" when she learns of Dr. John's interest in Polly (XXVII; II, 82). Alone in the garden of the Pensionnat, Lucy "recalled Dr. John; my warm affection for him; my faith in his excellence; my delight in his grace. . . . such kind looks, such a warm hand; his voice still kept so pleasant a tone for my name; I never liked 'Lucy' so well as when he uttered it" (XXXI; II, 141).
    Even when Lucy's intimacy with Paul is well developed, and she knows that Polly loves Dr. John, Lucy cannot hide her feelings. To Polly, Dr. John "seems now all sacred, his locks are inaccessible, and, Lucy, I feel a sort of fear when I look at his firm marble chin, at his straight Greek features. . . . Do other people see him with my eyes? Do you admire him?" Lucy's answer is this: "I never see him. . . . I mean that I value vision, and dread being struck stone blind" (XXXVII; II, 223). Polly and Dr. John are engaged, and Lucy very much occupied with Paul, but the sight of Dr. John brings this: "I believe in that goodly mansion, his heart, he kept one little place under the skylights where Lucy might have entertainment, if she chose to call. . . . I kept a place for him, too - a place of which I never took the measure, either by rule or compass: I think it was like the tent of Peri-Banou. All my life long I carried it folded in the hollow of my hand - yet, released from that hold and constriction, I know not but its innate capacity for expanse might have magnified it into a tabernacle for a host" (XXXVIII; II, 265).
    Lucy's love of Dr. John does not prevent her from loving Paul Emanuel, a man who is everything Dr. John is not. Paul is older, poorer, and anything but handsome. While his motives are impeccable, with his relatives and those of his first love he is submissive and self-denying. The excitement and passion he does display are primarily associated with the school, and have the flavor of childishness, as does the delight he finds in being ostentatiously in the forefront of public events. The secrecy with which he arranges for Lucy's future, and his arrangements themselves, remind one of a child's way of planning, with an obsessive care for detail, some cherished event, or the fixtures of a doll's house. None of this denies the fact that there is great warmth and tenderness in his actions, and much charm too. With Paul are associated gifts of candy, flowers, and books, a faithful dog, and a love of gardening, and of nature generally. He is a man of consummate kindness, but there is nothing of that "strange, sweet insanity" in Lucy's response to him. He is the fitting Paul to travel off on the Paul et Virginie.
    The contrast between Paul and Dr. John is somewhat complicated by the fact that Dr. John ministers regularly and with intelligent tact to indigent patients, surprising behavior for the man whose most obvious traits are his personal attractiveness and a callous, unthinking, and unwise selfishness. We never see Dr. John in the guise of the Samaritan, nor do his charities ever interfere, as with Paul, with his pleasures. We are never shown Dr. John from his own point of view, but he awakens strong interest as well as the suspicion of faithlessness in Lucy, young Polly Home, Madame Beck, and Ginevra Fanshawe. Lucy even suspects that he may be courting Rosine, the portress. Dr. John is thus characterized indirectly, rather than from the "inside", and this itself suggests that he has no "inside", no self-consciousness, but is merely an attracting force. We are led to suspect that his hospital work is not really altruistic, or to see it as an attempt to justify Lucy's love of him on moral grounds. Lucy goes so far as to call Dr. John "good" as well as "beautiful" (XXXI; II, 142). The novel consistently denies this: Dr. John is beautiful, Paul is good. Lucy's attitude toward the two men is a paradigm of the moral ambiguity of Villette, and of the less apparent ambivalence in the earlier novels.
    The foregoing attempt to illustrate the Angrian elements in Villette has of course been anticipated by Fannie Ratchford's excellent study of the Brontës' "web of childhood". Miss Ratchford called Villette "the most Angrian of Charlotte's novels", and Dr. John a more faithful incarnation of the spirit of Zamorna than was Rochester. (56) This identification she most convincingly supports by the quoting of "innumerable verbal parallels" in phrases and epithets

used to describe the two characters. Lucy's ambivalence toward Dr. John is seen as the result of the fact that Lucy was herself an amalgam of two Angrian characters whose product was necessarily inconsistent.

This would not deny an ambivalence in Charlotte Brontë herself, but Miss Ratchford's view is that she, like Lucy, was like "all of the wives of Angria, (who) kept secret shrines in their hearts for the worship of this divinity (i.e. Zamorna), and certainly no woman who came under his notice, as Lucy came under Dr. John's, could ever put him out of her heart." "There is no doubt that John Graham Bretton was, in Charlotte's mind, the real hero of Villette, for Zamorna could have no rival." (57)

I believe I have demonstrated the moral component of Villette's content and structure that makes this last an over-statement: Dr. John is only the secret hero of a part of "Charlotte's mind". The attraction of Dr. John and of Angrian violence and amorality is undoubted, but the novel can also be seen as Charlotte Brontë's last attempt to exorcise this world of "Imagination", to counter it with a stern, moral Protestantism made the sterner because of strongly felt and disquieting doubts about it. The investigation of human justice and suffering, that is so important in Shirley and Villette, is the philosophical side of the conflict between Zamorna and Paul Emanuel. Faith in Divine Justice, if one really had it, would negate that awful appeal of Zamorna. There is a scrupulous and conscientious honesty in Charlotte Brontë that forbids a rash or simplistic choice, and which results in emotional anguish, and in convoluted, painful, and intractable ironies. This, I submit, describes the tone of the ending of Villette more justly than does Miss Ratchford's suggestion that its "ambiguity" is related to Miss Brontë's Angrian "habit of resuscitating her hero". (58)

The precedence of the Angrian tales to the later novels is far from being a simple question. We may be excused from believing that Dr. John was modeled exclusively on Miss Brontë's publisher, George Smith, (59) but the resemblance to Zamorna does not end our search. Branwell's red hair and Grecian features, Scott's John Grahame of Claverhouse, and Byron's Cain and Don Juan, are some of the possible prototypes that lie behind the fascination with the flawed but insistently attractive hero of Angria. That seemingly autobiographical reference to Lucy Snowe's "three times", three domestic tragedies, may in fact be a relic of an Angrian tale, for the phrase, and in the same association with omens, appears there too. (60)

Even Lucy's emotional anguish and hypochondriac dreams may owe less to the tragedy and loneliness of Miss Brontë at thirty-five than to her temperament at fourteen, for there is this in a manuscript of 1830:

> I was racked by a dull torturing pain in my forehead which prevented me from sleeping. Sometimes my limbs were icy cold, sometimes burning hot. I could hear the violent throbbing of my temples; thrilling pain ran through my body from head to foot; a knot was in my throat and I felt dreadfully thirsty; my tongue was as dry as a dusty stick; and all my teeth were aching as if they were in want of the dentist's instrument and skill. . . . I rose and, tottering to the washstand, seized the ewer and drained its contents. Then I reeled back to bed and flung myself almost fainting upon it. After midnight, I fell asleep . . . dreamt many troubled, confused dreams, all of which have faded from my memory except . . . one . . . . Excruciatingly horrible is the remembrance of that frightful dream. . . . But to think of it is insupportable agony. (61)

The confusion in Villette between traumatic and temperamental causes of Lucy's malaise has its analogue in the questions this passage's existence raises. Which came first and mattered most, the temper of the trauma, the real life, or the life of Angria?

There is an extraordinary irony in the fact that, despite Charlotte Brontë's repeated and aggressive insistence on the "real" and the "true", despite her dedicated attempts to avoid the conventional in life and literature, we can in the end suspect that her prime sources were literary sources. We have seen how, verbally and rhetorically, her reading is echoed in her style. The Bible, Bunyan, Shakespeare, Richardson, Dryden, Milton, Watts, Sand, Lamartine, Scott, Fielding, Austen, Dickens, St. Pierre, Thackeray, Cowper, and others, appear again on Charlotte Brontë's pages. If this were limited to the borrowing of names and plot incidents, it would be no more than a curiosity, but phrases and images, moods and modes, seem to be so impressed on Miss Brontë's ear and imagination that her own voice and style, her own passion and reality, is sometimes obscured.

Not the least of the books influencing Miss Brontë were her own books. In large measure she was indelibly fascinated with her own Angrian tales. Parallels of technique, characters, and phrase, are probably beyond counting, and as much could be said of the relationship between the four novels. Her work is a theme with variations. With <u>Villette</u> Miss Brontë succeeds in creating in Paul Emanuel, a moral hero, an "anti-Zamorna", who is preëminently believable and a triumph of realism. Yet <u>Villette</u> also creates Miss Brontë's purest "Zamorna" in Dr. John, (62) and there will always be those who detect the hesitancy in the celebration by Lucy Snowe and by Charlotte Brontë of Paul's supremacy. <u>Villette</u> is her most realistic and most fantastic work. She vigorously closes her <u>Radcliffe</u>, only to open her Byron.

In her refusal to be conventional, Miss Brontë commits the ultimate Romantic heresy - the belief that art is at last irrelevant to life, that life is more true and more real than art. Her own literary life exhibits the impossibility of the attempt to eschew convention, even tradition, in favor of originality and spontaneity. She did not realize how little of these last two qualities there really is. She could not and would not revise her work after completion; probably her insistence on "truth" made it distasteful for her to manipulate her tales, to try to control their effect on the reader. The work suffers because of this. Despite her intentions, her insight, her integrity, Charlotte Brontë was a most derivative artist, and an imperfect artist.

This is not to deny that the technical expedients to which Miss Brontë's convictions forced her did not in fact produce much that was new. Simply in her choice of subject matter her work represents a milestone in the history of the novel. Thinking herself a different sort of pioneer than she was, she aimed to oppose the "romance" with the realistic novel, and at the same time, to make good her "Farewell to Angria". Instead she became perhaps the most romantic English novelist. The nearer she came to realism the more potently did she reproduce the charms of Angria. She was irretrievably enmeshed in that "web of childhood", and her crusade against romance was foredoomed to subversion from within.

The effort to disengage from that "burning clime" however was a real one, enlisting traditional sanctions and unusual energy. It accounts for much of the communicated honesty that makes us believe and believe in Charlotte Brontë, although we can less often and less readily believe in her characters, or in her style, or in her larger artistic achievement. Vigorously, with a reformer's zeal, she looked to see things, sometimes very terrible things, as they really were, and if, in the end, she saw no further than men have ever seen, she did confront and expunge what she found to be false. Drugged and distraught, Lucy Snowe wandered among the midnight revelers in Villette's illuminated park:

> There are many masks in the Park to-night, and as the hour wears late, so strange a feeling of revelry and mystery begins to spread abroad, that scarce would you discredit me, reader, were I to say that she is like the nun of the attic, that she wears black skirts and white head-clothes, that she looks the resurrection of the flesh, and that she is a risen ghost.

> All falsities - all figments! We will not deal in this gear. Let us be honest, and cut, as heretofore, from the homely web of truth. (XXXIX; II, 274).

But that feeling of revelry and mystery was true too, and, even after discounting the meretricious solace and comforts of the romantic imagination, in life and in art, Miss Brontë was as true as she could let herself be to the mysterious energies that poured from Zamorna's eyes. From this conflict came, as the rational George Eliot said, "a still more wonderful book than Jane Eyre. There is something almost preternatural in its power." (63)

NOTES:

(1) The Atlas, 12 Feb., 1853, quoted by Robert A. Colby, Fiction with a Purpose, Major and Minor Nineteenth-Century Novels (Bloomington and London, 1967), 106.
(2) The Athenaeum, XXVI (12 Feb., 1853), 186.
(3) (G.H. Lewes), Westminster Review, LIX (1853), 486.
(4) Christian Remembrancer, XXV (April, 1853), 428.
(5) Victorian Novelists, 134.
(6) "Form and Substance in the Brontë Novels", in From Jane Austen to Joseph Conrad, 117.
(7) "Charlotte Brontë's 'New' Gothic", 127.
(8) p. 210.
(9) "It is Currer Bell speaking to you, not the Circulating Library reverberating echoes", said The Leader, "Currer Bell's New Novel", IV (Feb., 1853), 163.
(10) Athenaeum, 186.
(11) Colby, 210.
(12) The same writer's "Villette and the Life of the Mind", PMLA, LXXV (1960), 410.
(13) Lewes, 485.
(14) Watson calls this "false emphasis or improper proportioning", 116.
(15) W.A. Craik, The Brontë Novels, 172, 194n, and E.A. Baker, History of the English Novel, VIII, 56. The Christian Remembrancer had much earlier noted the difference between the autobiography and the novel in their opening comparison of Villette and Lady Georgiana Fullerton's Lady Bird.
(16) Margaret Lane, The Brontë Story, 327-329, and introductions to Everyman eds. by May Sinclair and Margaret Lane.
(17) E.D.H. Johnson, " 'Daring the Dread Glance': Charlotte Brontë's Treatment of the Supernatural in Villette", NCF, XX (1966), 325-336.
(18) Heilman, "Charlotte Brontë, Reason, and the Moon", NCF, XIV (1960), 283-302.
(19) Georgia S. Dunbar, "Proper Names in Villette", NCF, XV (1960), 77-80. The early review in The Leader had noted the apt designation of Belgium as Labassecour.
(20) Wroot, "Sources of the Brontë Novels"; Gérin, Charlotte Brontë; Mrs. Humphry Ward, Introduction to Villette, Haworth Edition (New York, 1900).
(21) K. Tillotson, Novels of the Eighteen-Forties; Colby, Fiction.
(22) Johnson; Craik; R.B. Martin, Accents of Persuasion.
(23) Paul Emanuel leaves Europe on the Paul et Virginie, and the scene of Lucy waiting on the shore for his return, as well as the scenes of their innocent fulfillment in the Faubourg Clothilde, seem direct allusions to Bernardin de St. Pierre; see Colby, Fiction, 206-208.
(24) Lewes does not consider the possibility that Virginie's death stands for a deserved retribution. She, with Paul's eventual agreement, left the island in the first place in order to please a rich relative, and in hopes of being well remembered in her will.
(25) Westminster Review, 474-475.
(26) Letters, IV, 54.
(27) Letters, IV, 55-56.
(28) Letters, IV, 13.
(29) Letters, IV, 16, 18.

(30) Arnold Shapiro, unpub. diss., pp. 179-180, takes the unusual position that Lucy, at the end of the novel, has not achieved love, wisdom, or any sort of "wholeness, completion".
(31) Letters, IV, 52.
(32) Such as IX; I, 106, and XXXVII; II, 220-223.
(33) The Brontë Novels, 200.
(34) Letters, IV, 16.
(35) Letters, IV, 18.
(36) It need not have been stressed that another personality might have reacted differently to Lucy's tragedies, unless, as I am led to suspect, the original plan was to have Polly Home's future a tragic one, and to then compare the effects of tragedy on the two different personalities. There are some relics of a comparison between them, and a strategically placed preparation of trouble ahead for Polly (XXX; I, 38). This may be a deliberately false lead, based on the theory that "the spirit of romance would have indicated another course, . . . but this would have been unlike real life - inconsistent with truth - at variance with probability" (Letters, IV, 22-23). Whatever the reasons for such false leads, the effect is confusion.
(37) "Thousands" is picked up significantly again, XVII; I, 225 and XLII; II, 312.
(38) Shirley, XXVI; II, 150. Using Villette as a gloss, one guesses that Shirley was mum about Lewis because of her affection for him.
(39) Aspects of the Novel (Harvest Books: New York, 1965), 92-93.
(40) "We hear of events only as they impinge on Lucy's consciousness as significant", says Craik (p. 191), who thinks that, were the reader to know so much about Paul too soon in the story, "the reader would soon be so much wiser than Lucy about her own affairs that he would cease to pay the proper attention to her relations with Graham, which are thematically still more important".
(41) Life of Charlotte Brontë, XXV, 366.
(42) The thematic importance of Miss Marchmont is discussed, with varying emphases, by Colby, PMLA, 415; Craik, 163, 185; and Martin, 153.
(43) There is an unfortunate verbal echo here of Polly Home's childishness: "I cannot - cannot sleep" (III; I, 35). Such echoes seem a mannerism of Miss Brontë, for they appear often, and are very rarely functional.
(44) Jane Eyre had similar doubts about her love of Rochester. See Eyre, XXIV; II, 45.
(45) "Chapters IV-VI serve only to get the heroine, however clumsily to Villette, where the real action starts in Chapter VII" (Watson, 115).
(46) Wuthering Heights is perhaps the prime example of such moral ambivalence. The moral reading, made early by Charlotte Brontë, is in the sharpest conflict with many modern critics who see it as a celebration of a love that is beyond morality, at least symbolically beyond life. See Philip Drew, "Charlotte Brontë as a Critic of Wuthering Heights", NCF, XVIII (1964), 365-381.
(47) Pp. 402, 434.
(48) Fiction with a Purpose, 192.
(49) See esp. chs. III-IV of The Bride of Lammermoor. Villette alludes to characters in Scott (VIII; I, 145). Mr. Home, like Hiram Yorke and Yorke Hunsden, probably owes something to Campbell of Rob Roy, esp. ch. XXIII.
(50) It is possible to relate this passage to the three catastrophes in Lucy's life: domestic loss, Miss Marchmont's death, Paul's death. But the remarks are made by the young Lucy, on whom only the first blow has fallen. The paragraph in question begins and ends with direct quotations, and the narrator's summary between these makes use of the pluperfect tense five times. Three disasters "had" struck Lucy at this point in the story.
(51) Letters, I, 297.
(52) Ratchford, 149, and above, II, 3.
(53) Letters, I, 81.
(54) The Spell, ed. G.E. MacLean (London, 1931), xi.
(55) "Angria was a completely amoral world", Ratchford, 102.

(56) Ratchford, 240, 230.
(57) Ratchford, 233-234.
(58) Ratchford, 240.
(59) Letters, III, 52.
(60) Ratchford, 226, quotes the Angrian lines among a number of parallels linking Paul Emanuel to Howard Warner.
(61) Quoted from Ratchford, 238.
(62) Rochester is much more compellingly realized, but he is very conscious of moral issues, as Zamorna is not.
(63) Letters, ed. Haight, II, 87.

A Selected Bibliography of Works Cited

1. Primary Materials

Brontë, Charlotte, Jane Eyre, Shakespeare Head Brontë, 2 vols. (Oxford, 1931).
_____, "The Keep of the Bridge", Autograph Manuscript (Berg Collection, New York Public Library).
_____, The Professor, Shakespeare Head Brontë (Oxford, 1931).
_____, Shirley, Shakespeare Head Brontë, 2 vols. (Oxford, 1931).
_____, The Spell: An Extravaganza, ed. George Edwin MacLean (London, 1931).
_____, Villette, Shakespeare Head Brontë, 2 vols. (Oxford, 1931).
Brontë, Charlotte and Patrick Branwell Brontë, Miscellaneous and Unpublished Writings, ed. T.J. Wise and J.A. Symington, Shakespeare Head Brontë, 2 vols. (Oxford, 1936-38).
Brontë, Charlotte and Constantin Heger, "Le Nid", Autograph manuscript (Berg Collection, New York Public Library).
The Brontës: Their Lives, Friendships and Correspondence, ed. T.J. Wise and J.A. Symington, Shakespeare Head Brontë, 4 vols. (Oxford, 1932).

2. Secondary Materials

Allot, Miriam, ed., Novelists on the Novel (New York and London, 1959).
The Athenaeum, "The Works of George Sand", XX (1847), 543-544.
_____, Review of Villette, XXVI (12 Feb. 1853), 186-188.
_____, Review of The Professor, XXX (13 June 1857), 755-757.
Baker, Ernest A., The History of the English Novel, 10 vols. (London, 1924-1939).
Blackwood's Edinburgh Magazine, "The French Novels of 1849", LXVI (1849), 607-619.
Bonnell, Henry H., Charlotte Brontë, George Eliot, Jane Austen, Studies in their Works (New York, 1902).
Booth, Wayne C., The Rhetoric of Fiction (Chicago, 1961).
Bradby, Godfrey Fox, The Brontës and Other Essays (Oxford, 1932).
Brammer, M.M., "The Manuscript of The Professor", RES, n.s. XI (1960), 157-170.
Briggs, Asa, "Private and Social Themes in Shirley", BST, XIII (1958), 213-219.
Burkhart, Charles, "Another Key Word for Jane Eyre", NCF, XVI (1961), 177-179.
Burns, Wayne, "Critical Relevance of Freudianism", Western Review, XX (1956), 301-314.
Cecil, David, Victorian Novelists, Essays in Revaluation (Chicago: University of Chicago Press, 1961).
Chase, Richard, "The Brontës, or, Myth Domesticated", in: Forms of Modern Fiction, Essays Collected in Honor of Joseph Warren Beach, ed. William Van O'Connor (Minneapolis, 1948).
Colby, Robert A., "Villette and the Life of the Mind", PMLA, LXXV (1960), 410-419.

_____, Fiction with a Purpose: Major and Minor Nineteenth-Century Novels (Bloomington and London, 1967).
Craik, W.A., The Brontë Novels (London, 1968).
Day, Martin S., "Central Concepts of Jane Eyre", Personalist, XLI (1960), 495-505.
Delafield, E.M. (pseud.), ed., The Brontës, Their Lives Recorded by Their Contemporaries (London, 1935).
Dobell, Sydney, The Life and Letters, ed. E.J., 2 vols. (London, 1878).
Dodds, John W., The Age of Paradox: A Biography of England: 1841-1851 (New York, 1952).
Drew, Philip, "Charlotte Brontë as a Critic of Wuthering Heights", NCF, XVII (1964), 365-381.
Dunbar, Georgia, "Proper Names in Villette", NCF, XI (1960), 77-80.
(Lady Eastlake), "Vanity Fair, Jane Eyre, and the Governesses' Benevolent Institution Report for 1847", Quarterly Review, LXXXIV (1848), 153-185.
Ericksen, Donald H., "Imagery as Structure in Jane Eyre", VN, # 30 (1966), 18-22.
Ewbank, Inga-Stina, Their Proper Sphere, A Study of the Brontë Sisters as Early-Victorian Female Novelists (Cambridge, Mass., 1966).
Forçade, Eugene, "Le roman contemporain en Angleterre", Revue des Deux Mondes, XXV (1849), 714-735.
Ford, George H., Dickens and his Readers, Aspects of Novel-Criticism Since 1836 (Princeton, 1955).
Forster, E.M., Aspects of the Novel (New York: Harvest Books, 1965).
Gary, Franklin, "Charlotte Brontë and George Henry Lewes", PMLA, LI (1936), 518-542.
Gaskell, Elizabeth C., The Life of Charlotte Brontë, Everyman Edition (London, 1960).
Gérin, Winifred, Charlotte Brontë, The Evolution of Genius (London, 1967).
Girdler, Lew, "Charlotte Brontë's Shirley and Scott's The Black Dwarf", MLN, LXXI (1956), 187.
Haight, Gordon S., George Eliot, A Biography (New York and Oxford, 1968).
Haight, Gordon S., ed., The George Eliot Letters, 7 vols (New Haven, 1954-55).
Hanson, Lawrence and Elisabeth, The Four Brontës, The Lives and Works of Charlotte, Branwell, Emily, and Anne Brontë, 4th ed. ((Hamden, Conn.:) Archon Books, 1967).
Heilman, Robert B., "Charlotte Brontë's 'New' Gothic", in: From Jane Austen to Joseph Conrad, Essays Collected in Memory of James T. Hillhouse, ed. Robert C. Rathburn and Martin Steinmann, Jr. (Minneapolis, 1958).
_____, "Charlotte Brontë, Reason, and the Moon", NCF, XIV (1960), 283-302.
Holgate, Ivy, "The Structure of Shirley", BST, XIV (1962), 27-35.
Houghton, Walter E., The Victorian Frame of Mind, 1830-1870 (New Haven, 1957).
Johnson, Edgar, Charles Dickens, his Tragedy and Triumph, 2 vols (New York, 1952).
Johnson, E.D.H., "'Daring the Dread Glance': Charlotte Brontë's Treatment of the Supernatural in Villette", NCF, XX (1966), 325-336.
Knies, Earl Allen, "The Art of Charlotte Brontë: A Study of Point of View in her Fiction", Unpublished doctoral dissertation, University of Illinois, 1964.
Korg, Jacob, "The Problem of Unity in Shirley", NCF, XII (1957), 125-136.
Lane, Margaret, The Brontë Story, A Reconsideration of Mrs. Gaskell's Life of Charlotte Brontë (New York and Boston, 1953).
Langbridge, Rosamond, Charlotte Brontë, A Psychological Study (New York, (1929)).
Langford, Thomas, "The Three Pictures in Jane Eyre", VN, # 31 (1967), 47-48.
The Leader, "Currer Bell's New Novel", IV (12 Feb. 1853), 163-164.
Lester, John A., Jr., "Thackeray's Narrative Technique", PMLA, LXIX (1954), 392-409.
(Lewes, George Henry), Review of Shirley, Edinburgh Review, XCI (1850), . . .

_____, "English Novels", Fraser's, XLIV (1851), 375-391.
_____, "The Lady Novelists", Westminster Review, LVII (1852), 129-141.
_____, Review of Villette, Westminster Review, LIX (1853), 474-491.
Lock, John, and W.T. Dixon, A Man of Sorrow, The Life, Letters and Times of the Rev. Patrick Brontë, 1777-1861 (London, 1965).
Lockhart, John Gibson, Memoirs of the Life of Sir Walter Scott, 7 vols. (Edinburgh, 1837-38).
Lodge, David, "Fire and Eyre: Charlotte Brontë's War of Earthly Elements", Language of Fiction, Essays in Criticism and Verbal Analysis of the English Novel (New York, 1966).
Maison, Margaret M., The Victorian Vision, Studies in the Religious Novel (New York, 1961).
Marchand, Leslie A., The Athenaeum, A Mirror of Victorian Culture (Chapel Hill, 1941).
Martin, Robert Bernard, Charlotte Brontë's Novels, The Accents of Persuasion (New York, 1966).
McCullough, Bruce, "The Subjective Novel: Jane Eyre", Representative English Novels: Defoe to Conrad (New York and London, 1946).
Miller, J. Hillis, The Form of Victorian Fiction, Thackeray, Dickens, Trollope, George Eliot, Meredith, and Hardy (Notre Dame and London, 1968).
(Mozley, Anne), Review of Villette, Christian Remembrancer, XXV (1853), 401-443.
Prescott, Joseph, "Jane Eyre, A Romantic Exemplum with a Difference", in Twelve Original Essays on Great English Novels, ed. Charles Shapiro (Detroit, 1960).
Ratchford, Fannie Elizabeth, The Brontës' Web of Childhood (New York, 1941).
Ray, Gordon N., Thackeray, The Uses of Adversity, 1811-1846 (New York, 1955).
_____, Bibliographical Resources for the Study of Nineteenth Century English Fiction (Los Angeles, 1964).
Ray, Gordon N., ed., The Letters and Private Papers of W.M. Thackeray, 4 vols. (Cambridge, Mass., 1945-46).
Read, Herbert, "Charlotte and Emily Brontë", Yale Review, n.s. XIV (1925), 720-738.
Sand, George, Consuelo, ed. Calmann Lévy, 3 vols. (Paris, 1878).
_____, La Comtesse de Rudolstadt, 2 vols. (Paris: Calmann Lévy, 1879).
_____, Lettres d'un Voyageur (Paris: Pierre Solomon, Libraire Larousse, 1936).
Schorer, Mark, The World We Imagine, Selected Essays (New York, 1968).
Scott, Walter, Caledonian Edition, 50 vols. (Boston and New York, 1913).
Shannon, Edgar F., "The Present Tense in Jane Eyre", NCF, X (1955), 141-145.
Shapiro, Arnold, "A Study of the Development of Art and Ideas in Charlotte Brontë's Fiction". Unpublished doctoral dissertation, Indiana University, 1965.
Sinclair, May, The Three Brontës (Boston and New York, 1912).
Solomon, Eric, "Jane Eyre: Fire and Water", College English, XXV (1963), 215-217.
Spens, Janet, "Charlotte Brontë", Essays and Studies by Members of the English Association, XIV (1929), 54-70.
Thackeray, William Makepeace, Centenary Biographical Edition, 26 vols. (London, 1910-11).
_____, Critical Papers in Literature, ed. Harry Furniss (London, 1911).
Thrall, Miriam M.H., Rebellious Fraser's, Nol Yorke's Magazine in the Days of Maginn, Thackeray, and Carlyle (New York, 1934).
Tillotson, Kathleen, Novels of the Eighteen-Forties, 2nd impression with corrections (London, 1961).
Tompkins, J.M.S., "Caroline Helstone's Eyes", BST, XIV (1961), 18-28.
Watson, Melvin R., "Form and Substance in the Brontë Novels", in: From Jane Austen to Joseph Conrad, Essays Collected in Memory of James T. Hillhouse,

ed. Robert C. Rathburn and Martin Steinmann, Jr. (Minneapolis, 1958).

West, Rebecca, "Charlotte Brontë", in The Great Victorians, ed. H.J. and Hugh Massingham (New York, 1932).

Whone, Clifford, "Where the Brontës Borrowed Books, The Keighley Mechanics' Institute", BST, XI (1950), 344-358.

Wroot, Herbert E., Sources of the Brontë Novels: Persons and Places, Supplementary Part No. 4, BST, VIII (1935).

INDEX

Addison, Joseph, 15
Aesop, 15
Allen, Walter, 11n
Arabian Nights, 15, 29
Ariosto, Ludovico, 38
Arnold, Matthew, 94

Bacon, Francis, 14
Baker, Ernest, A., 13, 82
Balzac, Honoré de, 6, 20, 21, 33
Bentley's Miscellany, 25
Bible, 15, 19, 29, 70-72, 80n, 111, 116
Blackwood's Edinburgh Magazine, 6, 22, 26
Blair, Hugh, 14
Boiardo, Matteo Maria, 38
Bonnell, Henry H., 11n, 29n
Bossuet, Jacques, 16, 18
Bradby, Godfrey Fox, 1
Brammer, M.M., 50, 62n
Bremer, Fredrika, 25
Briggs, Asa, 83
Brontë, Anne, 82, 111
Brontë, Branwell, 22, 111, 115
Brontë, Charlotte:
  "Angrian" fiction, 2, 6, 28-29, 38, 100-101, 110-117
  "Farewell to Angria", 18, 111, 116
  Jane Eyre, 4, 8, 12-13, 15, 19, 27 30n, 34, 35, 36, 37, 41-42, 64-79, 86, 100, 101, 110
  "The Keep of the Bridge", 38
  "Le Nid", 16
  The Professor, 19, 20, 27-28, 40-41, 49-62, 110, 112
  "Scheme for a May Tale", 5
  Shirley, 10n, 13, 18, 20, 36, 42, 43, 44, 82-96, 104, 110, 112
  "The Spell", 6-7
  "Tales of the Islanders", 47n
  Villette, 4, 15, 19-20, 23, 28, 35, 37, 57, 59, 98-117
Brontë, Emily, 3-4, 36, 65, 82, 111, 112, 118n
Brontë, Rev. Patrick, 9n, 10n, 15, 64

Brooke, Henry, 15
Bulwer-Lytton, Edward, 14, 22
Bunyan, John, 15, 116
Burkhart, Charles, 10n
Burns, Wayne, 10n, 65
Burton, Robert, 14
Byron, George Gordon, 6, 16, 29, 39, 115

Carlyle, Thomas, 8-9, 13, 21, 27, 31n, 69, 71, 96n
Cecil, David, 11n, 13, 98
Cervantes, Miguel de, 14
Chase, Richard, 9n
Chateaubriand, François, 15
Cicero, 15
Colburn's New Monthly Magazine, 25
Colby, Robert A., 11n, 98, 117n
Coleridge, Samuel Taylor, 15
Cooper, James Fenimore, 14, 21
Corneille, Pierre, 18
Cowper, William, 29, 109, 116
Craik, W.A., 10n, 39, 49

Day, Martin W., 9n, 65
Delafield, E.M. (pseud.), 1
Dickens, Charles, 4, 24, 25, 26, 53, 64-65, 83, 87, 88, 92, 116
Disraeli, Benjamin, 25, 65
Dobell, Sydney, 2, 64, 65
Dodds, John W., 3ln
Douglas Jerrold's Shilling Magazine, 25
Drew, Philip, 10n, 118n
Dryden, John, 15, 39, 116
Dunbar, Georgia, 3ln

Eastlake, Lady, 12-13, 29n
Edgeworth, Maria, 14
Eliot, George, 8, 11n, 44, 117
Emerson, Ralph Waldo, 25
Ewbank, Inga-Stina, 29n

Fielding, Henry, 29, 38, 43, 116
Fontaine, Jean de la, 18
Forçade, Eugene, 42

INDEX

Ford, George H., 31
Forster, E.M., 106
Fowles, John, 4
Fraser's Magazine, 22-23, 26

Gaskell, Elizabeth C.:
   Life of Charlotte Brontë, 2, 10n, 30n, 49, 64, 82, 107
   Mary Barton, 83
   North and South, 46
Gérin, Winifred, 2, 30n
Gibbon, Edward, 14
Gore, Catherine Frances, 21
Guizot, François, 16

Hanson, Lawrence & Elisabeth, 10n
Hardy, Thomas, 8
Heilman, Robert B., 3, 8, 62n, 98
Heger, Constantin, 2, 16, 17, 18
Hogg, James, 39
Homer, 15
Hood's Magazine, 25
Hook, Theodore, 21
Hooker, Richard, 15
Horace, 15
Hugo, Victor, 16

James, G.P.R., 25
James, Henry, 1, 7, 45-46
James, Louis, 31n
Johnson, Samuel, 15
Joyce, James, 67

Kempis, Thomas à, 15
Kingsley, Charles, 64
Knies, Earl Allen, 62n, 83
Korg, Jacob, 10n, 96n

Lamartine, Alphonse de, 16-18, 20, 69, 111, 116
Leavis, F.R., 8
Lewes, George Henry, 33, 38, 82, 95, 99
Lewis, Matthew Gregory ("Monk"), 39
Leyland, F.A., 10n
Locke, John, 14
Lockhart, John Gibson, 21, 39
Lodge, David, 3
Lyell, Charles, 14

Martin, Robert B., 10n, 13, 62n
Martin, John, 19
Martineau, Harriet, 4
Miller, J. Hillis, 80n
Milton, John, 15, 116
Montesquieu, Charles de Secondat, 14

Murray, Lindley, 15

Nicholls, Rev. Arthur Bell, 2, 50, 63n
Nussey, Ellen, 14, 16, 19, 20, 23, 25, 45, 82, 83, 100

Ossian, 15

Paley, William, 14
Park, Mungo, 15, 39
Parry, William Edward, 15
Pascal, Blaise, 18
Pope, Alexander, 15
Prescott, Joseph, 65
Punch, 23, 24

Racine, Jean, 18
Radcliffe, Ann, 6, 15, 34, 67
Ratchford, Fannie Elizabeth, 3, 39, 62n, 114-115
Ray, Gordon N., 13
Read, Herbert, 8
Reynolds, Joshua, 14
Richardson, Samuel, 5, 6, 8, 15, 29, 37, 53, 116
Richter, Jean Paul, 25

Sand, George, 20, 21, 29, 33-37, 46, 65, 116
Schorer, Mark, 3
Scott, Walter, 1, 6, 15, 21, 26, 28, 29, 35, 37, 38-46, 83, 88, 111, 115, 116, 118n
   The Bride of Lammermoor, 39-40, 79, 111
   The Fortunes of Nigel, 5
   Guy Mannering, 40
   The Heart of Midlothian, 1, 5, 42-44
   Kenilworth, 37, 45
   Old Mortality, 41
   Waverley, 38
Seneca, 14
Shakespeare, William, 15, 116
Shannon, Edgar F., 37
Shapiro, Arnold, 79n, 118n
Sherbo, Arthur, 97n
Shorter, Clement K., 2
Sinclair, May, 1, 62n
Smith, Adam, 14
Smith, George, 115
Smollett, Tobias, 14
Solomen, Eric, 10n
Southey, Robert, 39
Spens, Janet, 96n
Spenser, Edmund, 38
St. Pierre, Bernadin de, 18, 19, 36,

99, 108-109, 116
Swift, Jonathan, 14, 15

Taylor, James, 4
Taylor, Martha, 83
Taylor, Mary, 16, 82
Thackeray, William Makepeace, 2, 5, 21-22, 23, 26, 29, 31n, 42, 43 73, 83, 85, 88, 92, 116
Thomson, James, 15
Tillotson, Kathleen, 29n, 66
Tompkins, J.M.S., 82
Trollope, Anthony, 72
Trollope, Francis, 14, 25

de la Vigne, Casmir, 16
Virgil, 15
Voltaire, François de, 15

Walpole, Horace, 38, 67
Watson, Melvin B., 62n, 98
Watts, Isaac, 14, 15, 29, 81n, 111, 116
West, Rebecca, 9n, 11n
Willey, Basil, 9
Williams, William Smith, 2, 28, 50
Wilson, Rev. Carus, 30n
Woolf, Virginia, 8
Wordsworth, William, 14, 29, 39